From Foot Soldier
to College Professor

{ A Memoir }

James C. Ma

Respectfully Dedicated to the Memory of My Parents

The author was 9 years old (far left) with uncle, younger brother, Zhongxin, father, mother, and eldest sister, Zhonglan.

The author (front center) with his army comrades after he passed college examination (1960).

Army friends from left, the author (in rear), Wang Jingfan, Sun Jingfu, Kuo Guangren, and Wang Yuhuai.

Fellow aspiring writers: (back) from right to left: the author, Zhu Guangxi, and Sun Jingfu. (front) from right to left: Li Chunsheng, Wang Yu huai, and Yang Zhenying.

From left to right: younger sister, Yulan, eldest sister, Zhonglan, the author, wife, Paolien, nephew, Jiankang, in Hong Kong in 1989.

After 40 years' separation, and during the Chinese New Year, the author had a family reunion with Yulan, Zhonglan in Hong Kong in 1989

The author with his wife, Paolien, son Tao Hung and daughter, Hungling (Carbondale, in 1975.)

The author and his family toured Lake Michigan in 1977.

A newly-minted Ed.D. in 1978.

The author took his first trip to the U.S. for furthering his studies: from left (front) Wang Bao-xia, wife, paolien, and Taohung, Wang Bao-hwa, the author and his mother-in-law (in rear).

The author and his wife with their son's family.

CONTENTS

PREFACE

This memoir consists of three parts. In the first part, I describe how I, as a teenager, ran away from home in 1948, how I escaped from a Communists' detention center located in the central eastern Shandong Province, how I survived by being a peddler selling shoes in Qingdao, how I was sort of student again, in an abandoned silk factory at a township, Changanzhen, and how I ran through the hilly lands to get to Fuzhou, and how I joined the army on the Penghu Islands. During the period of six years from 1948 to 1954, at one time, I was in danger of being killed falling off the rather steep cliff of a hill when retreating to the south in the Chinese Mainland, at the other, I almost died of typhus, the terrible disease spread on the Penghu Archipelago. As I ranked non-commissioned officer in the army, I once imagined that if I could be discharged from the army honorably, I would be content with very little living my life out as a nobody somewhere in Taiwan.

In the second part, education comes into focus of my life. With the amount of 940 yuan given to me when I quit the army, I got my undergraduate program done. And with the help of my friends, I got on two trips to the U.S. and earned two advanced degrees. And I was asked back to my alma mater to teach, and assumed many different university administration jobs from chairman of the Department of Foreign Languages and Literature through dean of College of Liberal Arts, chair of the Graduate Institute of Education to the Office of the Student Affairs, the highest position of my teaching career. During those two terms in office, I met with a lot of student protests due to the changes of political climate. I had never been frustrated by their demonstrations, nor did I look for the negative side of the students who had launched those movements. But they were often led by their own ideology, not considering the other students' points of view as a whole. Once I thought I was a troubleshooter, "untying all forms of the knots the students had tied for me." The most regrettable thing was that there were 26 students who died of car accidents and others when I was in office.

The third part is perhaps the heart-rending one. In it, I describe how I invited my sisters to Hong Kong for a family reunion in 1989 and how I paid a visit to my hometown after my 44 years' absence in 1992, and kowtowed to my parents' mound grave murmuring to them: "Your prodigal son comes back to see both of you."

I am a man who witnessed a part of the civil war between the Chinese Nationalists Army and the Communists Army when the National Government was retreating south and experienced the 713 Incident that took place in the Penghu Islands. It is called 713 Incident because it occurred on July 13, 1949. It is the cruelest but one, the 228 Incident at the beginning stage when the Generalissomo Chiang Kai-shek withdrew to Taiwan. In this 713 Incident, there are around 5,000 students from Shandong Province pressganged into the army, two principals and six students executed. And it is said that more than ten students who are carried on a fishing boat to the outer sea and put into burlap sacks and thrown overboard. This inhumane action is called "casting anchor." I was lucky enough to have gone through all of these proscutions as a private soldier and able to live to be an octogenarian man. I hope this memoir of mine can testify about a part of that historical era.

CHAPTER 1

AN ARCHAEOLOGICAL SITE —LING COUNTY

My birthplace is a small railway station named Huangqibao in Shandong Province, China, on the rail line called Jiaoji, from Qingdao to Jinan. But the place I have received education is in the capital city of Jinan.

It doesn't matter Huangqibao or Jinan, neither of them is regarded as my hometown. The word, "hometown" from the Chinese point of view, should be related to the following: there should be the ancestors' tablets established to be sacrificed, the genealogical tree kept to be checked with, and the ancestors' graves stood for descendants to pay tribute. Therefore, based on these fundamentals, my hometown should be Ling County.

If Ling County is mentioned, I am afraid that there will be a lot of people who don't know where it is. But if mentioning a historical figure, Dong Fangshuo (162 B C - 93 B C), no one doesn't know who he is. He is one of the behind-the-scenes strategists of the great emperor, Liu Che, of the Eastern Han dynasty, not only the greatest jester but also the forerunner of the blind man in the fortune-telling trade. Being sophisticated and witty, he is considered the best of the best among the Chinese intellectuals. This state-renowned figure is from the township named Shentou in Ling County.[1]

To this day, about 2 Chinese Li (one kilometer), to the west of Shentou, there is still Dong Fangshuo's tomb existing.[2]

During the Jin Dynasty, Xia Houzhan wrote a "Eulogy on Dong Fangshuo," in which Xia praised his exemplary conduct and nobility of character, and his intelligence and humor to the skies.[3]

The greatest calligrapher, Yan Zhenqing (709 - 785) in the Tang Dynasty, was the magistrate of Pingyuan County (the ancient title of Ling County) in the year of 753. When in office, based on Xia's work, he had the account rewritten in his own calligraphic art style and then, carved on a stone, named the "Yan's Calligraphic Art Monument."[4]

But the most pitiful thing was that when the Japanese troops occupied Ling County, the soldiers stationed there dismantled it and spanned it on a ditch as a road crossing flat stone slab. Because of the people's feet treading on it and the coming and going of the cart, some of the strokes of the characters became unrecognizable. Despite these damages, it is still stored in the Yan's Pavilion as one of antiques.[5]

When in office, Yan also wrote an epitaph for "Dong Fangshuo Tomb."[6] And that piece of work is still kept in the *wenyuan* of Ling County (Wenyuan is quite like a cultural center or art center nowadays, for writers, artists, etc. to meet or hold exhibits of their art works).

In the late 1980s, a group of archaeologists discovered that in Ling County, there were more than 70 ancient graves proved to be the Han Dynasty and the Tang Dynasty ones but only 38 of them are still kept there now. In addition, they found out that there were some Han Dynasty's pottery shards, and broken tiles, and some sections of wall built in the Tang Dynasty.[7] Consequently, it seems that Ling County becomes a holy place for archaeology studies.

Situated on the tract of about 1,120 square kilometers, the land of Ling is of fertility. Within its boundaries, there are neither high mountain ranges nor deep valleys. As far as the eye can reach, the land looks like a pancake unlimitedly enlarged.

The major agricultural products are: soybean, corn, barley, wheat, sorghum and cotton.

Farmers also grow clover with green leaf and purple flowers used as fodder for livestock. However, during the lean years when the food falls short, the farmers pluck the clover and mix it with soy pulp having it cooked in boiling water as sort of food.

There is a variety of famous fruits such as date, peach, apricot, pear and watermelon growing.

And one of its wine products called "Zhenqing" (after the name of the ancient magistrate, Yan Zhenqing) gets noted in the country and it can be regarded as Ling County's speciality.

Our home village is called Large Horse Village and shares the borders with the Quis' Village to the south and with Small Horse village to the east. Not far away from our village, there is a market by the name of Panhe. And right there, farmmarkets are regularly held on the first day and the fifteenth day of each month. During those days, equipped with an oversized sack slung on my grandpa's shoulder, he and I would have a donkey-back ride going there for shopping or selling. By then, I didn't know anything about what he wanted to purchase or sell, but one thing I did know was that once there, he always firstly ordered several hot and steamed dumplings from food stand for me to eat.

Our family had a large pear orchard producing a tremendous amount of green-colored and apricot-colored pears. When the pear trees were in full bearing, they bent low, and even lying on the ground under them, with the head tilted at an angle and mouth widely opened, one was able to get the tastes of these sweet pears.

In front of our village, there was a moat built with the purpose of protecting our village if attacked. When summer came, I was out of school and followed my parents from Jinan to pay a visit to my native village. And quite often, I jumped into it and stayed under the water until I couldn't hold my breath any longer or I played with my playmates of the same age by splashing water over one another.

Once when I jumped into it, I felt there was a severe pain in my right leg. Having climbed unto the bank, I found a two-centimeter cut down on my right shin from which blood was gushing. Without doubt, I landed that shin on something pointed like a piece of broken tile buried in the mud down there. Since then, a white scar has still remained visible.

Based on my immediate uncle, Ma Jiaxing's discription, the Ma clan in Large Horse village moved from Shanxi Province to Ling County, Shandong Province, and up to my father's time, there were fourteen generations having lived here.

My great grandpa, Ma Changchun, had obtained a *Xiucai* degree in the Qing Dynasty. What is *Xiucai* all about? *Xiucai* consists of two Chinese characters: the first character, "xiu," means excellence; the other, "cai," talent (Overall, *xiucai* can be referred to a person who has passed the imperial court examination at the county level). *Xiucai* can be classified into three catagories: *Linsheng, Zengsheng*, and *Fusheng*. My great grandpa belonged to the first one. The person who gets *Linsheng* can be paid from the emperor, not by cash money but by grains. And the other two catagories didn't get anything but the titles. Without giving any thought, one would know that this title, *Xiucai*, was considered a great honor to the Ma clan and fellow villagers. During the period of the late years of the Qing Dynasty, and the burgeoning period of the Republic of China, my great grandpa assumed a post as an education supervisor in the Education Department of the government of Ling County. Later, he was appointed a councilman to give timely recommendations to the county chief regarding how to run the county. And he had made great contributions. Unfortunately, he died rather young, at the age of 58, because of his kidney failure.[8]

My mother said that during my great grandpa's lifetime, it was the Mas' golden age. Besides there were tens of larger acres of farmland under his name, houses owned by him stood side by side, a whole block from the front to the rear. The houses became a great spectacle, namely, a big black mass viewed from the distance, and the whole thing was ours! He also had mules and horses in droves and traveled back and forth either in a horse-drawn carriage or on a horseback.

Up to the time of my grandfather, Ma Chuanxu, the family was in decline, no reason being known to anybody. Worse, years of drought plagued the crops on the wide plains of north China, and swarms of locusts flew across the county. Lots of people, who had been displaced and didn't have anything to eat, died of hunger while searching for foods on the road. Therefore, my father had to leave the native village heading for somewhere in the northeast of the country (the frontier-like area) in his teens and looking for the alternative to make a living.

The village called Zhangjia Miaokuo where my grandparents on my maternal side live in is about 5 Chinese Li (about two and half a kilometers) from our village. Ever since I can remember, this village has been etched on my memory because my mother took my older sister, younger brother and I to pay countless visits to my grandparents'. In colloquialism, we called these visits, "Visiting Grandma's home, instead of visiting Grandpa's." A pilot named Zhang Lianxu who flew the fighter aircraft in the Nationalists Air Force was from this village. And when my mother spoke of him to me, I said to her that one day when I grew up, I might join the air force, too.

Another village I often visited was Jiangjia Fangzi during my childhood. Because my second aunt on my mother's side had settled down there. The most interesting thing I can remember even to this day is that Uncle Jiang was so timid, scared of bandits that once he heard of bandits that were roaming in the neighborhood, he couldn't help pissing there. He hid himself under the table that one couldn't drag him out of his hiding place after the bandits were gone.

Later when I studied at the Municipal Jinan Secondary School, I came across a senior student named Wang Yuwen who came from the same county as I did. And based on his saying, in Jinan, the students from Ling County had done very well in terms of their academic performances. This could be considered one of characteristic features of the Ling people.

It is said that one of the ancient kingdoms by the name of Youge was situated near the prefecture of De Zhou, and Ling County was one part of it. Therefore, the so-called Yuge people might refer to the Ling people of today, too.[9]

CHAPTER 2

NICKNAMED: THE LITTLE MUDDLE HEAD

Based on my mother's statement, shortly after I was born, not even having the opportunity of getting cowpox vaccination, I contracted smallpox. At the beginning, I ran a temperature and then, fell into deep coma which lasted for seven days and seven nights. Accordingly, my mother, though in poor health, was not able to sleep a wink for the same time as the foregoing. She said that the family line on the Mas entirely depended upon me, and she tried whatever she could to keep me alive even at the cost of her life.

She had born the family a baby boy before me. But during those years, Chinese medicine fell far behind, and once an infant fell victim to sort of disease, there was little chance for it to survive. Later, she gave birth to a baby girl who is my older sister Zhonglan. Two years later, she gave birth to another baby girl, and though having grown big enough, it died of an unknown disease. The Chinese often say that there are three things against the principles of filial piety, and among them, the worst one is that one doesn't have any offspring. However, if one does, the offspring must be a male because only a boy that counts. Without doubt, my presence to the Mas was an unusual event.

After I came to myself, my mother couldn't let down her guard. She wrapped up my little hands with medical gauze scrupulously preventing me from scratching my face with the wrapped hands. She said the cowpox or smallpox would turn into the crust when dried. And it felt very itchy. If it got scratched with hand, the crust would be removed and the wound would discharge blood. When healed, it would leave a scar. However, despite the fact that she tried very hard to keep me from touching them, there was always a loophole existing. One day, at the time my mother was not that mindful, I touched my nose with one stroke of my hand, and only with this action, what a big difference it was! There have been two scars left on the tip of my nose since then. And they make me have a sense of inferiority for the rest of my life.

Because I had gone through high fever, my brain might be probably partially damaged. Thus, seemingly, I became muddle-headed in my childhood. My mother said that it didn't matter wherever I was taken to, I would sit there tranquil. And I could stay there a whole morning staring wide-eyed at something in the distance. And despite their calling or giving me any yell, I wouldn't react to them at all. Eventually, my family and others dubbed me "Little Muddle Head."

With the days went by, I awoke from that dreamy state, and a streak of stubbornness was clearly shown. If there was anything I wanted denied, I would cry loudly and use the crying as a tool to intimidate my parents. If what they had done or said to me was disagreeable to me, I would express myself by crying, the same way. From the recesses of my memory, the most significant event that made this character fully unfolded was that one day when my older sister Zhonglan did something nameless to me, I was crying loudly on the one hand, I relentlessly sank my teeth into her right forearm and did the biting ferociously on the other. In 1992, the Chinese New Year Festival was approaching, and we decided to return to our native village to pay tribute to our ancestors by way of Nanjing. When that event taking place in our childhood was mentioned, she rolled up her sleeve and showed me the scar on her white skin, though it was discolored, yet still visible.

I had a penchant for crying during my childhood, but when I vaguely felt that my self-esteem was insulted resulting from the kind of foolish behavior, I could stop crying right away.

In the 1930s when my father worked in the Department of Maintenance affiliated to the Jinan Railway Station, he had an opportunity of being transferred from Jinan to Huangqibao, and did the same kind of work there. And located in the middle between Qingdao and Jinan, Huangqibao was a third-class station. Small as it is, it is a beautiful small railway station in terms of its architectural style.

We lived in the dorm for the Huangqibao Railway Station workers. As far as I can remember, in front of our dorm, there was a rather large courtyard where several trees stood. After my father got off from his work, he usually sat having tea in the shade. My immediate uncle, Ma Jiaxing, also served in the same rail line and when free, he often came to keep my father company enjoying a few cups of tea and chat.

In 1937, the Marco Polo Bridge Incident took place, and the 8-year war against Japan's invasion was officially declared. And at the same time, the Communists intentionally tried to mobilize the peasants to do something as well. And the Chinese people were living in fear. The Huangqibao Railway Station was not a big one, and nor was a military strategic point the militants strove for, but it was located on the rail line. For the sake of safety, my father sent us back to our native village in Ling County to avoid the possible battle there between Chinese and Japanese armies.

That year, I was around six years old. If leading a normal life, I was school-aged and should be sent to school. Because avoiding risking our lives in the would-be battleground was more important than schooling, therefore, my father let me run wild and unruly in the countryside, year after year. Not until the beginning of 1940 when he was transferred back from Huangqibao to the Jinan Railway Station Maintenance Department having got all my family members back into Jinan again, did I get the opportunity to go to school.

The first school I attended was not a Western style of school but one-room schoolhouse with one teacher in charge of everything.

My father considered himself a man who belonged to the last generation. In his mind, his child should start with the Chinese Classical texts (referring to *Trimetrical Classic, Thousand Character Classic, the*

Analects of Confucius, the Great Learning, the Doctrine of Mean, and *the Works of Mencius.*) And after the studing of the Chinese classics for a few years, I might be sent to the so-called Western style of school. Being educated in this sequence deemed by him was the best of all.

That traditional school teacher's name has long been forgotten, but I still remember vividly what he looks like. He, who wore his long gown the entire year despite the changes of four seasons, was extremely lean and tight, waving a short-handled round fan called Putuan from one side to another (Putuan, a small pillow or pad filled with cotton or cattail or other soft stuff used by monk or nun who sits on it for meditation or use it as a praying mat, but here it refers to the size of the fan like Putuan). And he looked like a scarecrow erected in the field. When he spoke, he spoke gently; when he taught, he seemingly taught in a slow and easy manner, a real pedant, indeed!

One day, my father dropped by. And when he was about to depart, I caught sight of him who covered his mouth with hand and whispered something to my teacher's ear quite a while. That afternoon, even though I could recite the poems that I had learned, not fluently but stutteringly, I still got the taste of corporal punishment by the ruler. And I was wondering about what was going on there? (Having got the stuff right, I still got punishment). Later, from his indistinctly murmuring to himself, it began to dawn upon me that it was my father who asked the teacher to pay "more attention" to my studies than to anybody else.

I had a brother named Zhongxin four years my junior. He was a good-looking kid with willowy eyebrows and black bright eyes, but he was not in good shape. One morning when I was playing in the courtyard, all of a sudden, I heard my mother in the room crying loudly and simultaneously, yelling: "He is dying! He is dying! His face has been turning dark purple; eyes rolling, and body sporadically cramping. And there is no sign of breathing!" Having heard these words, we all rushed to his bedside, exploring what was happening to my brother. In time, as my father pressed his Adam's apple with one of his fingers, we saw my brother give forth a loud cough and a mouthful of phlegm shot out. And he got respiratory system back into normacy, and mother burst with happy tears in her eyes.

My mother thought this brother one of *xiwangmu's* children, or Queen Mother Wang of the west. And he was sent down into the world with a special mission. With this in mind, my mother often made pilgrimages to the Temple of Queen Mother Wang and paid tributes by burning incenses as offerings. She also bought a paper-made doll to be burnt as a substitute for my brother seeking Queen Mother Wang's permission to let my brother grow up in the world.

At present, Zhongxin was five years old, and he tagged after me all the time no matter where I went. One morning, I took him to a creek and strolled along it. Unconsciously, the whole morning was gone, and by the time we felt hungry and wanted to go back home, it was 2 p.m. And unexpectedly, this little adventure caused a big commotion back at home because my parents couldn't find us. And they were compared to a swarm of ants running on a hot pan rushing here and there. But when they saw us return home hand in hand safely, they ran up to us and hugged us tightly weeping and jumping for joy. Mother said that in a big city like Jinan, there were too many bad guys and numerous cases of child theft took place. And moreover, I was an inborn muddle-headed kid and easily fell to victim of child abduction. The consequences would be beyond imagination.

Our home being situated near a theater by the name of Beiyang, I often dazedly sneaked past the ticket takers. And as a standee, I stood by a red-lacquered pillar and watched the show.

One of four minor Peking opera actresses named Li Shifang was a residential one in this theater, and so was the one who was on rise in the field, Ma Lizhu, the mother of a noted movie star, Hu Jing, of Taiwan. Though I didn't understand what they were singing, I was totally mesmerized by their colorful costumes, their dramatic gestures and the beautiful sound of *erhu*, or Chinese violin.

If coming upon the part of repertoire about the story of the grand general, Guanyu, and upon hearing the sounding of gong, cymbal, and drum and the shouting of his men, I got quite excited. When I saw Guanyu's men brandish big banners, his horse groom who made several beautiful somersaults, and the grand general, Guanyu get in on the stage with the awesome steps, I couldn't be further excited. Once at home, with a broom held in hand and the sounding of the gong, the cymbal and the drum via my mouth, I practiced taking the postures of *Qing Long Yan Yue Dao*, or the broadsword with a blue-colored dragon and a crescent moon in relief. Since then, I have been fond of Peking opera for the rest of my life, particularly those operas adapted from the *Three Kingdoms*. One of the operas entitled: *Baimapo*, or the White Horse Hillside and another, *Huarongtao*, or the Hua Rong Pass, entrances me to the extent that even having watched them one hundred times, I will never get tired of them.

CHAPTER 3

ELEMENTARY SCHOOL DAYS

After studying in that one-room schoolhouse about one year, I was transferred to the western education system. The first elementary school I attended was called the Municipal Beitan Elementary School. Its educational facilities were remodlled, the conversion of a temple to a school. Therefore, once stepping into classroom, one could feel that the whole place had spooky atmosphere.

In the year of 1938, the Japanese troops had occupied Jinan for some time, and during this period of time, Japan was under the pretext of covering up its motive for the invation of China, and a great call, "The Greater East Asia Co-prosperity Sphere" was made publically by it. To "poison" the Chinese people, Japan had to start with education. I can still recall that on the first page of the textbook for the first graders in the elementary school is a big crimson sun with several little children. Alongside them are the words: "it is at the crack of dawn, little brothers and sisters get up hurriedly!"

With such a gloomy school environment that made my hair stand on end, and the simple textbook that I got, I wasn't able to develop any interst in books. Therefore, once I was free, I ran to "Grand Garden" located in downtown Jinan to get some fun by listening to a professional storyteller who recited many narratives, for example: *The East Expedition by Xue Rengui,* or *Xue Rengui Zhengdong, The West Expedition by Xue Dingshan,* or *Xue Dingshan Zhengxi, San Xia Jian, or The Story of Three Swords, Qi Xia Wu Yi, or The Seven Swordsmen and Five Knights,* and *Shi Kun An, or The Law Court Stories of Magistrate Shi's,* etc. Though I am muddle-headed, I have an exceptional memory.

To others, once the reading materials are browsed, they will never forget what they have read. But in my case, it is different. I have excessively retentive memory by ear. I will never forget what I have listened to even if I listen to it once. Strangely enough, having listened to a story only once, I can retell it to other story lovers.

On our Guangming St., lived a Mafia figure, Fan, the Great Uncle, who frequently had his head shaved and made his skull shiny, seemingly coated with a layer of oil. Being a man with a big stomach, he didn't have anything to do but to while away the whole day sauntering back and forth on the street with a caged thrush bird on one of his hands. He was spellbound by the stories that I had got from Grand Garden. In summer, when the sun was setting, and the weather was breezy in the evening, he, having a pot of good tea made and several platters of peanuts placed just on the sidewalk of the street, not far away from the entrance of the alley, asked me to tell the story that I had got. And "I was baking a cake and learning by doing." In another word, what I got in Grand Garden in the morning was repeated to him now. Having spiced the story up with antics while doing the retelling, I made him chuckle. He heaped praises on me by saying that I was a funny boy with the story-telling talent, telling the story well and acting well.

The Municipal Beitan Elementary school didn't leave me much favorable impression. But there were two figures that were etched on my memory, and I will not forget them for the rest of my life: one was my English teacher, a middle-aged man; the other, my Japanese teacher, a young girl. The former conducted English classes in summer and winter vacations, while the latter taught us Japanese three hours per week. Japanese was merged into the curriculum offerings.

Although I have forgotten this English teacher's name, yet his resounding voice, looks, and the way he chuckled are still kept in my mind. With close-cropped hair, full moon-like face, and bulky waistline and white shirt and black pants with black suspenders on, he didn't look like a teacher at all, but to resemble a rich man in a business world as if having accumulated a lot of money and deposited in the bank. There is a Chinese saying which reads: "A man can't be judged by appearance, nor can the water in the sea be measured by bucket." He bore no resemblance to a good teacher, but he was a really efficient one. He taught us from Daniel Jones phonetic symbol through grammar to Greek myths. Possibly, owing to his funny teaching methods, I became highly motivated to learn English or I might be an inborn foreign language learner. All in all, within a short span of time, I had a good grasp of the handouts he had given out. Seeing me make progress faster than anybody else in the class and love to show off, he dragged me to a corner of the classroom introducing me to a piece of ancient proverb once, *qianshouyi, manzhaosun,* or a modest person receives benefits, whereas a conceited person incurs losses.

My Japanese teacher was a young girl with two solid and thick braids. On her light skin face were two large bright eyes. If she didn't feel like talking, she remained silent all the time. But once she wanted to talk about something, she grinned from ear to ear, and showed a full set of white teeth shining. Though she was dispatched to China from the interior of Japan fairly recently, she and we clicked very well.

During my formative years, the only bullied experience I had got was from Japanese guards. When I passed the sentry box of a camp, I had to show my respect to them by looking straight at them without blinking eyes or making a deep bow to them, otherwise loud yells would be heard on the one hand, and on the other, they would brandish their glaring bayonets fixed at the muzzle of a rifle before my nose and bluffed me into submission.

I studied at Beitan Elementary for a year, too. Because the school district had to be rezoned, I had to change school enrolling at the Municipal Caishijie Elementary School. When registration time was due, I was told that I had to pass a screening test. And the result of that test showed that with the exception of the subject, Arithmetic, I got much better grades on the other subjects in terms of a third grader.

Therefore, the tester said that I might be placed in the fourth grade and given an opportunity to try out. If I couldn't catch up with others as expected, I would be demoted to the third grade as originally planned.

By then, the war launched by Japan to invade China didn't get anywhere. China was too vast to be conquered. And the Japanese troops could only control the cities they had taken. As to the rural areas, they had no security forces, strong enough to garrison them. Thus, being defeated is a matter of time. Furthermore, on the streets of Jinan, there was a sort of mysterious atmosphere spreading — the Japanese military personnel were still presumptuous and bossy to the Chinese, but its civilians were meanly submissive.

As time sped by, my brother, Zhongxin, reached the age of going to school. Every morning, mother took us to a "veggie market" to buy us breakfasts. She ordered "Shandong conge" made of soybean, and a piece of "fried twist" for each of us. After finishing them, she handed my brother over to me and told me to take much care of him. And loitering on our way to school was not permitted.

After the school was over, I took my brother straight home. In order to alleviate boredom while walking on the road, I made up the Robin Hood sort of story out of my mind. Upon getting home, I would carry two water buckets and a wooden pole to the Little Pure River to fetch drinking water for the family. Simultaneously, I gave my family members a "hint" triumphantly that "Fetching water by shouldering a pole with two buckets suspended on either end, full of water, is leg-training exercise. And it is in the scope of martial arts."

Mother loved living in the countryside. She often said that living in the rural area, she felt at home. If you were desirous of melons, you could grow them on a piece of farmland. By the same token, if you felt like having chickens on the table, you could raise them. And it seemed that there was nothing lacking there. In contrast to the lifestyle in the city, everything desired must have been purchased. Furthermore, your life was full of the hustle and bustle of the big city including the traffic jam, of course; living in the environment of this kind for a long time could make people feel upsetting and get sick. Consequently, we often accompanied her to get on a trip to our native village for a relief.

At that time, there were three forces alternately administering the rural area: No. 1 the force called *erguizi*, or the Japanese puppet soldiers or the Japanese' running dogs, No. 2 the militia force or the outer ring of the Communists Army, and No. 3 the guerrilla force connected with the Nationalists Army. These three forces fought the seesaw battle. And peasants were suffering. And we dubbed them "The Bearded." When we, the kids, were naughty or did not behave ourselves, mother always said, "The Bearded are coming!" to scare us. When they took turns to raid us, we hid ourselves here and there in the safest places we could find. When they were gone, my cousins and I resumed the games we had played on the threshing-ground. I was constantly asked to sing the songs that I had learned from the cinema. There are two songs that I can recall: one of them is "the Song of the Fisherman" sung by Ms. Wang Renmei, and it became a hit for some time. Even to this day, I can still remember the lyric of it; the other, "the Song of Selling Sweats," Ms. Li Xianglan. And by then, it got extremely popular, and almost everyone could sing it.

During the years I studied at Caishijie Elementary, luckily, I met two good Chinese teachers: one was Wei Zian; the other, Sun Dexin. Both of them were of slim build. And they had the bodily forms of window dressers' dummies in the window shop. During the winter days, they dressed themselves up in padded gowns with woolen scarves around their necks appearing quite cool.

When I was in the fourth grade, Wei taught us some essays written in the colloquial language by modern writers. However, he was suffering speech impairment—stammer. Frequently, for the start of a word, it caused his face to redden and his neck to tighten. Even to this day, I still remember some of his "pet phrases" which were stammered out like this: "Anyone who…is a man, no matter what he does…must firstly try to be a good man and…being a good man…takes precedence of all others." The other words sounded like verse lines: "The moon… is shining with the sparsely-strewn stars…and with many deaths on the battleground, can one ask who is not the beloved one of one's… mother?" Though with pauses and blocks in his speech disorder, he could sing songs as a different person. He has a beautiful voice. While singing, he doesn't stammer at all.

When I was in the fifth grade, Sun taught us Chinese classics, for example, *Wu Liu Xian Sheng Chuan*, Mr. Five Willows' Story by Tao Yuanming, *Ji Shi Er Lang Wen*, The Eulogy on the Twelfth Son by Han Yu, *Zhong Shu Guo Tuotuo*, Tree Grower, Mr. Hunchback Guo's Story by Liu Zongyuan, *Ai Lian Shuo*, On Lotus by Zhou Dunyi, *Ji Mei Wen*, Eulogizing My Younger Sister at Her Tomb by Yuan Mei, and *Ba Li Guan You Hua Ji*, The Tour of the Exhibit of the Oil Painting in Paris Museum by Xue Fucheng. Even now, more than 60 years later, I can recite some of the lines of these Chinese classical texts.

Sun was much more demanding than Wei. He said: "If you want to write good essays, you have to learn Chinese classics. Writing essays via traditional writing style is much easier than via the colloquial language in terms of word economy. In addition, the wording in Chinese classics is concise, neither tawdry nor tautological." He also added: "If you could manage to memorize one hundred pieces of Chinese classics, you can write any kind of essay with facility."

With the war going on, the mobility of students during my elementary school years was very high. I was transferred from one school to another. For this reason, I can remember few of my elementary school classmates' names. But at present, there are still two classmates whose names are still kept in my mind: Sun Daiping and Xin Yufang. The former also fled to Taiwan and settled down in Zhong Li, a city of Taoyuan County, while the latter is the prettiest girl in the class of mine in Caishejie Elementary. And she was compared to a yellow crane flying away and leaving no traces behind since Jinan was liberated by the Reds in 1948. In 1992, when a trip was made for paying the tribute to my ancestors at their tombs back to my native village, I stayed in Jinan about a week and paid a visit to Caishijie. Having tried to get someone who knew of any of my former teachers and classmates in my childhood, I found all my efforts were in vain.

CHAPTER 4

SECONDARY SCHOOL DAYS

In 1946, I graduated from Caishijie Elementary and easily passed the entrance examination held for those who wanted to study at the Municipal Jinan Secondary School.

At that time, it was the first year after the Nationalists Army had won the Anti-Japanese war and that war had lasted 8 years. We, the boys having just enrolled ourselves in the junior high progrm, were often sent to the Jinan Railway Station waving Chinese stick flags and greeting the Nationalist troops with shouts, "Welcome to Jinan!" On the streets, every door flew the national flag with its design attributes of "Blue Sky, White Sun, and the Wholly Red Earth." Chiang Kai-shek's portraits, the Chief Commissioner of the Military Commission, were pasted up on the power poles and walls. People were carried away by a fever pitch and the expectation of economic recovery. However, with the days gone by, the two Chinese characters phrase, *sheng li*, or victory, proved to be nothing substantive but an abstract term. Instead, the take-over officials, who were dispatched to Jinan for the administrators' jobs left by the Japanese, were foolish and undisciplined. Thus, the spell of great prosperity in Jinan became a flash in the pan, and closely followed were the commodity prices that were soaring, and life became very hard in this city again. Having returned to its official capital, Nanjing, the National Government, strong in will but weak in power, couldn't get the provincial chiefs under control. The country fell apart and was thrown into chaos again.

Despite such a mess of the country situation, life went on anyway. Since I was an individual, or just a teenger, I didn't know anything about the political or economic stuff. There is a short piece of saying, "*San gen deng huo wu geng ji, zheng shin naner dushu shi,* or under the oil lamp, from 11 p.m. to 1 a.m., during the middle night, the Third Watch, a hard-working young man dedicates himself to studying books, so does he do the same thing from 3 a.m. to 5 a.m., the Fifth Watch, when the rooster begins to crow."

Situated on a spot by the name of *Nanyen* was the Municipal Jinan Secondary school. It was roughly a five Chinese li away, two and a half kilometers, from my home. Every day, I went to school afoot as if having been driven to school. And I walked along right-hand sidewalk of a street close to the inner wall of the city and the left bank of Daming Lake going through Black Tiger Fountain to school. For a round trip, it took me one and a half hours, of course, in a casual walk way.

At that time, I became very much interested in English. Furthermore, I held that my English ability had already been higher than my other classmates'. Consequently, I went to buy a set of Kaiming English Readers, three volumes in total, edited by Dr. Lin Yutang. While walking, I began self-educating myself by reading the lessons loudly that interested me the most, for example: "The Match Girl," "The Woodpecker," "The King's New Clothing," and "The Kingfisher," etc. On the road, for the duration of one hour and a half in a round trip, I could learn one lesson by heart.

At the time the school was located in Nanyen, and the campus left me nothing impressive but a ruin. Barracks converted into classrooms looked wornout, and there were neither trees nor lawns. The whole campus was a large tract of gravel land. When windy day was on, there were sand grains and small rock fragments flying and hitting our eyes, and we found ourselves having difficulty breathing. Going to classes, students had to hike up their coats to cover their heads, moving towards their classrooms with unsteady steps. Under the circumstances, we could say that we lived in the terrible condition of sandstorm without any exaggeration. Nevertheless, in this junk yard, we found that there was a full-blooming flower—a girl student who lit up all our eyes. What we had seen was that she dressed herself up in a dark blue overcoat, long black boots and a felt hat crocheted from white wool rolls. With her flushing cheeks, she looked quite pretty. Therefore, students nicknamed her "Little Qingdao." The seaport city on the east coast is famed for its purity and cleanness.

From 1945 to 1947, within the duration of two years, our family underwent a series of crucial changes. My grandmother on my paternal side and my grandpa on my maternal side died in succession. Among them, my grandma's death came so suddenly. One night, I was sleeping like a baby and was waked up by my mother abruptly. As my eyelids were leaden with sleep, I was not wide awake yet, and my mother said to me as such: "Your grandma was suffering from a stroke and dying in her bed! Get up! Get up! Go to see her on this last occasion!"

Perhaps, because too much of housework and stress inflicted on my mother continuously, she felt tired from time to time. Her face turned pale as the color of Chinese cabbage, and her physical condition was deteriorating day by day. After the diagnosis by doctor in the hospital, it was proved that there was something wrong with her liver and gallbladder. Throughout her life, she believed in the traditional Chinese medicine, and seeking the help of a traditional doctor ought to be of significance. However, after going through several rounds of treatments, at one time, she felt better, at the other, she felt worse.

Another event that worried her too much was her younger brother, my uncle, Du Changde, who after working in Jinan for some time, he made a small fortune, well-clad, well-fed, and fancing girls. And consequently, got involved in extra marital affair. My mother tried every means to find out who that girl was and finally found that she was a hooker. And this finding made my mother dumbfounded. As a result, that night, she escorted this uncle to hop on a train telling him a lie that my grandma, his mother, was so ill that she might be on the verge of death, and as the only son, he had to return to his hometown, Zhangjia

Miaokuo. But when the train pulled up at the Tezhou Railway Station, she told him the truth.

Ever since my father was transferred back from Huangqibao to the Maintenance Department at the Jinan Railway Station, everything went well. Even though his position was not really better than anyone else's, yet in essence, he worth his salt is like a Chinese saying, "Yi ren de dao, Ji quan shen tian," or when a man gets to the top, all his chickens and dogs get to the "heaven," too. Therefore, our relatives living in the rural area, close or distant, came to us. Among these people, some of them, who were farm-for-a-living farmers through their entire lives, had never walked one step out of their villages. Unfortunately, they got years of drought successively and there were crops falling short, and without having any alternative, they were swarming to Jinan and trying to find odd jobs to minimize the impact of the natural disaster. Facing this kind of situation, my parents became speechless. What could my parents say to them if they wanted to stay for a while? Therefore, our home became their "footholds," and they burdened my mother, not only physically but also psychologically.

Coming also with them are those who don't fit in doing the odd jobs. They were the country gentries, who didn't have the big muscles to shoulder the carrying poles to transport produces around, and nor did they have the muscle strength to load and unload heavy stuff by hands. But they came to the city to make fortune by doing businesses. One of them was Uncle Zhu Mingting who had the knack of making money. Within the shortest span of time, he could rake in a lot of banknotes. And under the lamplight, I could see a look of pleasure on his face as he was counting the yuan and getting them into bundles. His mood was so high that seemingly, he was over the moon. Shortly after, he committed a fraud, getting caught, handcuffed, and locked behind prison bars. His imprisonment pained my mother too much and once in a while, she asked me to go with her visiting him with a basket of goodies.

As days went by, my mother's liver disease was deteriorating into the end-stage one that the traditional Chinese physicians couldn't do anything about it. There was no alternative left but to go back to see the doctor in the Western type of hospital. But it was too late, and her stomach became bloated having shown the sign of the retention of liquid. As we watched her thin day by day, it pained us excruciatingly to the extent our hearts bled. There was nothing for us to do but to behave ourselves and did what we were told.

When she was dying, she was courageous, neither having anguished looks nor whining. When she breathed her last breath, it seemed as if she were finally set free and had a look of inner peace. On the following day, we, firstly held sort of simple service for our own family, and then loaded a two-wheel working cart drawn by man with her body, and finally transported it back to our native village, Large Horse, for interment.

At the time father was tied down by his work, he couldn't go with us to our home village, but to be able to go to one of the Yellow River piers to see us off. While moving away from him, I saw him waving at us and looking away and sobbing.

When we got to Large Horse, my grandpa whose head was snow-capped now took over everything. And after the internment service, with the watching of uncle, Du Changte and two aunts on my mother's side and one aunt, the wife of my immediate uncle, Ma Jiaxing, and three of us, the casket was lowered down in the newly dug grave and buried in our pear orchard.

In the winter of 1947, my father was introduced to a woman named Zhong Shi and got remarried.

After I had studied one year at *Nanying*, the Municipal Jinan Secondary School was relocated to *Jinniushan*, or the Golden Ox Hills, a beautiful scenic spot. It is located on the outskirts of north Jinan, not far away from the Yellow River. No student was permitted to live off-campus.

The Students'dorms built on the slope of a hill face southward.

And the rows of classrooms are built at the base of the hill. As this hill stretches from east to west preventing northerly wind from hitting the dorms and the classrooms, and in winter, when we went to classes or slept in the dorms, we didn't feel bitterly cold as imagined.

There was one section of asphalt-paved road before our school entrance, and there were lofty white-trunk poplars growing on either side of the road. When the wind was arising, the big leaves were rustling, a spectacular sight indeed!

That was the first time I lived outside on my own, and I didn't have the feeling of loneliness. On the contrary, I felt there was much fun derived from it. I was learning to live a disciplined life and made a pact with myself: "When I should go to class, I never miss it; when I should play, I go to play. Every two weeks, I return home to be with my family. Always on Friday afternoon after the school is over, I go home. Next Monday morning, I'll return to school." For the duration of these days, I felt that I had got the living mode of my own.

In 1948, the Communists Army got the victory on various battlegrounds one after another, in Shandong Province: in March, they took the Zhous' Village, and the counties of Zichuan, Boshan; in April, Weixian, Anqui, Yidu, Anncheu and Changle; and in July, Yan prefecture. The next target would be the capital city of Jinan.

On the eve of the Mid-Autumn Festival, there was a huge, bright and full moon shining down through the foliage of the tree in the courtyard of our house complex. After having enjoyed pomegranates and moon cakes, we felt that there was a sort of uncanny stillness penetrating us as well as our home. However, this is just the lull before the storm. In the blowing of the cold fall wind, there was a sort of spooky atmosphere arising. All in all, we had a hunch that a battle of attacking Jinan was approaching.

Under my father's guidance, we dug a shelter in our yard and had our valuables buried in the varying corners of our house. When the battle between the Nationals Army and the Communists Army intensified, all of us hid ourselves in the shelter. When the battle slackened, we came out to get fresh air.

Overall, at night, there was fierce fighting going on, but in the daytime, the guns fell silent.

One morning, we firstly heard someone violently knock at our gate; and then followed was a loud voice shouting: "Open up! Open up!" and at last, we heard a bellow like this: "If you don't open, I will toss a hand grenade into the yard of yours!" In the circumstances, my father went to answer it. As soon as the door was opened, a "Nationalist solider" rushed in, with "a-not-knowing-what-to-do look," wielding a hand grenade and asking nervously and repeatedly: "Do you have any valuables?" and "Do you have any valuables?"

As my father was in his late 40s having had some of the worldly experience, he answered him in "a laid-back way": "No, we don't have any valuables, we don't have any valuables. All things we have had are all here, take whatever you like!" After he had made an inspection tour of all the rooms, he found nothing worthy of being taken. But at this juncture, he turned around to leave and saw a pair of the Jingang brand shoes laid behind the door. That pair is mine, and I had not worn them long, rather new so to speak. He hurriedly picked up the shoes saying: "Lend me this pair of shoes to me! Won't you?" Having finished his soliloquizing, on the one hand, he walked backward to the gate, but on the other, brandished his hand grenade. His red bloodshot eyes were staring at us all the time.

Afterwards, my father became much more cautious than ever to secure our all doors. What he had predicated was almost accurate, if not 100 percent, at least, 80 or 90 percent. He said that the Nationalists Army had showed the sign of cracking, otherwise, why were there stragglers roaming on the streets? One day, he said to us that the house-to-house fighting would be launched soon, and we could not stay at home any longer. To avoid getting trapped in the gunfire, he took us to the embankment of the Yellow River to keep us away from it.

In the middle of the night, my father lay prone on the Yellow River embankment, and gazed into the darkness at the direction of our home. The exchange of the gunfire took place as if it were right over our home, and the sound of artilleries and gunshots travelled with the wind and was heard by us intermittently. My father couldn't do anything but to think about the safety of our house. I think that one word could summarize what was on his mind, "That was he didn't like his property that he had spent his entire life having laboriously earned to be totally lost in a flash!" At dawn when they stopped shooting each other, he sneaked back home and saw what happened to it.

As the night was about to descend, my step mother sent me for my father.

Having been back and forth between the Yellow River embankment and my home several times, I didn't see the sign of the Nationalists Army's debacle, despite on the roads, there were several bodies scattered here and there. Nor did I see any triumphant Communist troops. However, I did see the new propaganda slogans posting: "Liberating the Big City of Jinan and Capturing the Commander Wang Yaowu Alive!"

On the streets, I saw people's houses stand on either side of the street with large holes on the walls. At first, I didn't understand what all these holes were for. After watching them a couple of days, I came to know that the Communists, having learned the skills of making holes from rodents, kept on making holes from one house to another all the way to the inner ring of the city wall of Jinan.

The fiercely defensive battle for Jinan began on September 16, 1948.[10] Though having outnumbered the Nationalists Army and used the overwhelming manpower called "Human wave tactics" and taken two outlying military strategic points, Yanchi and Maolin Knolls, the Nationalist troops fought the defensive battle very well, not as badly as thought of being in danger of losing this battle.[11] It was generally believed that if the defensive battle of Jinan held out a little bit longer against the fierce attacks, the Communists' strategy of "laying siege to the points (cities) and keeping the defensive forces from being reinforced" would fall apart. Because there would be a variety of reinforcements approaching by air or others, this strategy used by the Communists might be invalid. By then, neither the Nationalists nor the Communists were so sure that which side would have a certain win.

On August 19, 1948, the Commander of the 84th Division, Wu Huawen nicknamed renegade general rallied a group of "not well-trained troops" of twenty thousand men under the cloak of the Nationalists Army, waved the white flags and surrendered. Moreover, they evacuated Zhang Zhuang Airfield. Accordingly, this mutiny prevented the airlifts from reinforcing the Nationalists Army. And it caused the whole defending situation of Jinan to be a substantive change.[12]

Even though there were still several rounds of fierce engagements going on between the Nationalists' defensive and the Communists' offensive forces, the Nationalists Army's morale was gone. Consequently, the Jinan defensive battle held out only eight days, ending up with a total failure of the Nationalists' defending endeavors.

Garrison Commander, Wang Yaowu, had no strong willpower to defend the city to the last ditch, but to commit himself to the concept: "The Chinese should not fight with the Chinese." He saw the situation was not to his advantage, but he would neither surrender nor be a prisoner of war. And he was of his opinion that he could flee to Qingdao following the National Government and enjoying his generalship and emolument. Therefore, he disguised himself as a merchant, and made a narrow escape from the subterranean passage in the North Pole Temple of Daming Lake out of Jinan. Afterwards, on his way to Qingdao, in Shouguang County, he was identified as somebody in the Nationalists by one of the Communist militiamen,[13] because when he squatted in the outhouse, he was handed in toilet papers by one of his men. Overall, he, having once been ranked among the top 10 generals and cited by the National Government during the Anti-Japanese War, became the prisoner of the Chinese civil war in this way, shameful and regrettable, indeed!

CHAPTER 5

A GROUP OF FIVE ON THE ROAD
TO QINGDAO

Two days after Jinan was taken by the Communists, I stayed at home feeling extremely bored with nothing to do. Accordingly, I was like a mustang, not on leash, of course, running amok. I firstly ran to the new Jinan downtown area located on the outside of the outer ring of the city wall and saw what happened to it and then to the inner ring of the city wall where I saw bodies that were kept afloat in the Little Pure River. At last, I ran to the other side of the inner ring of city wall and saw bodies stacked up crisscross at the base.

Walking back to the new downtown area outside the outer ring of the city wall again, I saw nothing there but empty streets. In reality, what I had seen was a few of Communist militiamen dressed in peasants' garbs, with the rifles hanging upside down on their shoulders. On the one hand, they spoke to one another bursting out laughing, but on the other, seemingly, they were in a hurry heading for a place. The new posters such as the newly-issued city maps of Jinan, the new titles for roads and streets, and the newly organized administrative units, Bao (100 households) and Jia (10 households) were pasted up on the walls, and so was a fresh propaganda slogan: "The Chinese People's Liberation Army Won't Take a Needle and a Thread from the Masses!"

However, there was atmospheric pressure hanging over the city of Jinan and making people feel stifled.

One morning, I went to my school to see what happened to it. In front of the school entrance, and in the shade of the white-trunk poplars, I met a group of 10-some odd students who looked sad, and each one carried a simple piece of baggage. Asked what happened to them, I came to know that they rallied there and made themselves ready for going back to their hometowns. (Superficially, they left school on the pretext of returning home, and, in fact, wanted to go to Qingdao continuing to follow the National Government).

They were peasants' offspring. Originally, they studied at the local schools in their hometowns. After their hometowns had been taken by the Communists Army, they swarmed to Jinan, and enrolled at the school which had just moved back to the city from the "Home Front." With its original students and new arrivals from the rural area, the school was reorganized and renamed as the Provincial First Jinan Temporary Secondary School. When this school was fully filled, the 2nd, the 3rd, the 4th, and the 5th were set up. And when these newly established schools were filled full again, the new waves of arrivals, without any option, had to be placed either in the municipal schools or in the privately-funded schools temporarily. Within my knowledge, only one private secondary school named Yuying that accepted the students of this kind.

After Jinan was lost to the Communists, some students wanted to go back to their hometowns, others decided to stay put for a while waiting to see if there was any change under the rule of the Communists, and still others modeled themselves on their predecessors' doing in the Anti-Japanese War and wanted to go to the "Home Front" to be with the National Government against all the odds.

Moved by their patriotic passion, I didn't even let my father know what I would be doing, (Fearing if I let him know, he wouldn't let me go), and right in that afternoon, I went down on the road to Qingdao with them.

Having got out of Jinan, we walked on a road parallel to the eastbound rail line called Jiaoji, neither meeting with the Communists to stop us at the military checkpoints on the main road nor seeing the prisoners of war out of the Nationalists Army who looked dishevelled and dirty. What I had seen were the small groups claiming to be *laobaixing*, or the "ordinary people" who, with backpacks on their backs, heads hanging, went eastward one step after another. It seemed as if all of them were with pieces of rock in their chests, so was I. And there was one time that I had a feeling of remorse about running away from home and leaving Jinan and my family this way. And I questioned whether this sort of act was right or not!

All the way, my fellow students shared with me the food that they had carried so that I didn't get starved. When we got to the township by the name of Fangze, the militiamen stopped us, and herded us one by one into a disused and abandoned theater house. They asked us to be there patiently for just a temporary stay, waiting for further instructions.

The theater house was an extremely worn-out one facing the west. After being shut in, we felt extremely exhausted resulting from trudging on the road days and nights. Despite the squalid and damp earthen floor, we made our beds on it right away, and lay down to sleep with our clothes on. At first, there were a few of people living in there, and later when more and more people were locked in, it developed into an overcrowded situation: bed to bed they lay close-packed on the floor; the people slept next to each other.

To prevent those who had had the idea of getting away, they had all the windows and exits sealed with wooden boards except for one main exit where guards were mounted to watch. Owing to poor ventilation, the temperature was shooting high. And this theater-prison house, in turn, was getting hotter and hotter. We sat there half-naked letting the sweat pour down along the spine cord. Worst of all, there was only one rest room. After it had been excessively used, the bowls got clogged and then a tremendous amount of excrement and urine overflowed, and the offensive smell assaulted every nostril of ours.

Another thing that inflicted us was mental abuse. Since they had little knowledge of this group of refugees' backgrounds, they didn't know how to deal with us but to put us under the severest surveillance.

In the daytime, they kept us sitting still, no whispering with each other. At night, we were ordered to do the same thing. In case, we needed to go to the restroom, we had to report to the guard in advance, and if it got permitted, we might have a relief as wished.

Rumors began spreading in the theater-prison, and we heard that superiors were about to be here interrogating us, but in a minute, the rumor broke of itself. There was nothing for us to do but to idle time away. As we had stayed there long enough, we came to know their strategy—they wanted us to know there would be so many obstacles lying ahead of us that we might cancel our plan. In another word, those who changed their minds to return to Jinan would be immediately set free. However, those who insisted on going to Qingdao would have to wait.

In the days that followed, they began to single us out from other detainees. And those who were students were transferred from Fangze to the city of Wei County. And this change made an immediate difference in terms of the lodging conditions. One morning, there was an officer appearing before us. He was in yellow uniform, legging and wearing a service cap with a red star on the center. Stocky as he was, he lectured us: "After Jinan has been liberated, our liberating war is moving into the stage of winning side and the liberation army will be invincible in terms of offending. What you have stated: 'you are going home,' is true, that is fine. And if you go to Qingdao with other purposes, we are going to liberate Qingdao, to Shanghai, be sure we are going to liberate Shanghai, and to the horizon where the sky and the earth meet and every corner of the sea, we will definitely be there." In addition, he was a logician, endeavoring to elaborate the doctrines of new democracy and the theories of the dictatorship of the proletariat.

The most pitiful thing was that his lecture didn't produce good results as expected. Conversely, "the students who want to go home" became more and more in numbers! To stonewall this tide, deemed by them as "preventing students from going astray," they worked hard to arrange a series of recreational activities including taking us to tour a secondary school named Changwei, a university, Huadong, and had the volleyball team of ours set up to play against the counterparts.

In the city of Wei County, everything went well including board and lodging. What mostly troubled us was a reality that we were not allowed to leave. But "finding a way out of a predicament" is always possible. At this juncture, in a trance, I sneaked in an office without any man seen inside. That was a simplest office that I had ever seen. Besides an enamel basin and wooden tripod, there was only a desk and a chair. Having seen the drawer of the desk was locked, I took up a safety pin and put into the hole of the lock, poking and turning this way and that way. A miracle exploded right before my nose, and the lock clicked open instantly. I yanked the drawer out of its runners, and it scared me a lot because lying in there were stacks of green-colored yuan! And from my gut reaction, I snatched a handful of them and intended to run away. But just at that time, I cast my nervy eye downwards and caught the sight of a stack of travel papers, blank but officially stamped, beneath the money. Weren't they that I had dreamed of? I immediately returned the yuan back to its original spot and pulled out a sheet of the travel paper and fled. On the one hand, I was running, and on the other, I thought to myself that if I had been caught redhanded, I would be either beaten to death or placed behind prison bars.

In fact, what I had made away with was not one blank form of the travel paper but five of them on one sheet of paper, with a consecutive serial number on each one of them. These blank forms are dividable from the top to the bottom by dotted lines. Along the lines, one can tear them apart, and they can be filled out for five documents. I originally attempted to find four of my fellow students from the Municipal Jinan Secondary School to flee to Qingdao. Ever since we moved to Wei County, I didn't know where they were.

I stayed in a small alley being in the cold sweat and feeling my heart was revving up, "Boom! Boom!" I thought to myself what would be my next move! While puzzled, I saw four senior students out there on the main street walking to the opposite side of the street where a hot pot restaurant was located. I rushed out, pulled them into that alleyway, and sought their advice. Among them, besides Gao Weixu who studied at Shandong Agriculture College, the rest were all senior students from the Provincial Jinan Senior High. They are: Qi Fengjin of Laiwu County, Zheng Zunzhe of Changqing County, and Gao Dunchong of Rizhao County. When they saw me holding the blank travel papers, they were petrified. Initially they were dubious, and then their eyes sparkled with joy, and finally considered that this was the hardest-found opportunity to leave the detention center. Consequently, we set up a rendezvous with one another. And on the late afternoon of that day, we, five of us, fled Wei County.

Three decades later when Qi Fengjin, Zheng Zunche and I met with one another in the southern part of Taiwan, and recalled the old detainees' days in Wei County, we couldn't help heaving long and deep sighs, and wondered where did our guts come from to flee that county? As far as I know, Gao Weixu went to Sichuan Province when we were on our way south. The other two, Qi Fengjin and Zheng Zunche were admitted to Navy Corporal Academy through entrance exams at Hangzhou, the capital of Zhejiang Province, and with that academy, they retreated to Taiwan. Later, they, again, went through the screening process and this time, enabled themselves to get in Navy Academy. At last, they were graduated, having contributed what they could to the country for some years, and quit the navy. At present, the former has emigrated to the U.S. and is living in Los Angeles; the latter has thrown himself into the world of education at Kaohsiung County and resides in a township named Gangshan. As to the third one, Gao Dunchong, he and I have never had a chance to meet each other in Taiwan. All I know is that he also teaches kids in a school, somewhere in north Taiwan.

We, five of us, got out of Wei County at sunset. Going eastward, we tried to take paths instead of roads. To Qingdao, we ran at breakneck speed! At times, we slept in the daytime when we were exhausted; at other times, we kept on going on the path at night, and once in a while, we didn't care about what time it was, evening or morning, but to keep moving. While running on the path, we had reached a consensus on that if we were stopped and questioned by the Communists again, we would reply in unison: "Our homes are in Qingdao. And all of us have the travel papers because we have special missions to do in that city!"

When we got to a special zone, geographically called Jiao-Lai Trench, we suddenly became terribly nervous for this was the buffer zone between the Nationalists and the Communists, namely, neither side having the jurisdiction over it. In between, we saw neither villages nor any crops growing. All we had seen was the gravel land beneath our feet. Cradled in the trench was one low-lying tract of land in the middle by two heights sandwiching it. Once entering the lowest spot, we looked like as if having entered a jute sack. If any side, Communists or Nationalists, had come to get us, we would have had nothing to do but "to be at bay by sitting there to be arrested or killed!"

That the most terrible thing could happen to us was that if we were mistaken for the Communists to do some activities down there by the Nationalists, without doubt, they would blow our heads off. And the other way around, if we were mistaken for the Nationalists by the Communists, we would get shot, too. Given that any one of these two cases occurs, all our efforts made to go to Qingdao will become bubbles.

Thanks to the fact by then, we were young, especially, having good legs and feet. Sometimes, we walked at full speed and at other times, we went slow, and finally, we struck out at a bouncing trot. Within two hours, we entered the area controlled by the Nationalists.

As we looked back to the road we had travelled, we were in danger of being caught several times. However, with the blessing of God, all the fearful dangers became nothing.

As we got to the Nanquan Railway Station, the sun passed the meridian line. With the nodded approval of the station master, we hopped on a car of a freight train with no tarpaulin awning. We didn't go mad with joy nor did we feel so sad. And all we felt was that our hearts were still pounding quickly. But as the train was being drawn closer and closer to the city of Qingdao, and when we saw the national flag "with the colors of Blue Sky, White Sun and the Wholly Red Earth" flying, tears welled up in our eyes.

CHAPTER 6

SELLING SHOES IN QINGDAO

Among the five escapees of us, with exception of me, all of the others had some connections to turn to seeking helps either from relatives or friends in Qingdao. When we got out of the Qingdao Railway Station, and after bidding farewell to one another, I didn't know where I was heading. I had only two 10-yuan banknotes, the newly-issued currency called *Jinyuanjuan*, Gold Yuan Certificates with me, but one of them was borrowed from Zheng Zunche. And I got it estimated that this sum of money I had would only be enough for food for one week. As the sage-teacher said: "Man is able to live with what he has got." However, based on this kind of financial difficulty, how did this saying inspire me? But thinking the other way around and thanks to these two 10-yuan banknotes, and if I didn't have had them, I would try to survive. Wasn't that true or not?

I was walking around before the Qingdao Railway Station, not aware of the fact that it was getting dark. Though I was hungry, my stomach growling, I thought to myself that getting a "foothold" somewhere was the priority. Therefore, I walked to a road called Huantai which was only a stone's throw away from the station. And I was wondering if there was sort of hotel that fit in with my status, "a little refugee." At last, I went up to a hotel that bore the same title of the road, Huantai. Hanging around the hotel for some time, I watched what kind of people come out and go in, and couldn't dare to step into it bluntly. Fatigue and anxiety attacks sent me reeling. And as my legs were about to give way, I immediately realized that if I kept going like this, I would collapse and die instantly right there.

In a trance, I walked into that hotel and said to the hotel manager who was kindly-looking, "I am a student and made an escape from the city of Jinan, and I'd like to check in this hotel!" He gave me a sweeping gaze from my head to my toe and then asked me just one question: "Don't you have any baggage?" Not waiting for my answer, he led me through a flight of narrow stairs up to the second floor where there were *datongpu,* or platform beds, on either side of the aisle. And right on that floor, he pointed to the spot on the right-hand side platform saying: "You may sleep here!" In the meantime, he grabbed a piece of woolen blanket, and tossed it to me.

After settling in that hotel and resting a while, I decided to take a walk on the street seeing if there was any inexpensive food available for me to buy so that I could satisfy my stomach.

Out of the hotel, I walked southward on Huantai Rd. And I didn't dare to make any turn into the side-road. If I did, I was afraid of getting lost. I was strolling down, and involuntarily, I got to a night market.

As the night set in, all the lights were on. And it was also the dinner time. There were lots of people coming and going in the night market. Some of them went into the restaurants in small groups; others seated themselves around a variety of food stands enjoying their dinners.

As I walked in the crowd, I held on those two 10-yuan banknotes with one of my hands in one of my trouser pockets thinking about what was the cheaper food I could afford so that this limited amount of money could hold out longer? If I only ordered baked sweet potatoes or steamed buns, the money I had could support me about eight or nine days. But if steamed dumplings or Shanghai soup dumplings were ordered, I would certainly run out of this amount of money in five days.

At last, I sat at a food stand with a gaslamp on, the gas stove burning blazingly. And sitting on one of the stove burners was a big copper kettle from whose spout, a plume of steam escaped with whizzing sound. And the steam from the mouth in the darkness got very high as if "having reached the Aquila (Constellation)." After thinking for a while, I finally ordered two steamed buns and a bowl of watery stuff, its ingredients consisting of flour and tea.

Back to the hotel, there was no one on that huge bed but me. As I lay there, and though feeling extremely tired physically, I found that it was very hard to fall asleep.

The images of my father, step mother, Zhonglan and Zhongxin, like the waves of the sea, were crashing on me again. Thinking of a situation that they were anxiously combing the streets to find me in Jinan, I couldn't help weeping with tears coursing down my cheeks. Later, I tried to think the opposite. If a boy didn't get out to see the world, then "what kind of man he will be?" In addition, it was my belief that sooner or later the City Government of Qingdao or the Red Cross in Qingdao would come out to provide relief to the students who fled the city of Jinan. Once thinking this way, I was in high spirits. And shortly after, I fell asleep.

However, the reality betrayed the wish. The City Government of Qingdao didn't take our problems into account at all, nor did the Red Cross give a hand in time.

One day, as I used up those two 10-yuan banknotes, and there was absolutely no way out. Being so hungry, I resorted to a strategy called "sleep" to deal with this misery. However, with gnawing hunger inside, how could I fall asleep? Lying there wide awake, I had nothing to do but to sob under the blanket.

At the time the hotel had become crowded. Originally, there was only me who slept on that sort of bed, but owing to the deteriorating development in the battlegrounds on the Nationalists' side in the northeast of the country, the hotel was filled with "people from all walks of life" who had been retreated to Qingdao. While staying here, during the daytime, some of them went out to explore the possibility of locating jobs to survive at Qingdao, others were on missions for their units that were still on their way to Qingdao. Only at night, did they return for staying overnight.

Among them, there are two persons special to me: one is a captain from Hunan Province whose family name is composed of two Chinese characters, Ou Yang, and as to his given name I can't remember. With his bushy eyebrows, round eyes and resounding voice, he is quite open-minded and extremely outspoken when he is commenting on the civil war; the other, a woman, who has a curvy figure with slender waist and long legs, appears quite charming. During the nighttime, she saw the captain climbing up the stairs, she was thrusting her fair-colored legs out of her woolen blanket to pose sexy. But when she saw me running up, she was hurriedly pulling her legs in and having her head moved under the blanket to feign sleep. Ou Yang slept to my right; she slept to my left but to be several yards away at the corner of the bed. Sometimes, up to the middle of the night when everybody was in sound sleep, the captain crawled around my feet quietly from my right to my left to her and had that "thing" done. Afterwards, he got right back to where he had been. When this sort of thing kept on going long enough, there was a "rumor" spreading through the hotel that she was a whore with no underwear on, wide open, operating her business with no "prime cost" at all.

On the night of that day, the captain came back to the hotel, and when he found out that I was sobbing under the blanket, he had it rolled back from my head and asked what happened to me. After getting the whole picture of it, he couldn't help shouting loudly, "Ah! Ah! my little brother, why didn't you tell me earlier that you hadn't eaten anything yet? Get up! Get up! And come along with me, and we go out to get dinner together!" He also invited that woman, and together, we, three, walked out of the hotel. After we seated ourselves in an eatery, aside from *yangchun mian*, or noddles with a few pieces of veggies and ground pork, and a platter of double cooked pork belly with Chinese master stock, he ordered the small bowls of the Qingdao noodles made of lotus-root for each one of us.

While enjoying our dinner, the captain talked a little bit about himself. He said he had been a quartermaster in one of the units in the

Nationalists Army and stationed in the northeast. After the collapse of his unit, he made an escape firstly to Qinghuangdao and then to Qingdao. He further noted that if the military debacle of the Nationalists Army couldn't be stopped, he would return to his native village in Hunan Province to work on the farm. His talk was suggestive of pessimism regarding the ongoing civil war. In contrast to the captain, this "weak woman" was quite reserved, revealing much less than the captain, and throughout the entire dinner, she only said that she had lost her husband en route while retreating. Perhaps, with me, "no longer a boy but not yet an established adult," between them, she didn't make any pass to the captain. And using her chopsticks to try dishes, pick up the noodles, and spooning up her soup, she did conform to the table manners.

Anyway, after this dinner, the relationship between us became closer than ever. Being *tong shi tian ya lun lo ren*, or we are in the same situation as if those who are in exile.

Back to our huge bed, the captain used the fingers of one of his hands to scratch his head continuously. On the one hand, he kept on scratching, on the other, he said to me: "We have to find a way to get your problem solved! We must find a way to get your problem solved!" Suddenly, I saw him blinking his eyes, and then he said, "I've got an idea: why don't you go to sell shoes?"

During the times of turmoil and chaos of the civil war, anything so ridiculous could happen. As it was customary, *quiba,* or the servicemen and *quijiu,* or the refugees, especially, the homeless students, could take the train without paying any fare.

His thought-through idea was that he would loan me a 10-yuan banknote (Gold Yuan Certificate) to purchase the Wuhe brand shoes made of plastic, and then let me go by train to Lancun, not far away from Qingdao, and sell them there. These shoes were priced at 2 yuan per pair when I bought them in, 5 pairs totalling up to 10 yuan. When I sold them out there, each pair was priced at 2.50 yuan, and if all 5 pairs were sold out, I would get 12.50 yuan. The net profit would be 2.50 yuan. And this income would be the everyday money used for my three meals. Namely, I used the 10 yuan loaned as my principal, and the income made by selling shoes was used to defray the "daily expenses." The first day's business was very important. If it worked, for the rest of days, I wouldn't worry about the money for food.

He gave me a large-sized military towel and taught me how to carry the shoes. He also instructed me how a "territory" in the fair was chosen, how the shoes were displayed on the ground, and how a bargain was stricken with a customer.

I consider him the godsend from Heaven.

On the following morning, I went to the hypermarket to get the shoes, and not until the third day, did I get up earlier in the morning and headed straight for Lancun.

Sitting on the train, I felt that my thoughts were racing. And I was of my opinion that I ran away from home for doing something great, and now looked at what a business I got into, selling shoes as a shoe peddler. Once I thought of this, I couldn't help sobbing with tears rolling down my cheeks again. But as I thought the other way around, I calmed down. It was that even though I was stuck in the difficulty of this mess, I didn't die of starvation. And I should deem myself as one of the luckiest guys in the world.

I found the Lancun fair very quickly. In the hottest spot thronged with people, coming and going, I managed to take "a territory" under my control. I firstly spread my towel on the ground, and then had the 5-pair shoes arranged side by side, tidy and neat on the towel! And finally, I stood straight and coughed several times in the hope that the cough sounds might attract people's attention, and they might be aware of the fact there was a teenager like me who was waiting for the customers to come up to buy.

Unexpectedly, sooner than I expected, there were buyers coming to inquire the prices of the shoes. I initially planned to hike the price to 3 yuan per pair or at least held the originally-fixed price at 2.50 yuan per pair, but when an idea struck me—having them sold out at the earliest time as possible, I changed my mind. And I would like to make a deal with a guy when he bargained down the price. If there was anyone bidding 2.30 yuan per pair, I would hurriedly nod my head to have a deal with him. In the twinkling of an eye, I got all my shoes sold out.

That is the first time of making money in my life. I was more than happy with that kind of experience.

My shoes selling business held out no more than five days. In Qingdao, suddenly, there was a charity event held by Red Cross in a big temple for students. They were doling out congee. Up to now, my shoes selling job came to an end. When I returned the money borrowed from the captain, he declined firmly, and wanted me to keep it with the view that I might need it on my way southward in the future. He said that no one knew what would happen next!

At the time I left Qingdao, the number of the students from Jinan had got to a rather big one. Every morning, all of us went to that big temple together and queued up there getting "watery rice." After consuming our rations, we took to the street loitering and furthermore, ascertained if there were any other possibilities for getting some relief aids from other organizations. I followed some of the senior students once to get a sack of flour given out by the Salvation Army of the United Nations in Qingdao. Because I didn't cook by myself, I sent it to the manager of the hotel as a token payment.

CHAPTER 7

SHANGHAI! SHANGHAI!

With the situation of Nationalists Armys' side was deteriorating, the number of students who came to Qingdao was increasing rapidly. How to provide them with board and lodging became a problem. As the city authorities had seen such a worsening condition develop, they had to adopt emergency measure to deal with it. After several bouts of negotiations with China Merchants Holdings (International) Company Ltd., it came up with a solution finally. That is to transport this group of students to Shanghai. But an agreement has to be signed in advance. Since it was a passenger ship, and under no circumstances, were the students permitted to stay in the cabin once they went on board. However, given that the students managed not to block up the passages, they had the freedom of making makeshift beds as wished. When we heard this news, we were overjoyed at what had been done. This passenger ship named Jingxing is the luxurious one. As we were the students from the interior of Shandong Province, naturally, we didn't have any idea of what a vast sea looked like, let alone the experience of voyage. Now, we could take a ship like Jingxing, which would sail against the wind on the sea with waves trailing behind, and especially with the vision of the destination—cosmopolitan Shanghai, how couldn't we be excited?

The exact number of this group of students, who has fled Jinan and gone aboard the ship of Jingxing, was unknown to anybody. But based on my memory, at least, there were 200-some odd students. After getting on the ship, we packed the passages, forgetting "that agreement" that had been signed before. After putting belongings in any places possibly found, and in small groups, we went to the bow or to the stern of the ship to shoot the breeze.

Standing on the forward part of the ship, we watched the seagulls flying nearby and hovering high with their wings outstretched. Sometimes, they flew low slowly passing the bow of the ship, diving into the sea and staying afloat on the surface of the sea.

Turning our eyes to the horizon far away where the sea and the sky met, we saw nothing there, but unlimited imagination got us everywhere.

As I walked to the aft part of the ship, I saw Qingdao City just opposite me. The three-week stay made me fall in love with it because it was such an extremely clean city.

By then, Jiaozhow Bay Harbor was the *haikou*, or the sea gate controlling all the waterways from Shandong Province, an important harbor indeed. Now, I was taking my leave of Jiaozhou Bay Harbor as if I had bid farewell to Shandong, and by the same token, I felt that going away from Shandong was something equivalent to saying "Goodbye" to my hometown." How couldn't I feel sad?

Recalling the details of that voyage on that luxurious ship to Shanghai at the present moment, I, even though racking my brains, can only get a vague picture of them as if having appreciated flowers in the heavily foggy weather. However, there are two things that have never been misremembered. They are still there as if they had happened to me yesterday.

The first thing is the rice on that ship. Whenever the lunch or dinner was served, we saw two crewmen carry two big wooden containers of steaming rice, and place them on either side of the deck. And then all of us queued up and moved forward orderly to have our bowls filled. As well known, we are all brought up in the north and fed on steamed buns, noodles and dumplings made of flour, rice becoming a rare food for us. Not until the Chinese New Year Day, did we get a bowl of rice. On the ship, we were provided with the kind of rice cooked just right without getting gluey. Not only it was good smell, but it tasted quite delicious, able to satisfy our taste buds. To compare with the kind of "watery rice" served in the temple in Qingdao, there was a big difference between them, or not in the same breath.

The second thing I can remember is that when there were no waves arising, we could engage in chats, laughing a lot together. But when the wind designation was getting up to the level of gale, and the sea became rough, all of us began to feel seasick. Though feeling dizzy and extremely tired, we found it was hard for us to fall asleep.

When we got to Shanghai, we moved into Shandong Association Hall affiliated to the Provincial Government of Shandong. In the daytime, we were on the streets loitering; at night, we came back just for sleeping. The way of sleeping is nothing else but to lie on the concrete with sheets or old newspapers spread out beneath, and we sleep with our clothes on.

We were dazzled by the changing of the traffic signals in Cosmopolitan Shanghai. And we felt curious about trolley buses which were running back and forth, super fast. Like street boys, we, in groups, had nothing to do, but to walk back and forth unpurposely on the streets every day. Another frequently haunted place is the Huangpu River, and standing on its bank, we took a long look at those high-rises telling the differences from one to another.

Another way of having fun is to see the incense-burning in the Temple of City God. Following numerous male and female Buddhists' doings, we, having put our hands together, palm against palm, bowed to this local deity in the hope that this divine figure might not only protect the residents if the Communists came to attack Shanghai, but to keep us safe, no matter where this group of homeless students from the north would wander to in the future.

I also involuntarily followed some of the senior students to Grand Gold Theater to watch Peking opera. The opera entitled, *Yuzhoufeng,* was about a love story featuring the then-noted actress, Yan Huizhu.

At that time, I was just a mid-teenager, loving to watch Gong Fu show, in which warriors would engage in fighting with one another by using swords or lances, killing or being killed. As for the kind of the show acted by a "virtuous woman," I was a down-to-earth layman. And even concentrating on listening to the long-drawn tone for a long time, I was unable to grasp what she was singing even if I strained my ears. What she impressed me the most was that she looked great in colorful costumes and danced gracefully with some of the long, long, and long sleeve-throwing touches.

The Dancing Hall of *Bailemen*, or the Gate of 100 Pleasures is a very famous one throughout the country. Since we were in the city now, we didn't want to miss it. Thus, with several fellow students, we got there. Even though our life was not easy then, yet we had to find joy in hardship.

We saw Ms. Zhou Xuan's and Ms. Bai Guang's framed portraits hang on the wall, but what we had really got was not the songs sung by either of them: Ms. Zhou's singing is clear melodious; Ms. Bai's alto, soul-stirring and titillating. What we had got that day were the songs by minors. And though their singing skills were much and much inferior to those two, yet they were young, good-looking and charming.

We stayed in Shanghai about five days, and then, had to go to report to the Jinan First United Secondary School located in a small town, Changanzhen, in Haining County in Zhejiang Province.

CHAPTER 8

STUDENTS' PROTEST
AT CHANGANZHEN

Changanzhen, based on its size, is a typical of a small town, south of the Yangtze River. When we got to it, it was winter. Trees were stripped naked and lined on the either side of its sole street, and in the rice paddies, water was drained to the extent that only the dried clods presented. And all nature looked bleak; a scene of desolation met the eye on every side.

The Jinan First United Secondary School was established in two disused silk factories. The junior high program was in Changan Silk Factory; the senior high program, in Lianyuan.

Originally, I had finished the second year's and the first two weeks' studies in the third year of the junior high program at the Municipal Jinan Secondary School. But having gone through the battle of Jinan and due to the squandering of the days on the road south, I came to know that it was almost an entire semester gone. When it was the time for me to report to the school in Changanzhen, I seemed reluctant to accept the reality that one semester had been wasted this way. Therefore, as I registered with the Registrar Office of the school, I simply filled out the form based on the self-acknowledged level as the first-year student of a senior high program. In fact, during the civil war era, and the whole country was in chaos, was there any system to follow? One could fill in any grade in the form as wished. And any grade or year you wrote into the form would be approved.

After going through the registration procedure, I was assigned to Unit 9 (similar to the organization in the army).

Included in the same unit with me are the classmates whose names still kept in my mind are: Liang Eryu, Ma Nianyue, Liu Tailai, Liu Canyu, Wang Enjin, Chen Shihrui, Ding Lizhun, Mao Xuiqing, Zhu Lianye, Ding Weijie, Cao Aiyun, Guo Gang and Luan Qin. The last two classmates later assumed important posts either in the Ministry of Foreign Affairs or in the air force in Taiwan: the former took up posts as director, deputy minister and ambassadors, stationed in Colombia, Ecuador, and Dominican Republic; the latter, president of the R. O. C. Air Force Academy and deputy commander-in-chief of the Combined Logistics Command affiliated to the Ministry of Defense.

Nominally, the First Jinan United Secondary School is a sort of school. But in fact, its education facilities and equipment were dependent upon whatever was available. If we call it "refugees' camp," it may be more appropriate. Dorms were also used as classrooms. And at night, we spread our blankets or quilts out on the floor and slept on them; in the daytime, we just rolled up them on which we sat as study chairs during the class time.

The deepest impression left on me is my English class because my English teacher is the youngest one on the teaching staff. Though I forget his name now, his advice about how to learn English is still remembered. He said: "The secrets of English-learning lie in reading out loud, one paragraph after another. If one can read one paragraph fluently, one can move on to the next. Lessons should be done in the same way, one lesson after another. As time goes by, you'll find your pronunciation has been naturally improved." Furthermore, he noted: "Our school is surrounded by the rice paddies, and that perfectly fits in with the environment conducive to the practice of reading English aloud. And even though you read out in the loudest voice, you will not bother anybody else."

There is an interesting episode derived from doing that stuff.

One of our classmates was a veteran, who, having joined the Nationalist Youth Army, and in one of the battles against the Japanese, got hit by a flying metal splinter of a shrapnel blast. Aside from that he was suffering not only the physical injury but also the psychological stress. And the most heart-rending stuff was that he was hit mute. When we communicated with him, we had to use the body language most of the time.

He stuck to our English teacher's advice. In order to put it into practice, he got up very early every morning getting onto the causeway of a rice field to read English aloud, "Ah! Ah!" repeatedly. One day, a miracle exploded, and he got his voice back and could speak. He said: "One of the possibilities is that there is a tiny piece of metal splinter stuck in his vocal cord which dropped off due to the vibration that he had made while reading English out aloud." This was the way for him to unintentionally recover his voice he had lost many years. The news made the whole unit feel more than happy for him.

Another story spread through our unit was that one of our classmates, who being averse to the learning environment of ours, too noisy to study in our dorm, often went to a local temple by himself studying there. When he was about to leave, he usually scraped some burned wax residue from the base of candle holders into a bowl and brought it back for another bout of studying in the deep of night. Unfortunately, he was being seen by a native girl when he was doing the scraping. And the girl accused him of stealing the property of the temple saying that "I will suit you." However, no one expected that this kind of "country lore" about "a rich girl" and "a penniless boy" would develop into a love story. More than a decade later when I was admitted to the Base Hospital 52 in Taoyuan County in Taiwan, and in order to kill time, I wrote a short story entitled "The Candle Karmic Relationship" based on this episode and got it published in the *Wild Wind Literary Magazine* edited by Tian Shi.

During those days, we were at that sort of school at Changanzhen. As to the food, rice was firstly rationed to per head at 18 taels (675.18 grams) daily. And later, as the school authorities found that the ration couldn't satisfy our hunger, they, this time, increased the ration to 24 taels (900.24 grams). And the fee for the vegetable, meat and others was set at only three yuan per day, per head.[14] Although both the principal staple food and the fee for the greens and meats at the Jinan First United Secondary School were much better than any other schools of this kind, yet we were at the age of puberty. And after taking our meal for less than half an hour, we became hungry again. Therefore, I often went to the fields after being harvested in fall looking for something left there and gleaning the residues of Chinese radishes and carrots to be cooked as snacks.

I had no cooking experience. After getting the fire started on a makeshift hearth which is made of a few pieces of stones and broken tiles, I even didn't pay any attention to which direction the wind was blowing. At a time, I hunkered down there, on the one hand, cooking, on the other, scooping out some bits of the stuff to enjoy. And in the meantime, I was wondering why between my legs, there was something warm. When lowering my head to take a look at what was happening, supprisingly, I discovered my padded pants were on fire, and that made me get in the consternation of jumping to my feet and putting the tongues of flames out with both of my hands.

Because of the wet weather, south of the Yangtze River, I suffered from skin disease, scabies. There were pimple-like rashes beginning firstly developing on my inner thighs. Later, they became bumps with pus sealed in. After getting lanced, the yellowish-white pus was discharged firstly, and then, it was bleeding. When aired out, they became scabs. They felt firstly itchy and then burning. And I had never felt extremely bad like this before.

The civil war was raging and the living condition was deteriorating at Changanzhen. Thanks to our principal, Liu Zemin. With him in charge, we were at ease.

Liu is a native of Hoze County, Shandong Province. He is graduated from the Department of History at Furen Catholic University in Beijing. Throughout his life, he likes to play basketball. During his undergraduate years, he was one of the best players selected into the Beijing University Basketball Alliance Team organized by Beijing University Basketball Association. And this basketball team was sent to compete against different university teams across the country. Later, it was sent to Japan, Hong Kong, Thailand, and Vietnam to play against its counterparts on their home courts.[15]

In 1937, he graduated from the university, and there was the Marco Polo Bridge Incident taking place. He returned to his hometown helping organize the peasants to defend it against possible Japanese attacks. In the meantime, as the bandits ran rampant and with sorghum plants as tall as men in the farmland, he was entrusted with rendering a big cash escort service. After Jinan was taken by the Japanese Army, the Provincial Government disintegrated. The newly appointed governor of Shandong Province, Shen Hunglie, escaped to Cao County to assume office in exile and held Liu responsible for taking care of two official seals, namely, the seals of the Provincial Government and the Province Security Forces Headquarters. In addition, he was also charged with the cash money of 50,000 yuan and a telegram set with a copy of code book. Afterwards, he went through from the terrible ordeal of bombardment at Donglidian, the bloodbath on the hillyland area in southern Shandong to the imprisonment in a place named Zuantiangu. The event mostly extolled by people was that he was once kidnapped by the bandits and threatened at the gunpoint to dig a pit with a long-handled shovel for burying himself alive. While facing with such an extremely dangerous crisis, he managed to calm himself down and took advantage of their negligence and used the shovel to break their craniums one by one.[16]

In the year of 1943, Liu was transferred from the job in the Provincial Government to the field of education. He was firstly teaching PE classes and then history at the National Secondary School No 22. And later, he assumed a new post as director of discipline at No 21. Finally, he became a pick to lead the Jinan First Temporary Secondary

School after winning the victory over Japan.[17] His life was marked with vicissitudes. And consequently, he accumulated a lot of experience in running school, especially, the school set for those students who were homeless and in exile.

As winter was approaching, students still wore summer clothes shivering in the freezing wind. With such gloomy views before his nose, he felt sad in his heart and mind. Therefore, he ran to wherever it might be, getting help. Despite his utmost efforts, he could only collect 80 percent of winter clothes. The rest, 20 percent short, remained unresolved.

The Commander-in-chief of the Shanghai-Nanjing Garrison Headquarters, Tang Enbo, was stationed in Shanghai. He went there to get an audience with him seeking help. Unexpectedly, Commander Tang, consented without one minute's hesitancy that he would like to make the shortage of 20 percent up. And in addition, 4,000 pieces of mosquito nets were donated.[18] With the date to be fixed for dispensing them to students, a demonstration suddenly broke out and screwed up the whole thing.

At the time there was an eerie atmosphere spreading through the campus, and a kind of rumor was going around that our principal was accused of grafting. They said that the principal not only included the "ghost" students but allowed *chikongque* or conducted massive payroll padding. Furthermore, that he took advantage of keeping the padded clothes in the warehouse was a stratagem. By doing so, he could restrict the students' accusations. Otherwise, why didn't he distribute the padded clothes to us, now when they were all here? Was there any justification for the act of his that the winter clothes would rather be stored in the warehouse than be dealt out to the students and let them freeze in such a chilly weather?

This bunch of protesting students was rarely seen on the campus. And we didn't know where they came from, let alone their backgrounds. Our gut feeling was that they were older than ordinary students, their language, cutting; they were characterized in the character of being presumptuous and daring.

One evening when I was coming back from that one-street town after taking a walk there, I saw a military training instructor who was being marched by a group of students on the road from the Changan campus to the administration building located on the Lianyuan campus. They adopted the stop-and-go method. While walking, they gave him loud shouts. While stopping, they condemned him for his wrongdoings, surrounding the officer and seizing him by the collar. And I saw a tall guy suddenly slap him and get his service cap down to the ground. Once violence began by a starter, all the rest students tried to throw him to the ground, and he was pinned down there. When he got out of "the mob," I saw his face full of blood.

They finally got to the principal's office. Because that day, the principal was out of the town and led the school basketball team to Xieshizhen, a township, for a basketball match, they were unable to see him and had no one to argue with. The only vent for releasing their resentment was to chant slogans and stomped their feet on the floor rhythmically. Up to the middle of the night, their spirits rose to the highest point that "Hit them and kill them" was in the air. They began not only striking bystanders but also turning the desks and chairs upside down, and furthermore, smashing the doors and windows. In a moment, the principal's office was left in a heck of mess.

The "students" in charge of this protest found it hard to swallow the anger and led the group to tear open the door of the warehouse, pulling out bundles and bundles of the padded clothes to be given out, saying that anyone who was on the scene would get a suit. This news spread as fast as the wind, and in a wink of the eye, the Lianyuan campus was swarming with "ten thousand" of bobbing heads. And everyone was struggling to get a padded jacket and a pair of padded trousers.

The students' protest came as quickly as it went away. Within a very short span of time, the campus was restored to its normacy.

However, we didn't resume classes. As we had nothing to do, we chatted in small groups. Or we stood against the wall outside the school to watch the southbound or northbound trains passing. And some students strolled on the street of Changanzhen; others went to tour *Xihu*, or West Lake, in Hangzou, the capital city of Zhejiang Province.

In a week or so, there was word spreading through the campus that the principal would launch a campaign with a large group of students acted as a kind of protective force to return to school. And another sort of rumor was that each member of them would carry a stick claiming that they returned to school with "firearms." Added to these rumors was that once the principal got this operation successfully done, he would severely punish those troublemakers. Simultaneously, the students and teachers who remained staunch to the principal in the school didn't keep quiet any longer having organized an "army" to welcome the principal back. They served as a sort of "inner circle" coordinating with the principal's campaign under the leadership of some teachers.

Mr. Liu and his security force staged an easy come-back without resorting to much effort.

Though he didn't rally students before him to give a talk, the students immediately gathered around him on the Lianyuan campus in the hope that he would say something about this incident. He is a man of integrity speaking his mind. Firstly, he rebutted the rumor that he "had padded" the payroll. Even to this day, more than six decades later, I can still recall his resounding voice:

"Our school has 2,463 students. If one short, you can chop my head off!"

Closely followed was his clarification why he put the clothes on hold.

He asked a series of questions: "Who is not willing to see his students put on the padded clothes as soon as possible? But with 20 percent short of those padded clothes, how could I give them out? If insisting on distributing them to you, who has got the priority? If ignoring the consequences, those who have got them are happy certainly. How about those who have not? And they would nurse grievances against me. If they come up to me to protest, I'll become speechless to them."

"All of you have been with me since our hometown was taken by the Communists. Do I have any ground to prefer this student to that one in terms of distributing clothes? Haven't I filled the gap of the shortage yet? There was nothing seriously wrong there, but to delay a couple of days. Look at what they have done now? What a mess has been made? How can I clean it up?"

Further, the principal in his speech indicated that he would mete out severe punishments to the leaders and forgive those who were just ignorant followers.

That the civil war situation on the Nationalists' side was deteriorating so rapidly got everyone befuddled, and in another word, there was no way to predict what would happen next moment. After winning the Hsupen Campaign (referring to the Hueihai Campaign in the term used by the Reds), the Communists' invincible forces moved south fast like the lightning speed. The days for crossing the formidable barrier, the Yangtze River, were numbered.

The Jinan First United Secondary School was put under duress.

One afternoon, all of us were summoned to the Lienyuan campus for a pep talk. The speaker was our Chinese teacher, Hu Bitao. The contents of that talk I can't recall now, but after his talk, the look of his as to reciting a piece of poem entitled: "Marching Out to the Frontier" by Wang Changling is still vividly kept in my mind:

> *The moon of Qin shines yet over the passes of Han;*
> *Our men have not returned from the distant frontier.*
> *If the Winged General of Dragon City were there,*
> *No Hu horses could cross the Mt. Yen.*[19]

Where were those "winged generals" in the Nationalists Army under the National Government? They are graduates from Whampoa Military Academy. And the number is too big to count like *guo jiang zhi ji*, or a large school of the carp fish teems in the Yangtze River trying to swim across. These generals either became turncoats or captives one by one while fighting the Communists Army. To die a patriotic death in the campaign became a rare thing. As the rumor was in the air that our school would move south to Guangzhou, I made a good use of this opportunity to head for the Maintenance Department of the Longyou Railway Station to see my immediate uncle.

CHAPTER 9

THE TRIP TO LONGYOU

My grandfather, Ma Chuanxu, and my grandmother, Zhu Shi, raised two sons and three daughters throughout their entire life: my father, Ma Jiafan, uncle, Ma Jiahxing, and three aunts. These three aunts left some impressions on me, but as to their names, I don't remember any one of them.

When my father worked at the Maintenance Department of the Huangqibo Railway Station, though my immediate uncle, Ma Jiahxing, often paid visits to us, yet at that time, I was very small. What he looked like left nothing on me at all.

When I grew older, he had left Shandong Province and worked somewhere, south of the Yangtze River.

Because I lived in Large Horse Village for some years during my childhood, I still have some memories of these three aunts.

My first aunt is ladylike born of a good family. She is great at doing housework, often seen giving orders to the juniors of the family to do this or that. She could be compared to *pigjisichen*, or a hen crowing in the morning in place of a rooster. Her way of giving orders to do the household chores was seldom seen during that patriarchal era.

My second aunt is a traditional Chinese woman. She shuts herself in her chamber every day, seldom going beyond the threshold, not to mention going out of the gate.

That my third aunt is etched on my memory is the most impressive one. Because when she was being married, I, a small boy, was assigned a task sitting on an ox-drawn cart and among her her dowries to be a "cart boy." Unluckily, less than a year after her wedding, she contracted child fever and died while giving birth. She left a baby girl behind.

This uncle I was going to visit had been married during the years when he stayed in Large Horse Village, and his wife bore him two daughters: the older one is named Qin, the younger one, Qing. Perhaps, he felt that the marriage was an arranged one, and she was not a good match in terms of marriage because she was illiterate. Therefore, after working at the Jinan Railway Station for several years, and without bidding farewell to anyone of the family, he went to work at the Maintenance Department on the rail line from Hangzhow, Zhejiang Province to Nanchang, Jiangxi Province. And there might be a lot of reasons for him to do so but that arranged marriage, I firmly believe, is the major one of them.

After this uncle left for Zhejiang, my father took us to Jinan. Later, after my three aunts got married one after another, there was no one left in Large Horse Village to take care of the family house, farmlands, and my aged grandparents but this aunt of a traditional woman. With two little girls by her side, she lived in that big family house watching over everything without bearing anybody any grudge. Though she is a little bit unrefined, she is really being herself. I can still recall that in the early fall of 1947 when my mother' body was carried in the cart drawn to the family house in our native village, and put on a bier, she was with us to keep vigil days and nights. And she mourned for the deceased to an extent that the tears streamed down with a handful of mucus blown out from her nose. The way she mourned over my mother's death truly moved three of us.

Now, I was on my way to see this uncle. Thinking of this "disowned" aunt in my native village, I felt so bad.

Situated in the central-west of Zhejiang Province, Longyou County borders Jinghua County on the east, and is bounded on the west by the Qujiang River. And Qujiang City is contiguous to Jian De County in the north within the jurisdiction of Hangzou.[20] Rice, tea, and tangerine are major products of Longyou.

The Longyou Railway Station is a medium-sized one on that rail line. And that afternoon, when I got off the train, I discovered that vendors on the platforms sold neither fruits nor tea. What they tried to sell were spiced bean curds.

"Delicious bean curds!"

"Delicious bean curds!"

The vendors held wooden trays with straps going around their necks, and on the trays, there were dark purple-colored bean curds stacking. When trains stopped, they ran up to do businesses with the passengers who sat on the window seats. Regrettably, by then, I was *ruannang xiuse*, or having no money at all. *Ruannang xiuse* is a proverb referring to a guy named Ruan Fu in the Jin dynasty, whose sole belonging was only a black sack. And with it, he toured Kuaiji County in Zhejiang Province. Asked what was in his sack, he answered that there was only one copper in it. Because of that single copper, the sack wouldn't feel ashamed of itself, and at least, it had something to be watched for. And since then, *ruannang xiuse* has been used to refer to a guy who is in extremely financial difficulty.[21] Otherwise, I would get some and have tastes of them.

I stood around the exit waiting for the crowd to tear out. Afterwards, I asked a guy who collected the train tickets from the passengers how I got to the Maintenance Department. As he saw me, a teenage student in rags, giving me the cold shoulder. But when he heard my uncle's name mentioned, there was an immediate change from a poker face to a smiling one. Instantly, he passionately drew a simple map on a piece of paper and said that my uncle lived in a public dorm complex, though there was some distance from the railway station, it was really not far away.

Guided by that simple map, I easily found the address with the plaque hanging on the wall with the words "Dorm for Longyou Maintenance Staff." Standing on the doorstep, I put my head in and saw a man who bore a resemblance to my grandfather sauntering back and forth in the courtyard. Furthermore, his big frame made me more believe that it was he who was my immediate uncle I was coming to visit. Therefore, I asked him bluntly: "Excuse me, are you uncle, Ma Jiahxing?" This question caught him off guard but only for a second, and then he seemingly understood what it was all about. He denied it repeatedly, and in the meantime, said to me: "Follow me!" He led me toward a wooden building, and on the way, asked me: "You are Old Ma's nephew, aren't you? He has mentioned you to me before!" Surprisingly, he was the immediate boss of my uncle's.

My uncle's countenance is quite different from the one imagined. In comparison with my father, there are few likenesses between them. My father is tall; he, short. My father's face is rectangular; his, square. And around the age of 50, my father is a man with full head of black hair; he, several years younger, white hair like snow. However, on his face, there are two dimples like my grandmother's. And the way he smiles is like the way my grandmother does. When I firstly saw him, I felt awkward. Shortly after, I was melted by his native dialect spoken in Ling County.

When he was in the South in the earlier years, he worked at the Maintenance Department in the Yushan Railway Station in Jiangxi Province. He got remarried to a native girl there and right now had two kids: the first one was a boy; the second, a girl. He named the boy Chensheng, two years old now; the girl Guangyun, just a few months old, still wrapped in swaddling-clothes.

Long time ago, he was baptized a Christian and because of Lord's grace, it was said he was able to have gone through numerous hardships and difficulties.

That night, he and I talked about many memories of my hometown. Some of them were old stories I had heard of; others, I had no knowledge of at all. He was in high spirits and made an exception to have a few drinks with me.

This aunt is southern bred, at least, twenty years his junior. She has a sunflower seed-shaped face with two brilliant black eyes. She is a good-looking woman glowing with a sort of childlike charm. Up to now, when I recall the days I was in Longyou, I still feel so sorry for what she did for me. With her delicate hands, she washed my dirty clothes with blood stains resulted from the scabies I had suffered from. The language she spoke was the dialect of Jiangxi Province, and though I did listen to it carefully, yet I didn't understand it at all. However, a word that was clearly made out by me was: "If you are not my nephew, I will definitely not do the dirty laundry of this kind even if you pay me a plenty of money!"

My uncle put me up on the second floor in that building.

In the daytime, it was okay with me to tour the neighborhood or talk about the hometown with my uncle when he was off work. But as bedtime was up, I lay on an antique bed with the dimmed lights on the ceiling and the unrelenting spring drizzle (weather pattern in the South in this season), outside the windows, and felt extremely lonely. Thinking of the fact that I had been with my uncle one week already, and what I should talk with him, it had been done already; what I should say to him, it had been done, too. I figured it out that it was the time for me to go back to Changanzhen. If I further delayed my return to school, I wouldn't be able to catch up with others—getting on the train for moving to Guangzhou. As a result, I would be left behind like a bird that was doing the wild goose chase.

No sooner had I expressed myself that I wanted to go back to school than my uncle shook his head violently and said "No!" to me firmly. He further explained: "China's ruling party, the KMT, is doomed, and the whole picture of the civil war is getting clearer and clearer. No matter where you go, you are difinitely to be 'liberated' by the Communists Army." As he saw me stick to my own course, he made a special effort by inviting two engineers in his department to talk to me for a detailed analysis of the civil war going on in the country. What they had implied was that "the civil war is nothing but a change of the dynasty. After being 'liberated,' we will follow the decree issued by the new ruler as obedient subjects, and everything will be all right. As days go by, we will be able to get ourselves accustomed to his rule."

I still held on my own view: "As a boy, I should 'dash around' and do something greater!" Since I did not get to the end of my "odyssey," I would never give up that dream. Finally, my uncle found out that there was nothing he could do about the principled obstinacy. At the end of his tether, he gave me a piece of paper and a pen and forced me to write a note to my father: The contents should be: "Today I am going to leave my uncle's out of my own accord, not out of my uncle's."

He said to me that with this note in his hand, he would have no problem to explain what had happened to me to my father in the future. In addition, judging from the potentially retreating rail line southward to "The Home Front" we might take, he made a list of the railway stations along the said line saying, "When you get to any of these stations and if you have changed your mind, you can go to see Mr. so and so, a friend of mine, who will help you get a train ticket back to Longyou!"

When I said "Good-bye" to my immediate uncle, he stuffed into my pocket with five silver coins. He said profoundly that he had a family to take care of, and this extra amount of money given to me was just the sum he had saved up to this moment. And it was also his maximum amount of money he could afford. Furthermore, he repeatedly told me that once I settled down somewhere, I would have to visit the church.

CHAPTER 10

ROUGH ROAD TO FUZHOU

Quite unexpectedly, the train that took me back to Changanzhen was the last southbound one designated to ship the last group of students of the Jinan First United Secondary School to Guangzhou. When the train chugged in the station, I was still sleepy and bleary-eyed without noticing the platform was swarming with what sort of passengers. After I got off, I found out right away they were the students from my school. They jostled their way to the front and those who cut in line got on the train easily. Those who fell behind threw their belongings through the windows and then tried to climb into the cars. And they landed their waists on the window tracks letting their upper parts of bodies wiggle forward and their legs dangle outside, thrusting and kicking. What they were doing were as if they were conducting the frog style in the swimming pool.

Shortly after the whole train got filled including the door landings and the buffers.

At last, they began climbing up the train unto roof, and in a trice, the roof got filled, too.

As all the students fought desperately to get on the train, I was the only one who was foolishly and motionlessly standing on the platform watching this getting-on-the-train scene. Suddenly, out of nowhere, I was slipping back and realizing that if I couldn't get on this train, there wouldn't be "another chance for me to flee the danger of the forthcoming battle."

Having settled on the train roof and when I said indistinctly to my fellow students: "I have my belongings left in the dorm on the Lianyuan campus," they said: "There is no time for that. If you are going to fetch them, the train might leave any minute!"

When I got my head together on the train roof, I was seized by deep remorse! I thought to myself that If I had been on the alert for the development of the situation earlier and figured out that the train taken by me back to school was the last one for us to retreat, no matter what happened, I would have sat on that seat there. If that had been the case, I wouldn't have sat on the train roof and "been left in the open." Furthermore, I could have comfortably sat on that seat all the way to Guangzhou. Look at what I had done! Now, it was too late crying over spilt milk.

As night descended and as we were in a trance, the train started moving.

There are only several calls between Changanzhen and Hangzhou. In a flash, we got to Hangzhou. And at this juncture, the Hangzhou Railway Station became overcrowded with all walks of life. It included: civilians that wanted to flee the possibility of a battle, troops withdrawn from the battlegrounds, a few bunches of military dependents, and homeless students. That these people sat, stood, and milled around in the station reflected nothing short of the chaos of the wartime. The all these groups surrounded the station master, screaming and shouting at him and asking for him to get more trains to send them out of Hangzhou.

As we saw such a mess was going on, who dared get off the train? There was nothing for us to do, but to sit where we had been motionlessly, waiting for the train to be refilled with water and refuel. And we anxiously wished the train would have switched to the Zhegun line from Zhejiang to Jiangxi, the sooner, the better.

Eventually, the train chugged out of the Hangzhou Railway Station. Unluckily, after it went through the Qiantang River Bridge, it drizzled incessantly. At first, we improvised tents out of our blankets covering our heads and keeping us from getting wet, and then as the blankets got soaked and lost their protective functions. Consequently, we simply rolled the blankets up and put them under our buttocks readily receiving the baptism of rain.

On the retreating journey this way, we became exhausted, either dropping off or entering the dreamlands. In a half-conscious state, we heard something falling off the train roof and hitting the ground, a thud echoing back. And we immediately knew what this was really about! Nevertheless, during the fleeing period of time, everyone was for himself and nobody was able to give a hand.

When the train was drawn closer to the Shangrau Railway Station, word was passed down from the front car to us saying that the Communists Army had crossed the Yangtze River and already taken Ichang County, Jiujiang County, etc. We were cut off in the middle of our retreating route. Being so, there was no alternative for the operator to do but to back the train to Jiangshan County in Zhejiang. As the train made a clanging stop, the operator ran away at the first opportune moment.

We had sat through more than ten hours on the train, though feeling that we had sore sides and pains in our backs resulting from the long sitting, yet we were not out of Zhejiang. Right now, we were dumped into the wilderness by the train operator and had no idea of what to do and where to go! Therefore, we had no choice but to get off the train for stretching our limbs, the boys running to the faraway places for relieving, while the girls squatted themselves down under the opened-up umbrellas or the covering of the coats for pissing.

We voiced a lot of different opinions and after carefully studying for a while, we decided to go to Fuzhou, the capital city of Fujiang Province. And from there, we would take ship to Guangzhou. This is the only way for us to rejoin the "mainstream" in Guangzhou.

We were arranged in two columns and under the guidance of Zhao, a military training instructor, we started marching toward Fuzhou.

At the beginning of our march, students carried rather heavy backpacks, and afterwards, when climbing up the zigzag highway, we felt unbearable and threw away the items considered non-essentials. Walking on and on, and when our muscles for carrying this sort of load became weaker and weaker, we discarded some of the items again. At last, only the woolen blankets were left and draped over our shoulders slantwise.

Pucheng, a county city, was the first stop after we stepped into Fujiang. As we got in, we found it had been a ghost town already. Every door was locked, and there was neither a soul nor a wild dog seen.

Right there, some of the students, being unable to tolerate such a long march, gave up, and wouldn't take any steps farther claiming that they would stay in this city until it was to be liberated by the Reds. And after that, they wished they could go back to their hometowns in Shandong. Though others followed us and kept walking on and on, yet, they firstly became stragglers, then, each one of them being left alone, and at last, we lost the sight of them.

We kept walking days and nights. While hungry, we plucked wild greens in this hillyland to satisfy our hunger. While thirsty, we cupped our hands to get water from the springs in the hillsides to slake our thirst. In the month of May, it rained all the time in Fujiang, and the road became thoroughly soaked up and extremely slippery. On it, we were stumbling. If distracted from our walking, we might make heavy falls on our all fours with faces downward. And in a prone position, we were compared to a wild dog with its outstretched limbs enjoying "human wastes." Or we might be sent flying out and landing in the mud in a supine position, with our arms and legs outstretched in the form of a Chinese character, "大," or *da* equivalent to the word, "big," in English.

The most difficult part of this journey is the one when we climb up a monastery.

It didn't matter from which part, the eastern side or western side in terms of going up and coming down the mountain, we had to climb ten Chinese li or several tens of Chinese li. Between the base of the mountain and the monetary, there was neither a village for us to get a break nor an inn for us to get something to eat. All we saw was that there was a lonely huge monastery standing on the top of the mountain. Having got drenched with sweat, we not only felt cold but hungry desperately dragging ourselves forward. When we finally got there, we couldn't help collapsing before the gate of the monastery.

The monastery is the largest one incomparable to any other one that I have ever seen. Along its axis line from the front to the rear: firstly, the gate, secondly, the grand palace, thirdly, the library for housing Buddhist Sutras, and finally, the east and west wings. A lot of monks came out to meet us. The lead monk saw us in such a mess and chanted "Amitabha! Amitabha!" repeatedly. And then he led us into one room of a wing asking us to take a good rest there, and ordered young monks to start a fire in a red brick-made stove to cook a dinner for us. When he left us, he warned us not to walk around at will because this is the divine and pure land of Gautama Buddha, and nonbelievers are not permitted to inadvertently profane it out of ignorance. He told us that if we needed any other thing for them to do, we just made a request to anyone of them, and they would cooperate with us.

As to us, a bunch of refuge-like students who fled the horrors of civil war, what else did we need but a good night sleep and a meal?

On the following day, we, led by Zhao, walked down the mountain and marched toward Fuzhou.

The city of Jiangyang had been taken by the Communists Army already. And the highway leading to Fuzhou was cut off again in the middle. Right now, there wasn't anything else for us to do but to wade across the Min River. And then from the opposite bank of the river and on the uphill trail there, we might detour two county cities, Shuigi and Jiango. By doing so, we could get back to the highway again leading to Fuzhou.

We were hand in hand to get down into the river. Despite the the snags hidden in, treacherous whirlpools and the bone-chilling water, we were wading forward in the river unsteadily. The repeat falls and repeat rises in the water made the wading speed slow. When we climbed up unto the trail on the other bank of the river, I saw a male's body floating down from the upper river with his face downward and limbs outstretched in the form of a Chinese character, "大," or large. And it was being swept round and round on the surface of the currents.

There is a saying which can be interpreted as such, "the daunting route into the region of Shu, Sichuan Province, is more daunting than climbing the sky."[22] However, by then, to me, I felt disheartened by the route to Fuzhou. And it was hard to a certain extent that it would kill one while climbing.

In the daytime, walking on the trail called *yangchang xiaojing*, or the trail is "as narrow as a lamb's intestine," we were at ease. All we had to do was to stay in control of our steps having the pressure evenly distributed, and keep ourselves poised so that we could start climbing uphill. But as night set in, we felt forward on the trail in pitch-dark as if having walked on the brink of death. And on the one side was the high steep mountain, and on the other side, "the ten-thousand feet abyss." If we hadn't come into the focus of walking, we might have fallen off the trail, either getting broken arms and legs or getting the bodies torn up into "hundred pieces." For safety, each one of us got a length of bamboo stick in hands. You held one end of my stick with your hand, and in turn, I held the end of the other's stick, and so on till the last one. This way we formed a long line of bamboo sticks. The "lead sheep" used his bamboo stick to strike the trail. If the sound of 'Pu chi! Pu chi!" was heard, it meant that he hit nothing but the leaves of bushes. If the sound of "Bang! Bang!" was produced, it meant that what he hit was the solid ground. By so doing, we moved forward, one step after another. No one knew how many Chinese li we had covered that night and all we knew was that we could fall asleep while walking.

When it was at the crack of dawn, we had climbed up the top of a hill. We were so exhausted that we couldn't walk any more. Seeing this, Zhao had no alternative, but to let us take a break. However, he remarked significantly: "This is the crucial moment that can be regarded as the time of life and death. We must grit our teeth to move forward and keep on walking. If the route is blocked off by the Communists Army again, we'll never have another chance to join the "mainstream" in Guangzhou!" Upon finishing this, all of us slumped down to the ground, lying there topsy-turvy, and on a quite large area on which we slept.

In a flash, the rumbling of big guns was within our earshot. I felt that I got several powerful kicks on my thighs, very painful. Suddenly, I woke up and saw that not far away, there were artillery shell explosions going on, grey clouds of smoke spreading. Within sight, I didn't see a fellow student nor Zhao. In panic, I was running amok trying to find them from this side to another side and vice versa on the hilltop. Alongside the circumference, I ran around and around. At this juncture, there was a shell descending from the sky and landing behind me with an explosion sound. The smoke, clods of earth, and bits of rock flew to me overwhelmingly. I felt soft beneath my feet and was thrown off the balance and fell off the cliff, head first.

I was sliding down all the way on the downward slope.

When I stood up, I found my feet got deeply stuck in the rice paddy. Having got unto the causeway, I made a quick check over my body and found out that on my left shin, there were three bruises, each ten-centimeter in size; on the right thigh, there was a two-centimeter laceration, and down to the ankle of the same leg, a bruise there, too. In addition to these wounds, my pants were torn up to shreds. Luckily, my head didn't get any cut, nor did my face get any scratch.

By then, the panic of being left alone surpassed any wounds and pains, and worse than that, I felt that there were some ghoulies, ghosties, and long-legged beasties chasing me behind. Therefore, I desperately sprinted as fast as I could due south with the scorching sun overhead. After sprinting some time, I got to a spot where there was a path bisecting the landscape and stood there, not knowing what I wanted to do. Making a right turn or left might lead to a different fate. At last, I pointed to one of them, saying a prayer to God, "The Nationalist-held area or the Communist is totally dependent on you!"

Along the path that I had picked, I run through groves of trees one after another. Suddenly, loud shouts and yells scared me.

"Halt! Halt!"

I quickly made a stop.

"Hands up, and put them over your head!"

I did what I was ordered. And I saw several soldiers coming out from the opposite grove of trees with loaded rifles. As soon as I saw the military uniforms they had on, I was relieved immediately as if a piece of stone were dropped from my chest. On the one hand, I was thrilled; on the other, I shouted at them.

"I am a student from Shandong! I am a student from Shandong! Have you ever seen a group of students from Shandong?"

They continued letting me put my hands over my head, and this time, ordered me to move forward slowly to them. As I was at the close range, they commanded me to stop walking. And I caught sight of the truth that there were still several other soldiers hidden behind the trees with the rifle butts against their shoulders. They aimed at me and had their guns cocked as if they were going to press the triggers.

The one in charge sized me up for a while telling me that he didn't know where that group of students was from Shandong or from anywhere else but he did see a group of students go by about forty minutes ago. And he asked me to accelerate my step rate to catch up with them.

On the entire retreat route, as I had seen and experienced, this was the only one military operation that was "normally" executed by the Nationalists Army.

As far as myself concerned, I saw the worst debacle of the Nationalists. The miserable situation is in line with a Chinese saying: "An army defeated can be likened to a mountain collapsed."

As far as the military power concerned, just one communist

company could send a nationalist regiment to flee, chasing them as if they were herding a flock of sheep. Despite being equipped with the American weaponry, the Nationalists Army not only lost its power to fire back but also suffered low morale having lost its guts even to hear a word of: "the Communists Army is coming!" Along the retreat route, there were lots of stragglers hanging their best rifles on the trees. And they lay with their backs on the slopes of hills awaiting to be captured, and their faces were expressionless. Even up to the present moment, that scene is still embedded in my memory.

When we started our "Long March" from Jiangshan County, this group consisted of about three hundred students. After going through those trails in the hillylands and the mountainous area twenty odd days, we had roughly fifty-some odd students left.

Having entered the city of Fuzhou, we stayed at the entrance of a school and lay down there to take a rest.

That was a clear afternoon, and it was very swelting by then. Since we didn't have a bath for a long time, there were whiffs of ordor exuding from our sweat-drenched bodies. We sat or lay on the concrete looking like a bunch of beggars with disheveled hairs, our faces being coated with layers of dirt.

Fuzhou had entered the crucial time to prepare for a defensive battle. Here and there, we could see the propaganda slogans pasted on the walls, "We'll defend Grand Fuzhou to the last ditch and to the last drop of blood!"

A human being is always a human being. No matter what time it is, the human nature can always be seen. Instantly, people from all sides came close to and surrounded us. When they had seen us, a group of teenagers, in such a mess, aside from heaving sighs, they asked what had happened to us, and in the meantime, tossed in coins and yuan out of their pockets. Those who lived nearby went home and came back with teapots and cups to comfort us. Best of all, some people fetched rice and dishes to us.

There were such waves of warmth crashing upon us, homeless students who were dressed in rags. If there had been no sympathy of theirs, we could control ourselves for the sake of self-reliance and dignity. Once with their lovely words and comforts, we immediately had emotional breakdowns as if the Yellow River had made breaches in the banks during the flooding season. Tears coursed down our cheeks without stopping and closely followed were our sobs.

That was the scene we cried together. It was also the only saddest one in which I cried my head off during the days on the wandering road south.

CHAPTER 11

ON THE JIHO

Since banyan trees are everywhere in the city of Fuzhou, the city is also called *Rong Cheng*, or city of banyan trees. If there had been no war threatening the city, people would have sat under the one hundred years old trees with aerial prop roots, sipped tea and played *Xiangqi*, or Chinese chess. And if that had been the case, how happy would the people have been? However, during the times of the civil war, the Communists fought against the Nationalists severely, people felt panicky. Was there any spare time for playing that game and sipping tea under the banyan tree?

Although the defensive battle for Fuzhou was about to begin, yet the tempe enjoyed the booming pilgrimages. Following the senior students, I paid a visit to Nantai Temple. Though with panic-stricken faces, people still walked on their way to this temple incessantly. And they came to worship god or goddess for safety.

Our wishful thinking is, of course, to get on a ship which transports us from Fuzhou directly to Guangzhou. After contacting and negotiating with the shipping company several times, we found out that this sort of thinking was not practical. As we rethought about the situation when the city was to be attacked by the Communists Army, was there any shipping company accommodating us with a ship to get us to our destination directly? As a result, we modified our strategy to get to Guangzhou by medley relay. If there was a ship sailing south, we would like to take, one voyage taken, one voyage counted.

While staying at the seaport city, Xinmen (Amoy), on the southeast coast, we fell short of food. Luckily, there were some naval officers and blue jacks from Shandong at the naval base here. When they heard that we, students, from the same province had nothing to eat, they carried the left-overs to us. Our food problem was so resovled.

By the end of May, we took a passenger ship named Shihmen to Hong Kung. Because we didn't have visa, we couldn't get into Hong Kong except that we stood on the starboard side or port side to get a glimpse of the night view of it.

At daybreak, Shihmen, took us to Guangzhou.

We, 50-some odd students retreating to Fujian, suffered a lot to have gone through the hillylands and the mountainous area in the northern part of Fujiang Province but the groups of students who withdrew preceding us were no better than us—they firstly retreated to the city of Hengyang in Hunan Province and then to Guangzhou. It was said that their train travels from Zhejiang to Jiangxi were very difficult: sometimes, the trains travelled as fast as the wind; at other times, the trains crawled sluggishly like snails. Downpours occurred, and they had nothing to do but to sit there idling their time away. Those who sat on the train roofs got completely drenched to the skin. And as hunger and bitter coldness alternately gnawed and hit them, they became weaker and weaker as if they were dying. What made them feel more unbearable was the sponge cushions in their plastic shoes, soaked so long in the rain water and glued to the soles of their feet. In another word, the sponge cushions and the "calluses" on the soles were pressed together. Therefore, when taking off shoes, they found there were raw fleshes bleeding. Being so painful, they couldn't set their feet on the ground.[23]

More unbelievable than anything else was Hu Jiajian's stupidity and absurdity. He was the head of the department of secondary education in the Ministry of Education having just got to Guangzhou. He didn't speak anything praiseworthy for these groups of passionate teenagers who carried their simple belongings to follow the National Government despite the long journey and difficulties on the routes. Conversely, he rebuked us by using the most abusive language: "Our country is totally messed up and ruined by you, the groups of homeless students!" Upon hearing what he had said, our principal, Liu Zemin, grabbed him by his necktie giving him two slaps on the face. Furthermore, Liu, yelled at him outrageously: "I want to beat you to death, you, son of bitch!" Thanks to the Minister of Education, Hang Liwu's and the Deputy Minister, Wu Junsheng's coming in time to his rescue, Hu was set free. Because of this fight, our problems of the board and lodging in Guangzhou got solved.[24]

Initially, Sun Yat-sen Memorial Hall and the 53rd Elementary School in the eastern district of Guangzhow accommodated the students of the Jinan First United Secondary School, and then they moved into Donggao Elementary.[25]

When two military trucks carried us, the last 50-plus students in, and unloaded us onto the campus at Donggao Elementary, surrounding us were our fellow students on the scene who thought we had just crawled out of inferno. We, with dirty faces, were haggard, dressed in tatters, and repulsive indeed. When they finally recognized that we were their fellow students who had been through the most terrible ordeals on the way to rejoin them, they immediately came up to us, putting their arms around us and giving us hugs. And we were in tears, the mucus being blown out, alternating between joy and grief.

Sometimes, man is a very strange animal. While I ran desperately for my life in the mountainous area of Fujian Province, despite challenge trails ahead of me, and the Communist pursuers behind, I didn't get sick, conversely, being able to keep myself very strong. However, after stepping in the city of Guangzhou, I felt as if there were time for me going sick. Once relaxed, I felt as if my entire body were melted. And then I was stuck in fever with chills by fits and starts. Once I lay down on my bed, I couldn't get up. Some senior students told me that I had contracted malaria.

Guangzhou was one of the earliest trade cities described as a

00400

revolutionary Mecca against the Manchurians' rule once. And there were lots of scenic spots for us to visit. Every day, I saw my fellow students happily go out doing the sightseeing, and after returning, they depicted what they had seen such as: 72-Martyrs' Graves, the locale where the rebel general, Chen Jiongming, attacked Presidential Hall by big guns, and other geographical attractions, and I became extremely depressed because I missed the opportunity of doing the same sort of things as they did. I could create mental images of those scenic spots, but never be capable of visiting them in person.

At that time, it was in the month of June, temperature reading was very high. Sweating days and nights, I felt damp and clammy all over my body. Though provided with the wash stand right in front of our dorm (classroom), I was so weak that I didn't have any energy to clean my body even with a wet towel.

Some students saw that I was sick, and took me to the hospital to see doctor. In the waiting room, I reclined on an armchair, so feeble as if I were on the brink of death. With my eyes closed, I patiently waited for my turn.

As to when a woman and her child seated themselves nearby, I had no idea at all. Initially, in a trance, I vaguely sensed that there was the shadow of a woman there. And then gradually I saw her clearly who was covering her nose with a handkerchief and manifesting herself in her face full of contempt. I looked around and found that there was nothing which gave off this unpleasant smell. However, when I turned to my own bony body, I immediately realized that it was I who was the cause of its being smelly. This embarrassing scene I had experienced had a great impact on me that I would never forget it for the rest of my life. Thus, right at that moment, I made a vow that "If I have survived this malaria, I will make myself be 'somebody' in the future. Only when that happens, will I return to my home province—Shandong."

As the schools of this kind withdrawn to Guangzhou gathered together here, we came to know that there were still 8 of them in total.

Despite the fact that students were dwindling down on the retreat routes, there were still 8,000-some odd students who succeeded in getting to "the Lamb City," another name for Guangzhou.

The eight different schools were led, of course, by eight different principals. In many heated debates, they couldn't reach a consensus about what to do and where to go from Guangzhou. Some principals proposed that we should follow the way of those who had gone to the Great Westsouth during the 8-year Anti-Japanese War, and had the whole situation estimated—Su, or Sichuan is inaccessible in terms of the roads in the mountain region. Thus, it is easier to defend than to offend. The KMT might get the chance to recuperate there. Viewed from that perspective, the KMT might be with a bright future ahead.

Others noted that we could take train to get to Guiyang only, the capital city of Guizhou Province, and beyond that city, there was not any railway installation. As to the rest of journey, we had to go afoot. Because of the fact that the KMT had been badly defeated in the various battlegrounds so that there was no way for it to be recovered. We were not sure that the day when the schools got to the "Great Home Front," it was also the day for the "Great Home Front" to be liberated by the Communists.

The majority of principals agreed that we should go to Taiwan, especially, our principal, Liu Zemin. His famous saying sounded loudest: "The strategy to fight the Japanese Army is dependent on the mountain, while the strategy to fight the Communists is dependent on the sea."[26] Other comments of his were that "On the Chinese Mainland, the Nationalists troops have been demoralized and lost the fighting spirit; generals have had the ideas of surrendering. And not one piece of land on China Mainland can be defended. If we can go to Taiwan, at present, the Communists have no navy, and there is no way for them to liberate Taiwan despite their high morale in the Chinese People's Liberation Army."[27]

During that period, Taiwan was ruled by martial law. With the exception of the military personnel, the ordinary people who wanted to apply for getting into Taiwan were severely reviewed.

After withdrawing to Taiwan, General, Li Zhenqing, was appointed Commander of the Penghu Islands Defense Command. He saw his opportunity arising and negotiated with the principals to reach an agreement: male students who were above seventeen years of age were enlisted in the "the Youth League" in the Penghu Islands. It was stipulated that once in "the Youth League," the students would receive half a day's "regular education" as the curriculum set in the ordinary school, another half a day's military training as the military officers wished. If having passed the tests of a set of courses, the students could get senior high school diplomas. Those students under the age of 17 including female students would be placed in a newly established school named the Dependants' School for the Penghu Islands Defense Command personnel to continue their schooling.[28]

General Li is a native of Linqing County, Shandong. We thought that we had sort of closer relation with him for we all were from the same province. Originally, we had the idea that under his tutelage, we could get a good opportunity to resume our schooling as we wished. No one knew such a thought would be another inception of a horrible nightmare.

On June 22, 1949, we got on a freighter docked at Pier 5 at Huangpu Port. It was rebuilt from an amphibious assault ship and named *Jiho*. When we were boarding, each one of us was given 4-pound crackers.[29] And they made an announcement that this ration was the only food available in the course of voyage and there would be no more food catering for us.

In our expectation, Jiho weighed anchor.

When she was on the public sea the second day, we saw lots of sea dogs on either side of the ship. We couldn't help praising: "Almighty God whose magic power is unparalleled creates such a creature in the sea. Its agility is just marvelous." Simultaneously, we gave another thought that this might be ill-omened—a ship accident. If it had really happened, we would have drowned and landed ourselves in the stomachs of these sea creatures eventually. If it was not inauspicious, why did they go with our ship continuously?

Nobody could have proved that the hunch was right, but a fire broke out on the freighter suddenly. Firstly, we saw sparks shooting out all over, and then clouds of smoke and tongues of flames rising. Students became panicky immediately. Fortunately, the captain and his crew came to the rescue timely and put the fire out and within a short period of time, the mechanical problem of the boiler got resolved. And everything was back into its normacy again.[30]

When an amphibious assault ship is modified into a freighter and used as a vessel to transport passengers, the key problems lie in its water displacement and its huge flat-bottomed structure. When encountering high wind and huge waves at sea, such a type of ship will be pitching or rolling violently. And it may be led to danger of being capsized. To solve this problem, more than ten tanks are driven in to increase the water displacement and used as ballasts to ensure that the ship would be kept in good balance.[31] Despite all these efforts made, lots of students still got seasick.

We lay on the deck disorderly sleeping, resting, or leaning on the rails, and seemingly, thinking of whatever would be.

On the third day of our voyage, we ran into a rainy weather. Although it was not a downpour, it rained all the time. We retrieved our old tricks to pitch the blanket tents keeping the raindrops out. When the blankets got wet enough and the rain seeped in, we let the rain take its course and roll down us.

The worst thing was the cracker rations laid on our laps. The crackers soaked by rainwater became sort of batter. When I was not able to bear the gnawing pang of hunger, I would scoop it up with my fingers as a spoon to fill my stomach. This type of batter-like food though tastes sweet, yet diluted, and it is impossible to describe what flavor it is. It got stuck in my tooth cavities, sticky and gluey, I found words fail me regarding the feeling I had.

CHAPTER 12

PRESS-GANDED INTO THE ARMY
ON THE PENGHU ARCHIPELAGO

On June 25, 1949, the *Jiho*, carrying us, the students from Shandong, got to the waters of the Penghu Islands.

After a four-day and three-night voyage, we eventually steamed into our destination, and woke up from a sort of dreamy state, gathering on the deck to orient ourselves.

Looking eastward, we saw that there were the first rays of the rising shooting like golen arrows, and looking downward, we saw the expanse of the sea, deep and glossy smooth, and looking southward, we saw Yuwendao, or the Fisherman Island, that was floating on the surface of the sea, and seemingly, a lot of monsters haunting that entire mysterious area. And a pitch-dark mass of the land retained so still there.

When it was gradually turning into broad daylight, we saw fishermen rowing their boats towards our ship. And after they got their boats just right below our vessel, we became aware that they were coming to do businesses with us. Their boats were loaded with cigarettes, wine, bananas, candies made of peanuts, and anchovies.

Because of our long journey on the roads, we had no money left in our pockets but only a few pieces of clothes and quilts. Common sense be told that in Taiwan, spring stays all year round. And keeping a piece of woolen blanket, and a few of unlined garments could be good enough. Therefore, though having carried them all the way down to the Penghu Islands, some of the students traded their quits, padded jackets and trousers for the fishermen's few kilograms of bananas.

We waited aboard for an entire morning and almost half an

afternoon, and not until 4 p.m. were we allowed to get off and go ashore.

We were firstly led to the Neian Elementary School stadium for an assembly, and then put up at a barracks left by the Japanese army.

After settling down, we hurriedly got out and walked around. As far as the eye could reach, there was nothing else but the stretches of gravel land, bleak and barren. There were neither crops visible nor a lofty tree seen. The only thing that lit up our eyes was the towering lighthouse, thick and solid, in Waian village.

In the first few days, the "receptionists" in plain clothes maintained a lukeworm relationship with us, and then, we found out that there were progressive changes in their attitudes. Even though they treated us courteously, we found there was something uncompromising. At last, they took off their face coverings, indicating that when an order was once out, it had to be executed. And they expressed themselves suggestively through frowning and winking that they would be our superiors. We had been destined for being soldiers, and coercing us into the army was unavoidable.

Before they placed us in the units, they had us go through a screening process.

They made an announcement that those who were seventeen years of age came forward and lined up on the left; those who were not, on the right. (In China as well as in Taiwan, there are two ways of reckoning a person's age. One is called "Western age" starting the counting from the day one is born, while the other is called "Chinese age" from the day mother gets pregnant.) Because I was sixteen years old based on the Western way of reckoning, I was in a state of being on the moon walking to the right. But as I walked to the spot ready to move into the line, a robust guy quickly ran to me yelling at me angrily: "You can't go in there! You can't go in there!" and pulling me back. I was off balance, staggering. In the meantime, he grabbed my arms and marched me to the left-hand side line. In this way, I was forcibly placed into the army. In a few days, I was transferred from Waian to a unit called "The Third

Brigade affiliated to the Youth League" stationed at Bamboo Pole Bay.

Several days later, I heard about the news that the Penghu Islands Defense Command HQ summoned students to a stadium on the biggest island of Magong, and the process of placing students into the army was more violent and cruel than I had gone through.

Commander, Li Zhenqing and Commander of the 39th Division, Han Fengyi, had the students corralled in the stadium of the Penghu Islands Defense Command, and deployed the security forces around the stadium with the machine guns mounted. Standing on the reviewing stand, Han announced to the students with a deadpan face: "Welcome all of you to Penghu. However, our country is facing the crisis of life and death. I think that fighting for the survival of our country is much more important than receiving education." And he added: "Today is your best opportunity to serve your country. Because serving in the Nationalists Army as a soldier is a glorious calling, I don't think you'll refuse this opportunity."[32] Shortly after his speech, complaints were heard, and there was a few of students shouting protests loudly from the rows: "We don't want to be soldiers! We want to study! We don't want to be soldiers! We want to study!"

But the cadres implementing what General Han had announced lined the students up in the order of decreasing height. And they walked back and forth between the rows using a rope to measure them based on the length of type 38 rifle. Any one who equalled the rifle in height, and anyone who looked healthy should be placed in the army despite one's age, 13-year-old or 14-year-old. In another word, only stature and healthiness counted.[33]

The consequences of forcibly implementing the announcement to place the students into the army provoked more violent protests. However, in order to warn the students, soldiers began purposely shooting blank shots, and two students were bayoneted and got seriously wounded. And there were also some students whose buttocks and legs got hit by stray bullets. At this juncture, there was a great commotion going on, and the students were crying and claiming that: "we are not against military training, but we also want to keep our secondary school education going on as promised!"[34] But they just ignored what the students' outcry. Before many teachers' and principals' wide-opened eyes, they insisted on having students take off their clothing and put on military uniforms.

This event is called the 713 Incident because it happened on July 13, 1949.[35]

Bamboo Pole Bay is situated on the western coastal area of the Fishman Island. And the landforms of this area diversified by hills and vallies are criss-crossed. On the coast, scattered here and there are steep cliffs and strange coral grottoes. And the huge surf crashes into these grottoes echoing resoundingly the same tone today as well as in the distant past. Most of people's houses on this island are built on the gravel land with the coral fragments around them as fences or walls.

Overall, though the Fisherman Island is sparsely populated, it is an important military strategic point. It is also a good place for the field training program.

We were here firstly for military basics. After that, we had the field training program. Though we could stand physical abuses, yet mental abuses were the most unbearable of all.

Most of cadres, platoon and squad leaders, were illiterate, knowing few of Chinese characters. They not only spoke rudely but also acted tyrannically. Worse, they didn't have know-how and how-to to lead these student soldiers and thus, caused the interaction to deteriorate. We superficially obeyed them, but in the deep recesses of our minds and bottoms of our hearts, we defied them. However, how could the attitudes of this kind be concealed long and not to be detected by their mind's eyes? They began training us by using abusive language and corporal punishments. While dealing out blows to us, they insulted us by using the vulgar expressions: "What a country bumpkin you are!" Or they simply condemned us: "You are unhappy with this treatment, aren't you? When you are unhappy, you'll get beaten up, while I am unhappy, I'll beat you up!"[36]

The Headquarters of "The Youth League" was located at a village called Xiaochejiao, or Little Pond Cornor. It took about forty minutes to get there by marching. And the "regular rally" was held every Monday and we had to get there to listen to a pep talk by our "regimental" Commander, Han Bin. And occasionally, there was an officer from the political warfare department coming to give us a talk analyzing the international situation.

When Commander Li Zhenqing came to inspect the Fisherman Island, we had to go to Xiaochejiao to listen to his harangue. Originally, he was in General Pang Bingxun's poorly-trained army. By chance, he was promoted quickly from the rank of adjutant officer through assistant brigade commander, brigade commander, assistant division commander, commander of the 39th division, deputy army commander, to the highest position, commander of the 40th army. Luckily, in the Anti-Japanese war, he had scored one or two victories. At last, in Anyang County, Henan Province, he was captured by the Reds, and later, set free. By then, he collected some of the officers and soldiers who had suffered defeats, and retreated to Taiwan. Because of his loyalty to the National Government, he was recognized by Chen Cheng, the executive chief of the Military and Administrative Headquarters for Southeastern Region (referring to Taiwan) who gave him the second chance and appointed him the Commander of Penghu Islands Defense Command.[37]

As Li has received limited education, he often makes a fool of himself. His cliché on his lips is: "An egg equals ten peanuts in nutrition!" Therefore, he asked us to take more peanuts. Furthermore, he asked us not to smoke. Because of his little education received, what he had said showed nothing but trite expressions or numerous monotonous repetitions. In a speech he wanted to deliver, it always consists of "this is…" for example: "This is so." or "This is not so."

Amidst the student soldiers, there was a plenty of funny stories about him going around.

There was one derived from his talk like this: once, after giving a talk to the gathering, he was extremely excited, and tried to lead them to shout slogans. The first few slogans he shouted went well. However, the last one he shouted was originally composed of six Chinese characters such as: "Guo fu jing shen bu si!" (Our national Father's spirit is immortal!) But he shouted the slogan as follows:

"Guo fu bu si!" (Our national Father is immortal!) When it was shouted out, it caused the student soldiers dumbstruck.[38]

He, of course, immediately was aware that he had left two characters out, and redressed it: "He still has jing shen (spirit)!"

He looked like an honest man. And President Chiang Kai-shek is very fond of this type of general, staunchly loyal. Once he made an inspection tour to the Penghu Islands, General Li intended to make good use of this opportunity to please Chiang by pledging his allegiance to him to the utmost. When asked such a question: "What do you think of the present situation in Taiwan, General Li?" He replied:

"Mr. President, I don't have any idea. All I have had is that I am a draught animal of yours. I will go to wherever as I am told by you."[39]

I cannot remember how much money is fixed for food per head everyday. Overall, they fed the worst kind of rice and the worst dish to us.

There were 10-plus buddies in a squad. All of us squatted down in the open and surrounded an iron basin full of salty soup made from pumpkin, and a few drops of cooking oil and a few slices of white-colored pig fat were floating on the surface. The rice was not only unhusked but also mixed with grains of sand. Once in our mouths, and while chewing, we heard the sounding of *ga ba, ga ba*. And as I feared that there wasn't enough food, I had learned the skill of *da chong fento*, or lead the charge, not to the enemy but to the rice: "At first, I just get a half bowl full and after wolfing down the half bowl of rice, I quickly run back to get a bowl full!"

By then, I was very short, the second last guy in my squad when lined up, and ranked private, accordingly, getting the private solider's pay around 7.50 yuan per month, based on the Old Taiwanese Monetary System. By then, I was always craving for something edible to satisfy the insatiable appetite of mine and once a tea-colored envelope with cash money sealed in was handed over to me, I hurriedly ran to a small low-lying grocery store to get a few pieces of candies made of peanuts to eat.

The news that they had launched a "mole hunt" campaign spread out. And as we were lying on the bed in the night, we always felt that our whole camp was haunted. The following morning when we rose, we discovered that one or two of our fellow students had vanished from the earth. Having made an inquiry, we got nothing else but the same answer: "They have been transferred to another unit." "They would rather mistakenly kill one hundred innocent people than let one mole get away." This was the warning we had often heard in those days.

The news of principals Zhang Minzhi and Zou Jiang who had been arrested was spreading by word of mouth to us off and on. Zhang headed the Yangtai United Secondary School; Zou, the second branch of that school.

They were the ones who strongly opposed this shabby deal to have students illegally drafted into the army, and fought against vehemently that some of the younger ones were "ruined" this way. They sent out plenty of letters to seek assistances from everywhere. Furthermore, they invited the director of the Department of Education of Shandong Province, Xu Yiqian. to come down and get those 16 years olds and younger ones out of the army. These measures infuriated General Han, Commander of the 39th Division. On the one hand, he blindly accused them of "violating the martial law of army buildups" and on the other, labelled them as "communist agents," intending to get them executed.

Zhang was falsely accused of being "the member of Executive Committee of the Communist Party in the eastern Jiaochow region," and Zou, "the member of the Yangtai City Communist Party and the director of the New Democratic Youth League of the City."[40]

Allegations are easily made, but evidence is hard to get.

Han Fengyi is a crafty man aiming to keep his post as Division Commander trying very hard to avoid the embarrassing situation that cadres outnumber soldiers. Thus, he urged his henchman, Li Fusheng, to use every means to fraudulently get false confessions from the students. If not obeyed, they would be severely punished by sleep deprivation, hanging by the wrists and whipped, getting shocks from electrical generators, waterboarding, and rolling on the piles of dead and dried corals. Amidst these victims, one of the survivors named Liu Tinggong wrote one short piece of doggerel which could be exemplified to show the very true picture he had gone through. It reads:

> *"They stood me up there against the wall*
> *My hands were tied up behind and weighted down with stone*
> *Stone jabbed me till my ribs were bleeding*
> *And my legs were flogged by the rifle butt with the bayonet on*
> *Falling into unconsciousness due to numbness and cramping*
> *With bleary eyes, I entered the world of Hade*
> *A can of icy water was poured over my head*
> *Having woken up, I discovered I became a prisoner with blackened legs."*[41]

Those who had been transferred here were under the threat of these cruel tortures, and as a result, whatever the false confessions they wanted could be gotten. In another word, they could get whatever they wished. In addition, to legalize these "confessions," they asked these teenagers who didn't have knowledge of law to sign or affix their thumb-prints on the false confessions.

Once these false confessions were available as the evidence, the Taipei Security Headquarters got the two principals, at 10 a.m., Sunday, on December 11, 1949, executed at the spot called *Machangting,* or horse stable[42] When executed, there were five students who were, under the mask of the Communist agents, shot to death, too. (Originally, there were six students, but one, whose name was Wang Ziyi, got sick and died in the jail before the doomday) Among them, the youngest one was only nineteen years old.

Though these two principals and five students died of fake accusations, at least, they had been through a form of the kangaroo court during the period of so-called "the White Terror." One of the cruelest methods to commit the atrocity was that more than ten suspected students, "the Communist Agents," were arrested, shipped to the outer sea by a fishing boat, dumped into the jute sacks tied to a piece of rock, and thrown overboard, letting them go down to the bottom of the sea and drown there. They gave this "Death Penalty" a name: "Casting Anchor."[43] The rest of about fifty students of this kind were put into a program called: "The Newborn Camp." And they were under severe surveillance.

Though some of these unlucky students died with the principals, others died of drowning, and still others were detained for reform, yet those who had been gangpreesed into the army were not much better treated than those detainees. The tricks they tortured us were getting crueler and crueler. Included are: letting us learn the way of the turtle's crawling on the concrete floor; putting the hands atop our heads, squatting on our hunkers and doing the jumping as the frogs are doing, and under the scorching sun, getting us run laps around the stadium, 5,000 meters with backpacks on our backs and rifles in our hands.

When the session of military basics was on, the key points of "attention!" should be accurately executed. They are: keeping our heads erect and facing straight to the front, holding the bodies erect and shoulders back, arching our chests and lowering our chins. Even if we thought that we had these key points correctly done in terms of a good example of "attention!", we had to go through the unexpected tests inflicted on us. That means they would give us kicks upon the back parts of our legs, upper or lower, from behind. And if we could withstand the kicks without bending our knees, there was nothing for them to condemn of, otherwise they tongue-lashed us sarcastically: "What a country bumpkin you are! What a country bumpkin you are!" And under the cloak of training us to be absolutely obedient soldiers, they, in fact, revenged the contempt shown to them.

To me, the bitterest thing was the situation that I didn't have the availability of "that half a day's education promised." I couldn't learn new things, and further, what I had learnd that little bit of stuff in the past would fade away. Whenever I thought of this, tears coursed down along my cheeks.

CHAPTER 13

LIFE AND DEATH
ON THE PENGHU ISLANDS

After two principals, Zhang and Zhou, were executed, there was nothing else preventing them from doing whatever they wished to do. For that reason, making up the cases of "the Communist agents" was halted.

Though no one exactly knew how many of this group of Shandong students were drafted into the army illegally, yet the number that could man the following units were unquestionable: on the Fisherman Island, the units were the 115th infantry regiment, an assault platoon and an artillery battalion; on the main island, Magong, the 116th infantry regiment, a special task battalion and a communication battalion. I was placed in a mortar squad, the increasing order of my units being the 3rd platoon, the 5th company, the 2nd battalion and the 115th regiment.

In the fall of 1950, we were transferred from the Fisherman Island to a boot camp named Shiquan in Magong, the largest island of the Penghui archipelago. Once getting settled, we got another round of training started, of course, from the basics again, "Attention!" "At Ease!" "Right Face!" and "Left Face!" During the period of bayonet drill, we had to shout in unison, "Get them! get them!"

Suddenly, there were desertions taking place.

In my squad, there was a buddy named Wang Anshun who often absented himself from rigorous training sessions by asking for sick leave. But whenever there was an opportunity to gather together to have drinks, puffs, and chats, he suddenly came alive. Being possessed of wit, eloquence, and a sense of humor, he was greatly liked by all our company. We are of the same age and stature so that the other buddies of our company considered that we are *hengha erjiang*, or two guards of Buddhist temples. He considered me the closest comrade of his and I thought him the bosom friend of mine.

One night everybody slept like a tree, he quietly woke me up and took me by hand and led me outside our barracks. As I saw him behave weirdly, I felt a little bit restless. And he covered his mouth with one of his hands whispering to me: "*Xiao Ma*, or Mr. Ma, my dearest friend, since my older brother in Magong had got everything ready for me, tonight, I'll leave here!" Pausing for a while, he added: "When I'll get settled down somewhere, I'll surely contact you!" Up to this moment, I realized the whole story he was telling me was desertion. And I was dumbfounded there facing him and not knowing what to say. When I was just coming to myself and wanted to say something to him, he said nothing more than two words, "Take Care!" waving his hands to me and entering the darkness of the night.

On the following morning, the news of Wang Anshun's desertion spread through the entire company. Our company commander was extremely angry about this happening and vowed to get him back at all costs and have him severely punished. Since desertion might be contagious, therefore, getting him back could be served as a warning to others who had had such an idea. Conversely, we felt happy for him. Our Company Commander, Wang Yubing, was not capable of getting Wang Anshun back as he had vowed. And following suit, another one named Lu Mingshen, a student from the Yangtai United Secondary School, ran away, too.

To get in the ROC Military Academy by taking the entrance examination is another way to leave Penghu.

Lieut. General Li Zhenqing originally thought this group of students might be his own "assets." In the future, after launching a counter-offensive by the Nationalists Army successfully, he might use us as cadres to expand his own force in China Mainland. Therefore, we were not allowed to take part in the entrance examination held by the military academy.

Around 1951, President Chiang Kai-shek took an inspection tour to the Penghu Islands reviewing the armed forces. He discovered that there were such young and tall student soldiers (Shandong man is usually tall). Nodding to us frequently, he instructed both Li and Han to let us join the ROC Military Academy entrance exam.

However, both Li and Han superficially obeyed President Chiang's "edict" but actually they just let two or three in one company to sign up for the exam in a sort of formality. Totally, in our company, there were only three of our buddies, Liu Hehsin, Fan Zijing and Yang Diancai who had passed the entrance examinations. The first two enrolled in 1951 class; the third one, in 1953.

But thereafter, through a variety of channels to reflect the true picture of restricting students for getting the permission to participate in the entrance examinations held by a variety of military academies to the highest level of military hierarchy, Li and Han had no option but to loosen their grips on this matter. Consequently, all kinds of military academies or schools came to Penghu to recruit cadets: The ROC Military Academy got more cadets than any other school (especially the 1951 and 1953 classes); Political Warfare Cadres Academy ranked second; Air Force Academy, Army Communications School and Academy of Finance and Management also got a certain percentage of cadets respectively. Because my health was not that good, I didn't sign up for the exam held by any of these academies.

When we were stationed at a seaport called Suoguangang, President Chiang created such a propaganda slogan which reads: "In the first year, preparation is done; in the second year, counteroffensive is launched; in the third year, all the battlegrounds are cleared up in China Mainland; and in the fifth year, victory is obtained!"[44] He demanded that we should put our weapons under our heads as pillows at night, exercising vigilance until the crack of dawn and in the meantime, to step up our training without letup. If the Communists Army dared cross Taiwan Strait and attacked us, we would certainly deliver a hard blow to them defending Taiwan, Penghu, Kinmen, Matsu, and finally, taking advantage of the opportunity to launch a counteroffensive to recover the Chinese Mainland.

When political study session was on, we were demanded to study two booklets: *Junrenhun,* or the Serviceman's Guiding Principles and *Geminghun,* or the revoluntionary's Guiding Principles. By so doing, they inculcated in us the values of justice, integrity, and especially, courage.

When the fitness program session and the field training program session were on, we were highly demanded to run faster, jump higher and farther, and shoot better. Overall, they wanted to train us to be one Nationalist soldier who was worthy of ten Communist soldiers, ten, one hundred, and so on, an army of invincible troops as strong as iron and steel.

However, our shoes became a big problem. Made from poor qualities of plastic and frayed by the gravel land we trod on, a pair of black plastic shoes newly distributed to us was broken up on the soles for less than a month, so were the uppers of them, our toes were beyond the edges of the shoes. Henceforth, our squad leader taught us how to make straw sandals. Firstly, we were instructed to put our feet evenly on the ground, and then draw along our feet to get the measurements of our sandals with a piece of chalk, and at last, strike the wooden stakes along the lines of the blue-prints into the ground.

Produced in abundance on the Penghu Islands and deemed as the excellent material for making straw shandals, is the plant called agave. The first step was to get a bunch of agaves soaked in a pond letting them rot there. The second step was to spread them out on the ground under the scorching sun to be aired out. And the last step was to shake them clean by hands, and right before our noses, there were white agave fibers appearing. And as we had them twisted into the finger-like ropes, they can be used to make our straw shandals.

On the Penghu Islands, the sun in summer was as sweltering as fire. Stripped to our waists and with only red shorts and straw sandals on and rifles in our hands, we were severely trained on the rolling hills with the aim at getting the army ready and strengthening its power.

Once the training was off, we were sent to the seashore to build bunkers immediately. As a boulder, the basic material, was too heavy to be moved, we had to apply ropes and poles to carry it over. Each one of us was equipped with a hammer sitting on the sort of flat rock and breaking the boulder up into small stones, and then, having the small stones broken up into the smaller pieces. As far as the eye could reach, we saw nothing except that there were dense clouds of dust flying, and everyone's head and face were coated with a layer of dirt. And what we heard was the striking sound of "Da! Da!" together with the sounding of tidal waves, "Shua! Shua!" After getting the cube-like pieces, we poured water, sand, and lime into a mortar and blended them well. The last step was to carry shoulder poles from which suspended two buckets with this newly-made stuff in, and we got the layout filled. And every step had to be perfectly executed.

Owing to the long-lasting effects of undernutrition, non-stop rigorous training, and non-stop work on the bunkers, there were lots of buddies in our company suffering from night blindness. And I was one of them. In the daytime, my vision was normal. But as night set in, I saw nothing but a mass of yellow-colored opacity. When the time was due to turn in, I had to grope from the outside of our barracks into the inside slowly, step by step, also feeling in the bedroom for the doubledecked platform-like bed to the right spot where I enabled myself to climb up onto the upper deck of my bed.

In order to cure night blindness, our superiors distributed bottles of fish oil capsules to us, and furthermore, demanded the quartermaster of every company to purchase shark fish from the local fishermen to supplement the insufficient fish oil rationed.

Seeing those who had run away, those who had become cadets of a variety of military academies with bright future ahead of them, and worse, I got night blindness, I felt extremely depressed. However, the worse form of unluckiness befell me on the heels of my night blindness.

In 1952, there were two fatal infectious diseases spreading through the islands: No. 1 scrub typhus; No. 2 typhus.

One day, when we came back from our field training, I suddenly felt my limbs weakened. Firstly, I felt that I was running a temperature, but a low grade, and then followed was the high fever. And I also felt dizzy, eyes blurry. Worst of all, I couldn't sit bolt upright nor stand straight. Not until a day was over, did three or four buddies collapse in our company. The most horrible thing was that a private named Lu Shangyun passed away the following day. And his death had caused us so much panic that we were afraid of being infected, and all of our buddies were trying to keep away from us as far as possible. Our Company Commander quickly gave an order to have the inflected including me firstly carried out of the barracks, and then tried to locate one of disused houses owned by civilians to accommodate us.

I was dumped unto a sort of bed covered with straws under which there were coral fragments. At this juncture, I was in the state of coma due to the high fever. And in the meantime, I was raving.

The only thing that I knew was to drink water. The capacity for intake of water one night only, I was told after my recovery, was nine canteens. In another word, I kept drinking and simultaneously, urinating on the bed.

There were two close buddies of mine named Liu Bocheng and Yuan Lijuin who were not afraid of this infectious disease and took turns to get water for me. After delivering the water, Liu or Yuan, staying far away, watched how I was doing. In case, I was trying to stand up and do something dangerous due to my high fever, Liu or Yuan came to my rescue. If I was seen to have fallen asleep, they just stayed there watching for some time, and then left.

They are my saviors. Especially Mr. Liu to whom, I am greatly indebted, because only he who got involved in a heated debate with our company commander, "As Ma Chungliang is still breathing, you cannot have him carried out and buried alive!"

At that time, neither enough medicine nor enough doctors and nurses were available on the island. As I was abandoned in that small house by the seashore a week, I couldn't get admission to Magong Hospital, let alone the doctor's diagnosing. I thought to myself that there was nothing for me to do but to let mother nature take its course! I kept on drinking water for another two weeks. Though the high fever was still there, my case was not deteriorating.

One afternoon, I was in a sort of the condition of unnatural deep sleep. Suddenly, I felt that my eyelids were forcibly opened up. And in the meantime, I was blinded by the glare of a flashlight, and I was of my opinion that something bad would happen to me soon and that the little ghostly figures were sent out to get me by Yama, King of the Underworld. Shortly after, within my earshot were these words: "What he is suffering from is typhus, and it is in the peak period of its development. If he can hold out this way a week, it will turn better. I don't have any medicine for this kind of disease at home, and let him alone power through it!" When recovered, I became aware that he was one of the combat medical technicians trained in the Japanese Army during the Second World War. When Japan was defeated, he got the opportunity to return to his hometown and serve his own folks.

I totally depended upon the intake of water to have gone through this fatal disease. And one month after my recovery, that I was all skin and bones began plumping out, and downy hair began growing in the parts of my body from which the original hair had been lost. Shortly after, all the hair grew fully back as they had been before.

Though I was drilled to the bone and went through typhus, the matter of life and death, I survived despite all these trials. However, there was a buddy named Hu Chengye who was unable to get himself out of the deep black hole of depression. And during the hours, he was playing the sentry role for the security of our camp, and with the muzzle of his gun against his belly, he committed suicide by pulling the trigger of his rifle with one of his toes. The aftermath was that his stomach was blasted open; intestines exposed. His suicidal act left an indelible impression on me. Not until 2000, did I suddenly have the urge to write a piece of modern poem entitled: "Words from the Grave" to commemorate him. Because he is the only son in his family, I wrote this poem from his perspective. The whole thing is as follows:

> *At high tide*
> *At low tide*
> *In a wink of an eye, I have been buried here fifty years*
> *The monsoon wind blows over me once a year*
> *My bone and flesh become chemicals that have long eaten into the hardest rock of the cliff*
>
> *Martial laws have been lifted for several decades*
> *The wild geese have traveled back and forth countless times*
> *I am the only person who has been interred here*
> *Having no chance to see the leaves of the white-trunk poplars*
> *Nor do I have the opportunity to see the footprints on the snowy ground at my hometown*
>
> *Having come here, we are of the same fate*
> *Some are the sole trunks of their family trees; others, branches*
> *Only the family tree of mine is uprooted and withered away as the lean column cloud of smoke from an incense stick*
> *And it also seems as if I were the embarking light on the masthead of a sinking ship*
> *Having flashed on and off a few times, it goes down to the bottom of the sea.*

The stars are twinkling in the sky overhead
Silently I have been counting the mighty tides in my mind
Buried here, and acting as a "divine figure," I am watching days
and nights
As if I were watching the waves of barley in the field in my farmland

I contributed this piece of poem to *The Epoch Poetry Quarterly*, and the editor-in-chief, Zhang Mo had it run on the Autumn Issue, in the year of 2000. After the Mini Three Links were conducted between the PRC and ROC, I wish the spiritual being of Hu Chengye's, could pay a visit to his home village in Shandong Province and tend his barley or wheat field as he did in the Penghu Islands.

CHAPTER 14

LITERARY FRIENDS IN THE ARMY

In Magong, the largest island of Penghu, as the days went by, they loosened their grips on us in terms of the stringent rule, neither corporal punishment nor tongue-lashing any more. And even a cussword was hardly heard. Furthermore, though not publicly announced, "We can pick up our textbooks to study," yet at least when we studied them, they were not to be confiscated. Of course, the books written by the left-wing writers were still prohibited.

At this time, I saw a buddy named Wang Yuhuai begin writing. He was one of the students from the Yangtai United Secondary School and conversant with Chinese classics and especially, loving most the poetry of the Tang dynasty, the ci (another form of poetry) of the Sung dynasty, and the qu (a kind of song form) of the Yuan dynasty. To this day, I still can recall the look of his when he was teaching us a piece of poem entitled: "Pu Sa Man" or Buddhist Dancers by Li Bai.

He has a strange habit, snorting as the same as a donkey does. After speaking a few words, he cannot help contracting his nose. And when an inspiration strikes him, he can come up with a string of witticisms. His Mandarin is tinged with Yantai accent. With the exception of the Yangtai dialect, what he has said is not hard to be understood if you listen to him carefully.

When the fitness training session was on, one of the items he feared the most was *tiaomuma,* or jumping over a wooden box longitudinally. No matter how far the starting line was and how fast the speed he picked up, it came to the same result that he always landed his buttocks on that wooden thing.

We, the student soldiers from Shandong, got paid based on the ranks of *erdengbing* and *yidengbing*, the lowest ones called privates but there is slight difference between them, the latter is higher than the former by one rank in the Nationalists Army. There were few of us getting paid based on the rank of *shangdengbing*, the private, the first class in a company. Because this rank was, of course, higher than the other two, *shangdengbing* should possess good physique, impressive appearance and tall frame that qualified him to be ranged at the head of a squad.

By then, the pay for *erdengping* was raised to 8 yuan, *yidengbing* 9, and *shangdengbing*, 11. If further elaborated, our whole month's income was the value of less than twenty packs of the Banana brand cigarettes, each pack sold at 50 cents. If we wanted to buy *liangdao gaozhi*, or 200 sheets of manuscript papers on which we drafted essays, half a month's pay would be gone.

Every night, after the lights-out and all buddies had fallen sound asleep, Wang Yuhuai quietly got up and lit up half the length of a candle he had kept beginning to draft a short story on the bad quality of toilet papers. The title of that short story has long been unremembered, but a couplet as its subhead is still embedded in my memory:

"In the floral garden of the heavens, there is a flower blooming Simultaneously, there is one withering on the earth."

He was writing about a young tongue-tied guy with higher perspective. This guy had a great ambition. And in order to deliver the people of his home village from misery and want, he sacrificed his own life to have died in a pool of blood. In the 1950s, there were two popular *wenyi*, or literature and arts, magazines in Taiwan: one was the *Wild Wind Monthly*; the other, the *Wenyi Magazine Semi-monthly*. When he had finished his last touch, he mailed it to the *Wild Wind Monthly*. No sooner had his short story been published in that magazine than the whole company scrambled for it to read.

As Wang's handwritten thing of that short story was converted into that of a printed version and inspired by his example, thus, I secretly followed his way and wrote a piece of a sort of diary-style stuff entitled: "A Soldier's Diary" roughly 3,500 words. And I contributed it to the *Wenyi Magazine Semi-monthly.*

The education I had received on the Chinese Mainland only got to the level of having finished the second year and two weeks in the third year at junior high (which is roughly the equal of the eighth or ninth grade in the U.S.) That my Chinese was not good enough to do this sort of thing was clearly understandable. Fearing that my work would be rejected, and became a laughing butt in the company, I wrote a P. S. at the end of that thing: "Dear Editor, if it is not publishable, please dispose of it at will and don't send it back to me!"

Unexpectedly, in two months, when Wang Yuhuai serving as a "Mess Officer" went shopping for our kitchen stuff and came back from Magong City and told me that the piece I had written was published in the *Wenyi Magazine Semi-monthly*. In order to see what the printed version of my own writing looked like earlier, I asked for a leave and went all the way to Magong and bought a copy back out of my own pocket. The editor of that magazine didn't pay me for my work nor give me a free copy. He thought that my acquiescence to what he had done to me, a budding writer, was taken for granted.

Parallell to Wang in terms of "literary accomplishments" is Yang Zhenying except that Yang's Chinese calligraphy with brush and ink is beautiful and exceptional. He also possesses the gift of drawing. When the wall paper contest was held in the camp, he was held responsible for copying the more rigorously-selected works down on paper and drawing the "masthead" of the wall paper.[45]

Both had brought with them a lot of poems written by reputed poets from the Chinese Mainland. The poets include: Xu Zhimo, Yuan Kejia, Sun Yutang, Li Sha, Cang Kejia, Ai Qing, Bing Xin. Yang copied them one by one into a small notebook. You didn't have to bother about what the contents of these selected poems meant to you, only the beautiful art of his handwriting with the fountain pen would be greatly pleasing to the eye. When our training session was over, they took out the notebook to read. When they didn't read, I borrowed it from them.

As to their personality traits, Wang is outgoing and open-minded, while Yang tongue-tied and standing on his own feet. They firstly write short stories and then poems. I have found out that there are streaks of Chinese classics in Wang's poems. For example: "Has any forested mountain kept silent through my mind's eyes?" But Young's poems are tinged with the style of the modern times. However, I cannot recall any of his verse lines.

Overall, when they wrote short stories, I followed suit; when they wrote poetry, I did the same thing.

One night, suffering insomnia, listening to my buddies' rhythmically snoring, looking at the moon through the window, and worrying about the wretched condition in which I got trapped—being unable to continue pursuing my studies, I was so sad that I couldn't contain my tears in my eyes as if the flood had breached the river bank. However, as this sad moment elapsed, a piece of modern poem entitled: "Moonlit Night" came by itself, and I jotted it down. At dawn, I became impatient and hurriedly handed it over to Wang for reviewing. Having read it, he contracted his nose several times, and quietly had it polished as follows:

The tick-tock clock is compared to a whip whipping my heart
My eyes contain the tears of struggle
In the deep of the night, I quietly lie on my bed with the moonlight
Through the window, I gaze into the vault of the sky
A crescent moon takes care of the little sparkling stars
The night is likened to a decent lass
Quietly glowing with mysterious charming

The blue dream has just been woven but soon broken up again
I see a metric star gliding in the night sky
And I hear the footstep of spring silently go by.

There is no poet who does not cherish his virgin work. In fact, "Moonlit Night" is a half piece done by me; another half by Wang. I sent it out and got published in a magazine called the *Island Literature*.

On the Penghu Islands, the camps in which I have dwelt are: Waian, Neian, Bamboo Pole Bay, Shiquan, Suoguangang, Wukan, Aimen, Baisha, and the last one that I have lived in is called Jimowu.

I cannot recall the details of how and when I became acquainted with a poet named Li Chunsheng, but I can remember that at that time, he was a guy, extremely melancholic and quite passionate.

On Sundays, he frequently visited me. As soon as he saw me, he held my hand tight and called me by my given name in Mandarin tinged with strong Shanxi accent. We talked about literature and arts, modern poetry, life, etc. When I sent him back to his camp, I walked him along the coast line of Jimuwu. I was walking with him on the one hand, and listening to him to recite his new poetic works on the other. And once we were a stone's throw away from his camp, he would get an excuse by saying that he wanted to do the same thing as I did to him. Thus, I was accompanied back to my camp by him. And I repeated doing the same thing to him; he did to me likewise. As a result, sauntering along that coastal line back and forth, four or five times, a whole Sunday holiday was gone.

Zhu Guanghe usually wrote traditional poetry. After making friends with us, he began writing modern poetry. The creational inspirations of his were mostly from what he had observed on the islands: the sea of the Penghu Islands, the gravel land, the strong monsoon wind, the kids who gleaned seashells on the beach, and the girls who worked in the fields, with their half faces covered with towels, forearms and shins wrapped in motley fabric.

On one of Sundays, we met with one another on the street of the city of Magong by chance, and having reached a consensus, we went to a photo shop for having a group picture taken. And for that reason, since then, each one of us has kept a valuable photo. The inscription which is written by Li Chunsheng sounds poetic, simultaneously, revealing sort of our young wishful thinking: "We have sown the seeds of our faith in the desert of life, and we will passionately sing the song, 'Life is beautiful' over and over again!"

He sent this photo and our poetic works to his No. 4 uncle, Li Sha, a senior poet. Li Sha saw us, all teenagers in uniforms who were fond of literature and arts, accordingly, giving each one of us a pseudonym: Li Chunsheng (Li Qing), Wang Yuhuai (Wang Gu), Yang Zhenying (Yang Yi), Zhu Guanghe (Zhu Long), Ma Chungliang (Ma Ding). And another guy was Sun Jingfu who didn't write poetry, and therefore, he wasn't given any pen name. Further, Li Sha recommended our better works to literature and arts magazines to be published.

On the islands, I was acquainted with another group of literature and arts friends. They are: Guo Guangren (pen name, Guo Wu), Wang Chuanpu (Wang Pu), Wang Jinfang (Wang Shu), Cao Jizeng (Ji Wen), Zhou Yamin, Ding Chengzhong (Lu Ding), and Wang Xuekuan.

Guo Guangren, whose original pen name was Ziren, meaning an industrious person, was awfully hard-working in pursuing his writing career. Those proses of his, "the real thing, love me true," were within the limits of 1,000 words and published frequently in the supplements connected with the major newspapers in Taiwan and won great admiration of ours. Later he changed his pen name from Ziren into Guowu at the time he got his novelette, "Traces in a Dream" serialized in the *Central Daily News*. This work became so popular with readers, and was a must-read. Every morning, there were lots of readers getting up in the early morning to buy a copy of the *Central Daily News* to read this serial. It was said that the most renowned writer on the island, Suma Zhongyuan, was no exception. When the whole thing finally came to the end by installments, readers complained the story ended up in tragedy boisterously demanding that the writer should rewrite the last part of it into the denouement of having the hero and the heroine married and of "they live happily ever after."

Wang Chuan Pu is a talented essayist, novelist, and poet, namely, he can write prose, novel and poetry simultaneously. He is also great at translation, rendering English works into Chinese. He translated Pearl Buck's *Letters from Peking* and got it published in the *Crown Magazine* in installments. And one of the radio stations in Taipei had got it on the air. Among his novels, *The Everlasting Confessions* is an outstanding one. Later, he utilized video camera to have the more than 65 years old writers' biographies taped. The project was called, *The Videotaped Biographies of Senior Writers in Taiwan, ROC,* having got him to the acme of his career. Consequently, somebody called him the contemporary Su Maqian, the greatest Master of the Eastern Han Dynasty famed in the field of history and literature. At present, his unprecedented undertaking of this kind not only makes him reputed in Taiwan and the Chinese Mainland but the world. And lots of famous libraries have stored a set of his works—the *Videotaped Biographies of Senior Writers in Taiwan, ROC* (disk edition).

Wang Jinfang is a loner, not socialized himself with people at all. He holds himself so high that he is too opinionated to change his views even if he has been proved wrong. His modern poems are tinctured with newness and freshness. By then, we didn't know he possessed drawing gift. Unexpectedly, several decades later, he became one of the giant water colorists in the field. He relished the fame of being the top water-colorist not only at home but in the world. He is living in Australia, now.

Cao Jizeng's poetic works are rich in prose; Zhou Yamin is a versatile young man; his wife, Ai Ya, noted for her prose works. More than a decade later, Zhou got into the world of broadcast.

When the Chinese New Year Festival was in the corner, aside from enjoying our "feast" and setting off fire crackers for celebrating the occasion of saying "Goodbye" to the old year, Zhang Youn, from the 6th company, Gong Weiyang and Wang Wenxie, from the 4th company (Several decades later, Wang took up the posts, Commander, Combined Logistic Command and Deputy Minister of Defense), and I, from the 5th company, staged a "home-made" play. Based on the economic principles, we were the picks with the aim to get our buddies entertained. There was only one female lead role in the play. Wang Wenxie and I disguised ourselves as this girl, and he played the girl in the first part of the play; I, the second.

In 1952, without having had much of substantive changes, only the 39th division was renamed the 57th; the 115th regiment changed into the title of 169th. This time, I was transferred to a unit called Headquarters Company which was an affiliate to the regiment. The battalion commander and the company commander remained unchanged. Only the regimental commander, Colonel Han Bin was replaced by Colonel Yuan Zijun.

CHAPTER 15

MILITARY TRAINING BASE IN TAIWAN

In 1954, we finally got the opportunity to be transferred to Taiwan, the largest island in this region, and left the Penghu Islands where we had been stationed for five years.[46]

After getting ashore at Kaohsiung, we began marching toward Chenggongling, a military training base located in central Taiwan. On the road, while walking, we simultaneously conducted sham battles. When the night fell, mostly we borrowed classrooms from the middle or elementary schools for overnighting. We made our makeshift beds by pulling two or three desks together and slept on them with our clothes on. Sometimes, we were quartered in villages for spending nights. We made our makeshift beds there by firstly having the spots under the eaves of houses cleaned, and then putting the hay on as mattresses, and finally, spreading our woolen blankets out.

Once, our squad was assigned lodging to a family to stay overnight.

There are a few members in this family: an old couple and a young couple. After a good night's sleep, we discovered that all the household chores were totally dependent on a daughter-in-law. We saw that firstly, she did the cooking for the family; secondly, she did the laundry; thirdly, she fed pigs with pigswill; and fourthly, she went to the checkered vegetable fields to get some greens back. She got all the routine duties done one by one orderly.

She is a girl of few words and the look of grudging no one made me to admire her greatly. I thought to myself that if one day I could be discharged from the army working on a piece of farmland somewhere, marrying a country girl like her and spending my entire life in the countryside, I wouldn't feel discontented.

After the Dragon Boat Festival, the weather in Taiwan is getting hotter and hotter day by day.

With steel helmets on our heads, backpacks on our backs, the scorching sun overhead, and the steaming hot asphalt-paved road beneath our feet, we felt terribly bad, and the feeling of this kind was beyond description.

When the start of march from the Kaohsiung dock, we performed very well as crack troops. But after passing by the township, Tianzhong, the entire company was like sheep without a shepherd. Worst of all, after several days' walking on the road, some buddies suffered from blisters on the soles of the feet. As a result, with the going of frictions, the blood blisters appeared. And they became lame limping forward slowly as if snails had been crawling.

When a man is in pain, the best way for him to do is dreaming himself away from the reality of his suffering and thinking something else. Firstly, I let myself go wild dreaming of marrying a country girl and then, dreaming of being a poet. Walking on and on, I felt as if I were hit by electrical shock, and a poem, "Snail" was formed in my mind. When we got to our camping-place that night, I busied myself jotting it down as follows:

> *I am a snail*
> *Living in a shady and dark corner*
> *People ignore me simply walking by before my nose*
> *But I still remain happy even if nobody is paying any attention to*
> *my being there*
> *Though I have an ugly face*
> *Yet I have a shell to protect and defend myself well*
> *The antennae are my mind's eyes that could figure out when it is*
> *sunny or rainy and the rough path ahead*

You are a bird with wings flying as high as you can in the blue sky
Or you are a free fish in the river swimming as joyously as you wish
All glory and joy belong to you
Tossing your sarcasm and eye-rolling to me
I will be able to bear them all
Crawling on my own path
Though the wind blows or the rain pelts and the unknown is ahead
I'll definitely crawl on my journey ahead of me.

This is an easily-grasped piece of poem. The *Vineyard Poetry Quarterly* ran it on its 67th issue. Later, Mr. Wen Xiaocun, the chief editor, edited it into an anthology of poems entitled: The *Analytic Studies of 100 Modern Poems* which is used to teach young folks and teenagers who are interested in poetry. Through the editing of Wen's, it is arranged in the Chapter of Animals in the collection and because of this edited work, he was awarded a prize by the Cultural Bureau connected with the Provincial Taiwan Government.

It takes us a week to get to Chenggongling afoot.

As I recall when we got to Wu Ri, the sun stood very low. Though exhausted, we were curious about this new military training base.

All units moved into different barracks but in the same military base, of course. Thus, visiting each other became easier. Though belonging to varying units, we, the group of verse lovers, who had no verbal promise, gathered together at Guo Guangren's unit spontaneously. He worked at the regimental headquarters, a bigger target and easily to access. With Li Chunsheng's pushing, we decided to have a mimeographed poetry magazine published, The *Green Apple Poetry Monthly*, to spice up our daily life during that period of military training.

There was no shortage of poets who could contribute their works to the *Green Apple Poetry Monthly*. They are: Wangpu, Shulan, Jiwen, Zhulong, Wangshu, Li Chunsheng and me. However, only Guo Guangren, himself, rolled up his sleeves and did the entire work from editing through stencil-engraving to mimeographing.

We made a new friend with administrative secretary Shan Yizhen who had been writing poetry for years and his pen name is Shanren. He was also the immediate boss of Guo Guangren and ranked first lieutenant. We had to toe his line in everything. If he gave us his nodding approval, any problem would immediately be solved. In fact, the *Green Apple Poetry Monthly* is the sideline of the military newspaper the *True Words*, issued by the Headquarters of the 57th Division which is labeled, "The Great Wall Army." On principles, our "poetry magazine" is not for the reading public.

The *Green Apple Poetry Monthly* is not well organized in terms of its hierarchy nor are there any regulations for contributors. But we took it seriously getting the mimeographed magazine out on time. Once out, each one of us had a copy in hand and discussed with one another the strengths and the weaknesses of our works. And we got a lot of fun from it.

Even up to the present moment, I still can recall the argument with one another about accepting or rejecting one poem written by a senior poet named Chen Dong. Li Chunsheng said, "Despite the fact that Chen Dong is a senior poet, the piece of his is not publishable in the *Green Apple Poetry Monthly*, and the publishing of a work is completely dependent upon its quality, not on the repute of a poet!" But I refuted him by saying that the reason Chen Dong mailed his work to our monthly magazine was totally out of goodwill to encourage us, nothing else. However, from this argument, we could see how seriously we valued the *Green Apple Poetry Monthly* at that time.

Our poetry magazine was run for some time, and there were two of our buddies passing the entrance examination and enrolling at Fuxinggan Military Political Warfare Cadres Academy; another one or two friends were transferred to other units. "We were torn apart." Thus, our bid couldn't continue, and naturally it came to an end.

At Chenggonling, another event worthy of recording here is General Sun Liren's talk: "Firstly, throughout my life, I wear woolen socks because they absorb sweat and moisture so as not to be easy to contract Tinea Pedis—Hong Kong feet. Therefore, I ordered my quartermaster to have woolen socks distributed to you. Secondly, after the marching, no matter how exhausted you are, do not go to bed immediately, having to take a bath or get your hands and feet washed. Because of this act, you will be set free of fatigue, and further, made sleeping like a log."[47]

Our unit, after going through the training at Chenggongling, was transferred to Guguan, a remote mountainous area, for a sort of "mountain training." At that time, our company commander was dismissed, and the newly inaugurated commander saw that my penmanship and my writing skills were good, promoting me from corporal to sergeant. Actually, he let me do the paperwork that should be done by a senior sergeant.

The days at Guguan were the happiest ones in my entire serviceman's career. Perhaps, because of the fresh air in the mountain, I was being lifted up in terms of spirit, and my physical strength was boosted, too. After the dinner, I followed buddies to see the falling and splashing of a variety of falls, and the different birds sailing back to their nests. And I was amazingly productive in terms of poetry writing. The *Wild Wind Monthly* was the major magazine to run my works, and occasionally, a few pieces got published in the *Modern Poetry Quarterly* and the *Page of Poetry Weekly* connected with the supplementary edition of the *Taiwan Gonglun Bao*, Gonglun means public opinion.

CHAPTER 16

THE TAICHUNG INCIDENT

Among these 8,000 students, aside from those who were placed in a newly established school called Magong Military Dependents' School, those who passed the entrance examinations and enrolled in the various types of military academies, those who were discharged from the army because of chronic diseases,those who were dumped into jute sacks and thrown overboard and got drowned, those who were executed, those who committed suicides, and those who died of various diseases, at this time, there were only 900-some odd students left in the army. And they were either all non-commissioned officers or the private soldiers.

Of these 900 students, the vast majority of us didn't want to stay in the army to be professional soldiers. No matter how hard our superiors did the brainwashing, we made up 100 percent of our minds to quit the army. Our only demand was the reinstatement of student status. Going back to the school from which we came, we wanted to finish our incomplete studies there. However, this long-awaited wish finally developed into a *jitiqingyuan,* or a collective petition which really means collective protest to my way of thinking.

In the Nationalists Army, launching a collective protest to the authority is a big deal. The organizer whose case is considered less serious may be imprisoned. If the case is considered serious, he may be executed. Therefore, It was stipulated that firstly, each one of us should be an organizor and no one should show heroism in this protest; secondly, we should have the justification for this collective protest and be able to enumerate concrete examples to prove that we had been unfairly treated; thirdly, the present predicament we stuck in should have unbiased celebrities' sympathies regardless of the parties they belonged to, the ruling party or the opposition; and fourthly, every collective protest rally should adopt "non-violent means."

Besides, passing on to us were Four Proclamations as follows: 1. No gun-carrying; 2. No rioting; 3. No oath-taking; 4. No revolting against the country.[48]

On April 25, 1955, in Houli camp in Taichung County, suddenly, there was a news passing on to us by word of mouth that a collective protest rally was to be held in Taipei.[49] Our moving was swift as if the cloud were amassing in the sky or as if the sound were traveling in the air. We stepped out of our camp and headed for the Taichung Railway Station to assemble there. And we hoped that if there was any train available, we would get on, no matter what it was, passenger or freight. In another word, we thought of nothing else but to go to Taipei to protest.

As we were gathering boisterously together in front of the station, there was a lot of military police rushing in timely and laying siege to us immediately. We adopted the strategy of keeping our mouth shut and they dealt with us by the trick of pacifying us and kept us under sort of "flexible" surveillance. In order not to leave a way of escape to any netted fish to get out, they further gave an order to the stationmaster to postpone the northbound train so that they could run back and forth through the cars and have a thorough check.

In front of the station, we stood or sat around a small park in which there was a bronze statue of the late President Chiang Kai-shek. Initially, about 50-odd students were there, and later, there were 300 or 400 plus students getting in. Some students got down on their knees adopting the kneeling postures on the concrete silently protesting they were unfairly treated; others sat there with their eyes tightly closed and silently prayed. And the majority of students were sitting there and keeping their eyes downcast.

We had nothing else to do but to sit there whiling away the time.

More and more people were gathering around the park to see us. And certainly, no reporters were permitted to interview us, not mention to take a picture of us. But a piece of unjustified news was passing on to us that there was a correspondent of *The New York Times* getting involved in this. As stubborn as a mule, this correspondent kept on inquiring, and finally, he got an answer like this: "These soldiers are extremely patriotic and ask to go to the off-shore islands to fight the Reds! Because their requests have been denied, they have no alternative, but to stage a sit-in!"

As time sped by, second by second, minute by minute, more and more students were coming to join us. The order was: the students could get in, but not get out.

The crowds bursted with curiosity about it keeping on watching, standing around, and wholeheartedly wanting to see how this "drama" come to an end.

With the crowds' watching, the military authorities didn't dare to give an order that each one of us be handcuffed, fettered and carried into military trucks to be transported back to our camp, nor did they dare take us away by two-on-one or four-on-one from the scene by overwhelming manpower, not mention to have the guts to disperse us by firing guns. If they adopted any one of the above-mentioned hasty acts, it would cause a big commotion. The best way they could do to us was a repeat persuasion, "Having us understand the interest of the country and the essence of nationalism." Further, they advised us to return to our camp voluntarily. If the stratagem of persuasion didn't work, they would wait till the middle night, when people were gone, launching a brutal crackdown on us.

A five-point consensus of ours is as follows:

1. In 1949, the country was in a storm, and we were illegally drafted into the army having served the country six years already and defended Kinmen, Matsu, the Penghu Islands and Taiwan. Since the Sino-American Mutual Defense Treaty was signed, the

situation of the R.O.C. on Taiwan got steadier and steadier than ever before.[50]

2. Based on the same status, the students of colleges and universities, who followed the Nationalists Army's retreat from the Chinese Mainland to Taiwan, were not placed into the army, nor were the students of Changbai Teachers' Training College in the northeast China. Instead, all of its students enrolled at a school called the College of Administration established by the government, and were better taken care of.[51]

3. In the same case like ours, in 1953, the National Yuheng United Secondary School students, who returned to Taiwan with General Huang Ji's troops, were all admitted to the Provincial Yuanlin Experimental Secondary School. At the beginning, they fled the Mainland to Phu Quoc, Vietnam; several years later, they came to Taiwan.[52]

4. Again, based on the same status, those students retreating from the Dachen Islands to Taiwan in 1953 were totally accepted by Yuanlin.[53]

5. After the year of 1949, the students firstly stowed away from the Chinese Mainland to Diaojingling, a refugees' camp, in Hong Kong, and to Macau and then enabled themselves to come to Taiwan through different channels. They were all allowed to get in the school, Yuanlin.[54]

After contrasting the above-mentioned cases 2 to 4 with ours, and we wondered on the same status that why had there been such a huge difference between them and us? We were all angry at the government and thought that the government really mistreated us. Therefore, we felt that it was reasonable for us to stand up against the government. Under the circumstances, united, we stood; because of being united, we remained powerful; and only united, we could avoid being punished individually. And in case of getting punished, we would get collectively.

The people surrounding us kept on watching. Some came and

some went away. Around 1 a.m., director of the Department of Political Warfare in the First Army-group, Major General, Yi Jin, got to the scene.[55] Before he came, we all sat on the spots as wished. Once he appeared on the scene, we all adopted the tall kneeling postures and faced upward to the bronze statue of the late President Chiang Kai-shek. He stood on a military truck giving us a talk through loudspeaker:

"Brothers, I understand what your problem is, and will pass it up to my superiors. And within a very short period of time, I ensure that you will get an answer. But first you have to get up and return to your camp and wait there."

We didn't react to what he had said. Having seen this, he repeated what he had just said.

At this moment, it was extremely quiet, and the air was like lead.

Again, seeing us with heads down and tight-lipped, he pounded his chest and guaranteed us:

"I might be your older brother or your father. The protest you are doing now is tantamount to the kind of behavior murdering your older brother or your father. As you all know, solving the problem needs time. Let us get up, all get up, and go back to your camp, and I guarantee you, within the very short period of time, the answer will surely be given to you!"

As the hour was drawn to 2 a.m., the deadlock was still going on. The military authorities moved a division force to "wait on" us.[56] And they thought that if they let this group of soldiers be "monkeying" on and on, it did not only damage the repute of the army but also have the great impact on the image of the country. If the strategy of persuasive talks didn't work, they would forcibly drag us away.

Having been aware of the fact that we were surrounded, we knew that the hope to Taipei for protesting was disappointed. And we had nothing to do but to adopt the tactic of expedience to deal with this kind of situation. We had to beat "the metal-sounding call of retreating," temporarily going back to our camp, and waiting for another opportunity to stage a come-back.

In our judgment, the problem of resuming schooling at Yuanlin wouldn't be resolved within a short span of time. And we also predicted that the worst thing would happen to us. That was to use whatever the means available to disintegrate us and position us in different military units stationed in the various parts of the island.

Once they got this "attempted move" done, it was extremely hard for us to launch another collective protest. Therefore, thinking this might happen soon, we couldn't wait any longer, but to take action again to link us up launching another protest in Taipei.

The military authorities saw the developing of this kind rapidly and took measures to get the matter settled once for all by utilizing different military vehicles to transport us, groups of twos or threes to different units. The majority of us were placed into the 81st division. And there were 39 students arrested. And of them, four students were sentenced to different years' imprisonment: Chang Yongbin (10 years), Chang Yonggeng (7 years), Chang Songshan (7 years) and Xu Xiuqi (7 years). The others, 35 students, were shut up in a detention center and half a year later, they were transferred to a place for reform.[57]

Shi Liquan, Li Jilun, and I were dumped into a vehicle that carried us to a camp named Longgong in the Zhongli district of Taoyuan County, the Communications Corps of the First Army-group. After reporting to them, they had us sent down to the communications company right away. The company commander of that unit, upon seeing us, gave each one of us a sheet of paper and a ball pen requesting of us to write about ourselves. I can't remember what I put down on the paper now, but I am pretty sure that in the last paragraph, I put such a word in: "My ambition is going back to school and finishing my incomplete studies."

The new unit appointed all three of us to do the paperwork for the entire corps. Our job descriptions were clear, not complicated at all.

And a few days later, we were on track. Furthermore, our superiors were greatly moved by our stories, and they were sympathetic with us, and encouraged us to sign up for "the Classes in the Supplementary Education Program for the Servicemen in the headquarters of the First Army-group." These classes were designed to promote the qualities of servicemen in the field of humanities. This program is regarded as one of the good policies of the National Government.

Mr. Wang Yuanheng, who taught us English, is the most interesting teacher of all. Prior to his entering the classroom, he might have a couple of drinks. Once he was in, the whole room was filled with the pleasant smell of liquor, and maybe, under the influence of alcohol, he became long-winded. Aside from teaching us English during our class time, the anecdotes of the "English giants," Prof. Wu Bingzhong, a famous English teacher in Taiwan, and Gu Weijun, a prominent diplomat were vividly delineated.

There was one time that during the class time, he gave us a written test on a whim demanding us to write a piece of 300-word essay. We could pick up any topic to write but it must be a real experience related to everyday life. I wrote quite well and won me admiration and respect from the class. And he praised me: "You possess the ability to write something in English."

At that time, I also wrote two pieces of prose in Chinese, too. One is entitled: "Mr. Wei—My Elementary School Teacher"; another, "My Eldest Sister." I contributed them to one of the military newspapers, *The Jing Zhong Bao*, Jingzhong meaning allegiance, Bao, newspaper, issued by the Chinese Army HQ, in Taipei. This was the only newspaper available in our company, then. After their publications, I jumped for joy a few days. It is regrettable that the clippings of those two pieces get lost. Otherwise, I will certainly have the second one: "My Eldest Sister" duplicated and mailed the duplicated copy to Zhonglan who is living in Nanjing now.

CHAPTER 17

DAYS IN THE HOSPITAL

When I stayed in that company under the Communications Corps affiliated to the First Army-Group at Longgong camp, Zhongli, I lived rather a good life If I didn't think about the issue of the reinstatemint of student status. Simultaneously, I made a pact with myself: "Do not rivet my attention on that thing again." If incautiously, I let it pop into my head again, I had to make an immediate stop.

I clearly sensed that by then, I was pessimistic. If I let myself go unchecked, I would certainly get into a dead end, and became too angry to extricate myself from pessimism. Furthermore, I might go mad and at last, I would commit suicide.

I put everything behind my back simply thinking of that taking one day at a time. Enabling myself to keep living on was my calculation.

However, one form of unluckiness befell me, again. One day after having my lunch, I lay on my aluminum-framed bed in the room and relaxed myself for a nap by regulating my breath. Being humid and hot that day, and stripped to the waist and with a pair of shorts on, I fell asleep with my legs splayed apart towards the opened window and my head towards the aisle of the two rows of doubledecked platform-like beds sidelined. That was a sweet and sound sleep that I had ever had. When I awoke, I felt that everything around me was glowing. Flowers and grasses were smiling at me.

Gradually, I felt that there was a dull pain in my left knee. Getting up and taking a good look at it, I was shocked by what I saw—there was an egg-sized swell there. Clerk sergeant, told me that it was not a serious case. If I applied a hot towel to it, it would soon heal up.

In a few days that followed, it didn't turn out all right as wished, conversely, it got worse. Being so painful, I couldn't set my foot on the ground. And I was rushed into the 805th Field Hospital. After the usual procedure of X-ray examination, blood test, and raps and taps, the doctor diagnosed it as rheumatism, and the X-ray film also showed that my heart was one finger larger than it should be. It is called cardiomegaly. Therefore, I needed hospitalizing and treating for some time.

In the 805th Field Hospital, I made two friends: one is Gao Wu; another, Sun Zongliang. The former is a nurse, the latter, a resident doctor. And they are also verse lovers. The former has her poetic works published by real name; the latter, in the supplements connected with newspapers or magazines by pseudonym, Lu Song. At that time, they were in love and seemingly had intimate relationship, and even when making the rounds, they went hand in hand together.

Originally, I was greatly optimistic about life. Even though I was dangling between life and death on the Penghu Islands, I never gave up. At present, facing the hopelessness of going back to school, and lying on the bed in the hospital, I felt as if I had been thrown in the lowest mood. And in turn, I came up with some of the so-called "modern poems" tinged with negative infinity. One piece of poem entitled: "My Poetry" could be served as an example of the degree of negativity in my life at that time:

Perhaps, one day I'll pass away suddenly
Crossing a river at fords
And in the woods, I'll live in a grave forever
By then, I think my poetry might be transformed into a talking bird
Fluttering its wings in the foliage of a tree
Merrily singing the sweetest songs of the world
Only at that time, will I smile heartily with my eyes closed
Despite my mound grave is covered with thistles and thorns
And the base covered with the thick moss

Perhaps, I think my poetry might resemble the yellow leaves
Rustling firstly in the wind, and then, one leaf after another,
falling off
Crushed under the feet of human beings, and run over by the
vast wheel of time
My poetry and the sludge will be a blend
Like me, my poetry will be forgotten
Perhaps, my poetry doesn't look like anything
As I am deceased, my poetry will be entombed with my remains
there.

The *Page of Poetry* on the *Gonglun Bao* published it in its issue No. 162 on August 16, 1957.

During the period of my being in the 805th Field Hospital, Wang Chuanpu, Guo Guangren, Wang Jinfang, and Zhu Guanghe from different camps in Taiwan came to see me, and sharing the woe with me. Truly, a friend in need is a friend indeed.

Wang Chuanpu had just graduated from the Department of Journalism at Military Political Warfare Cadres Academy and got the know-how of photographing. Since we gathered together, we were certainly glad to have a group picture taken. Therefore, Wang picked a tree as the setting. Coincidently, that was a very strange tree with branch-branch crotches, one of its boughes growing sidewise, so low that we could either stand or sit on it posing for the picture. While it was being taken, "Smile everybody! Smile everybody!" Wang shouted at us. Afterwards, he told me privately, "Chungliang, you look so depressed!"

Suffering "unluckiness" the same as I did, but in a different form, was Li Chunsheng who had passed the entrance examination and got admitted to Military Political Warfare Cadres Academy already. Having dressed himself up in the cadet's uniform with service cap on, he had a picture taken in the photo shop and mailed each one of us his head shot to share his glory. Holding it up, I took a long look at it feeling that Li in the picture was a different guy now who looked ambitious. Between his bushy brows, seemingly, there was pride hidden there. And it looked like the way that nothing on him was relevant to the former Li, the poet afflicted by melancholia in the past, didn't it? I immediately wrote him a letter congratulating him on his marvelous achievement.

What a pity it was! He was at Fuxinggang, the locale of the academy, for just a month. The school authorities found out there had been some of "misconducts" recorded in his personal information. And he was kicked out of school without any postponement. The expulsion from that academy was a great blow to him as if a lightning out of the blue hit him. And this led him to nursing more grievances against his superiors. His bizarre behavior was going from bad to worse. The denouement was that he was transferred to the off-shore island, Matsu. On that island, he became more impervious to reason and advice than ever. At last, he was viewed as a "bad apple" to be prosecuted, and firstly, handed over to a reform center located in Yilan County, and then, sent to Yanwan Reform Center in Taitung County for correction.

In a letter to me, he asked for a copy of the Holy Bible in the hope that God's words might pacify his emotional turbulences and heal his traumas: "A bruised reed he will not break and a smoldering wick he will not snuff out."[58] And I mailed the sole copy I had had to him.

The 805th Field Hospital is the frontline one, on principles, only receiving the wounded or patients who need treating in ICU cases. If recovered, patients must be discharged and returned to their respective units; if not, they must be referred to the base hospital for further treatment. Because I suffered from the kind of chronic disease, I needed to stay in the hospital for a longer treatment. And coincidentally, I had a classmate named Liu Tailai from the Jinan First United Secondary School who was working in the 52nd Base Hospital in Taoyuan County as a resident doctor, and I appealed to the person in charge in the 805th Field Hospital to send me there.

The size of the 52nd Base Hospital is larger, equipment and

facilities being better. Aside from the three rows of the wards in the rear accommdating patients who suffer from tuberculosis, the other three in the front are assigned to receive "elective patients." I was sent into one of the wards in the second row where there are several trees in the courtyard. One ward has six beds, either side lined with three beds. They all stand against the walls. In between, there is an aisle.

My bed is between an old patient's (an old soldier) and a young patient's (a raw recruit) beds. The old one suffered from duodenal ulcer while the other, kidney failures. Although their cases were serious, they were more active than the other patients in the ward. By then, on Sundays, the movie theaters throughout Taiwan were required to schedule an extra early morning show, free for the armed forces servicemen. After taking their breakfasts, they were in a haste to head to the largest movie theater in the downtown area of Taoyuan City.

On one of the Sunday mornings, they came back from the show. And this old guy complained of stomachache. The on-duty doctor came to check him rapping and tapping on his stomach. After examining his vitals with his stethoscope, the doctor thought that he might suffer from appendicitis or perhaps, he was poisoned by some contaminated food. He let him take the prescribed medicine and waited to see what would happen to him.

The following day, the attending physician came to see him. He went through the same procedure as the previous doctor had done before, and came to the same conclusion of the previous diagnosis. However, this old guy still complained of the stomachache incessantly. Up to the noontime, this doctor brought another two doctors in for consultation. One of them said that he "might" suffer from appendicitis but in a progressive inflammatory process. The reason was that when he pressed the spot on patient's appendix hard with his hand, the patient indicated that he felt the pain became a little bit less. But the third doctor was doubtful about this kind of tentative diagnosis and claimed that based on this patient's account, on his way back home from that free show for the servicemen, he took a bowl of beef noodle. And that bowl of beef noodle with spicy ingredients in might cause all of this trouble.

At last, these three doctors made a decision to conduct an operation on him and saw what it really was.

When these three doctors were getting themselves ready, he was suffering severe pain, and drenched in cold sweat. When the paramedics saw him roll eyes and the involuntary muscular contraction of his entire body, they hurriedly put him on a stretcher and rushed him to the operating room. Alas! It was late, and one step short of that operation, he died on the way.

After conducting an anatomy, the cause of his death is "fecal impaction." This old guy died from a disease that can be cured!

The young inmate sleeping to my right-hand side was 23 or 24 years old of age. When I first saw him, he didn't look like a human being any more. His face was sallow as the yellow waxed paper. His hands resembled chicken's claws. His spindly legs looked like bamboo sticks. And there was no hair atop his head. His whole body shrank except that his belly swelled out with the retention of liquid. On the skin of this tautly-stretched part of his body, there were dark blue blood vessels spreading like spider's web, every "silk" seen clearly. Despite all these, there were two bodily organs functioning well: eyes and mouth. The former registered wisdom; the latter, intention of smile. The doctor and other patients didn't hold any hope for his recovery but he himself was never seen frustrated. When talking about his case, he had quite confidence in saying:

"I am not suffering from cirrhosis or at the final stage of the scarring of the liver. What I have got is kidney disease. If I take the right medicine and follow the right regimen, it will get better and better!" He looked rather optimistic and carefree.

"How do you know?" asked the doctor.

"Because this is a genetic disease. My mother told me that!"

"If it is something wrong with your kidney…." The doctor couldn't continue.

"Don't worry about it! Doctor, I will be all right! And I will be recovering!"

What surprised us the most was that he was a patient with a big belly of edema getting on a walking tour of the hospital from one ward to another and making small talks with other patients. When the attending physician was making the rounds in the ward, he always answered the doctor by using the same kind of words, confident and straightforward: "Certainly, I will walk out of the hospital alive!"

One day, he complained: "Last night I ran to restroom four or five times, and now I am almost tired out." This time, he behaved himself diametrically different from the usual way with confidence gone. And he lay on his bed groaning in self-pity.

As he took the medicine prescribed by the doctor less than two days, a miracle happened to him, not only his diarrhea was completely controlled, but also the retented fluid in his body was gradually reduced day by day. The doctor didn't believe his eyes simply shouting repeatedly: "It is incredible!" He suggested to him that a food allowance should be practiced: "Many meals are taken but less quantity in each meal." By doing so, he could regulate his digestive system. Consequently, in a space of less than one month, he plumped out gradually. And the soft fine hair grew back atop his head and elsewhere on the body.

Less than half a year, he was able to get to what he had said, "I will certainly walk out the hospital alive."

In the 52nd Base Hospital, as I had seen the young patient's struggle for life, and the Death gained the upper hand of an old guy, I came to know instantly that life is not permanent. I recalled my uncle's words, "No matter where you will be, once settled down, you should go to the church."

In 1958, I was baptized in a small church affiliated to Lutheran denominations in the city of Taoyuan. The biggest difference between this church and others lies in the baptizing ceremony. The pastor of this church baptizes the persons by using the water-soaked fingers to sprinkle the water droplets on their heads; the others baptize the persons by immersing their whole heads or whole bodies in the water tanks. The pastor who baptized me is an American named Anderson. He was born in Henan Province, and got educated there. Prior to 1949, he spread the Gospel in Henan. And he can speak down-to-earth dialect of Henan Province.

CHAPTER 18

MR. LI PINGBO'S WISDOM

At the time we, the students from Shandong, still served as non-commissioned officers and privates in the army, and if there had not been a guy whom we dubbed "idea man" like Li Pingbo, the date for our discharging from the army would have been further delayed, and the plan to carry out such a collective discharge from the army wouldn't have been mapped out so perfectly.

Li Pingbo is a native of Jining County, Shandong. In earlier years, he didn't go by his first name, Pingbo, but Yuanfeng. And I really don't know when he did have his first name changed. When the "Youth League" was reorganized as the 39th Division, he and I were placed in the 5th Company whose increasing order of the units is the 2nd Battalion, and the 115th Regiment. Though we were in the same company and had dined in the same mess hall for years, yet we were in different platoons and different squads. And there was neither a chance for me to socialize with him nor a chance for me to say "Hello" to him. In 1952, I was transferred to the Headquarters Company affiliated to the 169th Regiment, and he and I were drifted further apart in terms of camaraderie.

One day, he was admitted to the 52nd Base Hospital, too. And as we had been in the same unit before, and right now, unexpectedly, met with each other in this hospital, we had no words to depict the happiness that we were enjoying despite both of us were in patient clothing.

At this time, what Li had demonstrated was: he exercised caution and euphemism in doing and saying anything. And every sentence, he wanted to speak, was weighed again and again in his mind. He churned out words, one by one with the excellent command of the Chinese language. He was characterized in the character of the greatest strategist, Zhu Geliang, in the classic novel of *The Romance of Three Kingdoms*.

As we had stayed in the same ward for some time, I came to know that he single-handedly engaged in a self-imposed job running back and forth between Taoyuan and Taipei trying to resolve the problem of reinstatement of the Shandong students' status. Every few days, he made a trip to Taipei always leaving in the early morning and returning in the late evening. When progress had been made, I was unable to see the happiness of his being revealed, and when no progress had been made, I was unable to see him crestfallen, either.

Based on my observation, Li Pingbo's strategy was: (1) reminding the authorities concerned to pay much attention to the real situation. Though they "disbanded" the group of these student soldiers by placing them in different units, the problem still remained unsolved. And without doubt, there would be some "guys" trying to relaunch a series of demonstrations in Taipei continuing to make collective protests to the authorities involved. (2) having the injustices and mistreatments the Shandong students had suffered put down on the paper and sent to the print media, creating the force of public opinion.

When he saw the stand of the Ministries of Defense and Education melted and both ministries were in earnest desirous of establishing a channel for dialoguing with students through him regarding the problem of our returning to school, he firstly took their word for it and looked at the problem in their shoes and then elaborated the standpoints of the students' and spoke for them. He tried to untie the knots these officials had had on their mind. And it doesn't matter how complicated the knots were, he did his utmost trying to get the knotty points unraveled one by one.

The problems for going back collectively to the Provincial Yuanlin Experimental Secondary School are nothing else but to be: No. 1 classrooms are not enough; No. 2 the equipment and facilities are inadequate; No. 3 the school lacks financial resources; (4) the problem for the placement of this sort of older students in school. Do all of them enroll in a specifically designed teacher-training program or is there any other alternative? And (5) with such a large number of students collectively returning to school, Yuanlin doesn't have such a space capacity, and how do they get the problem of this kind to be solved?[59]

After racking his brains, Li made some of the practical suggestions for resolving these problems to them.

Meaningfully, he told the authorities concerned that the student soldiers staying in the army were "dregs," neither being able to get themselves in various military academies due to their poor academic performances nor being able to carry out the full-time services in the army because they were either physically disabled or mentally retarded. If still kept in the army, they would only be there to waste the provisions, and there would have also some impact on morale. This kind of saying, "self-depreciation" made the officers in the Ministry of Defense feel that the student soldiers from Shandong were as worthless as "Chicken rib bones," meaning that though with a little bit of meat on, nothing inviting left. To solve the problem, the earlier, the better, would be a good policy. Otherwise, to have them stay on would have harmful impacts on the army.

Li Pingbo used a "carrot and stick approach" or talk soft and act tough strategy. However, he made himself extremely modest in his attitudes, especially during the time when the Garrison Headquarters investigated him why he, not other guys, engaged in doing this sort of stuff. He used the stratagem—admitting that it was his fault first, and then saying regrettably, "Certainly! I must straighten myself out!" [60] This soft tone of his speech was proved to his advantage that he could command the sympathy of all the officers of the Garrison Headquarters that why he got himself involved in this Shandong student soldiers' case.

As he had met with these "superiors" innumerable times, a sort of "friendship" was born and growing. And he had won them over in terms of sympathy and forgiveness. And thus, the officers of the Ministry of Defense, the Vice Minister of Education, Legislators of Legistive Yuan and he together made a concerted effort trying to solve the problem.

The biggest concern is who should be held accountable for our discharge from the army.

In the past, President Chiang Kai-shek had once been to the Penghu Islands and was aware that there were these student soldiers. If there was a day, on a whim, he asked where these student soldiers were, and who would be the one that was held responsible for giving an answer to him?

At last, it developed into a situation in which the legislators stood up saying, "the whole Legislative Yuan (judicial branch) will be held accountable!" Accordingly, the biggest bottleneck for the case of the Shandong studens' resuming schooling was finally resolved.

The case regarding the student soldiers' discharging from the army is called "The Mu Lan Special Project."[61] Though there were some nuts and bolts to be dealt with, overall speaking, it got settled. One day, Li Pingbo told me quietly that "the probability of our honorably discharging from the army is 80 or 90 percent of success, but we cannot call it a complete success unless we have held our Discharge Certificates in our hands. And that piece of paper counts!"

CHAPTER 19

THE WAISHUANG STREAM

At the time I was in the 52nd Base Hospital for convalescence to the summer of 1959, I was neither getting better nor getting worse. In the meantime, As I felt that there was hope for going back to school, I would rather be placed into a new unit waiting for the order quietly there than continue living in the dark cloud of the hospital and waiting for the same thing. Accordingly, with the help of a Shandong man, I was transferred to Military Administration Academy at Waishuang Stream Park in Taipei. After reporting to the school, I was sent down to a supporting unit called Services Company. And I was appointed clerk sergeant, doing the paperwork for this unit.

The commander named Pan Peitian is from Anhui Province. As soon as he saw me, he told me bluntly that he had already read my personal information and said to me that I had two choices to make: "No. 1 is that in our unit, there is a vacancy of a warrant officer between staff sergeant, and second lieutenant. You rank sergeant now. If you like to stay on, you will, firstly, be promoted to the rank of staff sergeant, and then, advanced to the higher position of warrant officer. Finally, to qualify yourself for that rank, you must go through a training program, and the place for getting that training is nowhere else but this school. No. 2 is that you can take part in the Joint College Entrance Examination (JCEE) for going to university."

I told him without one minute's hesitation that I liked to take part in the JCEE.

The paperwork of this services company was the simplest one compared with that I had done in my former units. There is neither the planned training program for me to make a copy of nor many documents for me to sign my name on. The real duties of mine are: making a pay-sheet when it is due for buddies to get paid, rationing the packs of cigarettes for those who smoke, and filling out the requisition forms when tools such as shovels, spades, brooms, dustpans and the others are needed.

All the buddies in this company are from the Chinese Mainland, and naturally, their backgrounds are different. They are not on the same level in education. Some of them even haven't got one day's education.

There is a wide variety of jobs for them to do: cooking, driving, gardening, guard duty, couriering, switchboard operator duties and cleaning. To them, the most challenging job is to clean up the mess after the hitting of a typhoon. The school stands on a large tract of acres, and there are lots of dark and out-of-the-way places that need not only all the company to do the cleaning, but also several muscular guys and their agility. And being able to climb up and down the walls of buildings is a must.

In our unit, there was a guy named Dong Tianchao from Sichuan Province, who was the best of the best, having brawny arms, worthy of several guys combined to be used. He was being seen climbing up and down the walls of the buildings easily, and not until the duration of finishing smoking a cigarette, did he get all the broken branches off the roofs and have all the fallen leaves on the ground raked in. His only "hobby" is smoking. He was so addicted to tobacco that he could consume two packs of cigarettes a day. Whenever there were some cigarette leftovers after rationing out, I often gave them to him free.

One day, I discovered that the money I had locked in the drawer for paying the cigarette ration was gone. Being greatly shocked by this unusual theft, I immediately reported to our company commander, Pan, who initially frowned at this stealing but then, said to me calmly, "Leave it to me! Leave it to me!" When the time for the roll call was up in the evening, he announced this theft to all of our buddies:

"How is our staff sergeant Ma doing for our company?" Our

commander tossed out such a question, and our buddies didn't have any idea of what had happened, and got lost somewhere.

"He is doing very well." All of them replied in unison.

"Is he a good man or a bad man?"

"He is a good guy!" Following the reply, all the buddies asked the commander puzzlingly:

"What has happened?"

"The money he has collected for paying the cigarette packs is gone!" Our commander raised his voice and continued to harangue the whole company about the theft: "I don't want to investigate this. And among you, anyone who has made away with this money, is aware of what you are doing. I give you three days to think about it. No matter what kind of method you use to return it, no punishment will be meted out, and it seems as if there were not anything happening at all. Otherwise, if I have found out who did it, I will give him…."

When the first day was passed, there was nothing stirring. After the second day, no one owned to having made this theft. But all the buddies felt as if there was a sort of air pressure force remaining to stifle them. And they had nothing to say but to have a lot of pent-up anger, having difficulty in breathing.

Our commander, Pan's warning not to mete out any type of punishment had the greatest effect upon the offender. On the third day, he secretly handed a yellowish official envelope over to me, and hinted to me that he, Dong, was the guy who did the stealing.

Among all the buddies, there is a guy named Wang Guishan who is 15 or 16 years, my senior. He is very reserved, just speaking few words a day. He didn't get along well with others but me.

He often dropped in my office. Once he was in, he just sat there and took a few cups of tea quietly watching me do some of paper works. He waited there until everything got done and if time permitted, we usually went out and took a walk along the Neihuang Stream toward the mountain area. We often made some pauses to appreciate the scenery on either side of the road.

He told me once: "When I left the Chinese Mainland, I had been married. Now, since the hope for launching a counter-offensive war to recover the China Mainland cannot be fulfulled, what should I do?" On the one hand, he spoke with his eyes glistening with tears, but on the other, he heaved deep sighs.

But I told him, "The case like yours is countless, yours is the only one of them!"

The Waishuang Stream Park is a scenic spot famed for its ranges of greenery draped mountains and crystal-clear water. Upon getting to it, I wanted to write an ode to it. However, many aspects of its beauty are: natural landscape surrounded by mountains; cultural stuff: institutions of higher learning—Suzhou University and Military Administration Academy; and the designated place for constructing a national palace museum. And I was of my opinion that based on my so-so talent, no matter how hard I racked my brains and searched for the appropriate word, I didn't think I could get its beauty fully unfolded by my poem. Almost on the brink of giving up, a piece of prose came to me by itself. It is entitled: "Strolling along the Waishuang Stream." When I had finished writing, I counted the number of words, less than 800. Because it involves a story, I must get the whole thing down here:

If the city could be compared to a "complex symphony," and then, the countryside could be likened to a "serenade." Based on my own calculation by fingering the days, I have been transferred to Waishuang Stream Park in the Shilin district, more than three months. Every evening, when the sun is setting, I always take a walk along the bank of the Waihuang Stream watching the sun going down and the birds returning to their nests. The red sun now has finished travelling the whole day's journey, and seemingly is not willing to let go of the world, struggling to the last minute to hang on there. The rays sent out by the sun are the colors of red, violet, yellow, and blue, etc., not only making something beautiful such as sunset clouds in the evening sky but resembling the eruption of a volcano with flames shooting randomly. The sun setting scene provides people with unlimited imagination, and certainly the imagination can take people everywhere.

Those awesome birds you have never heard after one day's work sail low above the tops of trees circling and circling and darting into the bosom of the forested mountain. And at last, everything goes quiet. Beneath feet is the "causeway" between the green rice paddies. When a gust of wind is arising, the rice stems fall and rise as the sea waves crash upon you. After a while, when the wind dies down, they return to their upright positions staying as quiet as they have been. If you stare at them, you cannot help giving them a huiyidi weixiao, or a smile of understanding because they look like nodding their heads, "welcome to you!" repeatedly. Keeping silent, they could be personified as a group of shy country girls. They do not understand the ugliness, hypocrisy, and fraud of the mundane world, but always to glow with exuberant vitality.

Behind me is the Waishuang Stream with its crystal-clear water in. Added to it is the springwater from the depth of the mountain area. And it becomes a real stream flowing slowly and benefitting the residents on either bank of it. Owing to many a M-shaped boulder in the upstream, there are rapids rushing against it, and then, the sounds made by the currets of this kind are quite pleasing to the ear. Bubbles are formed and then broken up. In the downstream, somewhere in the deepest part, there are small groups of soldiers keeping their heads above the water by treading water, floating on the surface of the water or staying under the water. They are swimming around each other and doing the splashing battle, and so do they pinch their noses diving, laughing, hooting, and yelling like kids.

On the opposite bank of the stream is Suzhou University. The high-rises standing on the base of the mountain are very impressive. Though during the summer vacation, there are no traces left by human beings on the campus, and the school still has the solemn air of an institution of higher learning. From somewhere afar comes a shrill siren, and that is the yellow-skinned bus No. 29. Behind it, there are clouds of dust rising, and on either side of it, street boys are racing with it. They are yelling and shouting. And since there is no way to beat the bus in running, eventually they are returning languidly. Thereafter, everything goes deadly quiet and harmonious.

I am gazing at the scene with my wide-opened eyes and indulging in unlimitted imagination. And I don't know when there have been several silver stars hanging over the dark green vault of the sky. I have made a stretch with a yawn. Along the path that I came from, I am walking back to my nest. On my way back home, I think of the saying by one of the unknown Western philosophers named Jiaerbin in Chinese. It reads: "One hundread percent of quietness can broaden one's mind and generate the swelling feeling of happiness."62 I think that is the feeling I have had now.

I contributed this short essay to the supplementary edition connected with the *Young Warriors News*. And in about three weeks, I got an answer from the editor without signature, "Strolling along the Waishuang Stream has been accepted, and it will be published shortly." However, in the P. S. of that notice, the editor promoted his book to me. After I mailed the money to him, the essay I had contributed was published. The book that he mailed to me was something like The Outline of Western Literature. And because I had made several moves, that book got lost. I have no idea of where it is now.

CHAPTER 20

WAY TO HIGHER EDUCATION

In Military Administration Academy, for the whole season of fall, I did nothing but to keep myself, *tao guan yang hui*, or keep a low profile. Gradually, I was pondering over taking the Joint College Entrance Examination thing seriously. All the subjects that needed testing, such as Three Principles of the People (of the people, by the people, and for the people), Chinese, English, Chinese and World History, and Chinese and World Geography could be studied by myself except that Mathematics must be prepared systematically under the guidance of a teacher. At the time, it didn't matter what programs, A, B, C, and D you wanted to get in, (A is science and engineering, B, humanity studies, C, medicine, and D, agriculture and biology), Math test was a must for all college goers. If you got a zero on Math, you wouldn't be admitted to any university despite the fact that you did well on other tests. Therefore, I decided to go to the after-school program to see if I could sign up for the Math class only. After exploring it, I came to know that the teachers in that sort of school had special "skills," and within a very short span of time, could get the key points in the test subjects arranged in order. This way, it was easy for students to enhance their reading comprehension and memory power. Overall, they played the key roles to help students get in universities. After weighing the pros and the cons, I decided to sign up for all the classes on offer.

In the academy, there were buses shuttling back and forth between Taipei and Waishuang Stream Park during the weekdays. When I was off in the afternoon and the bus was leaving for the downtown area of Taipei, I took it to go to Jianguo After School Program located on

Guanqian St. When the school was over around 10 p.m., I took Bus 10 to Shihlin stop first. And from there I caught Bus 29, the end bus, back home.

Jianguo After-School Program was touting its business by claiming that all of its teachers were the best of the best. They said that the classes they had scheduled could guarantee each one of the enrollees to be able to get in one of the universities in Taiwan. Even up to the present moment, I can still recall some of those well-known teachers' names: English, Lou Zifeng; Chinese, Ba Hutian; History, Zhu Gui; Geography, Wang Hungwen; and Math, Wu Gongxun (also a famous physics teacher). Of them, two of them whose teaching was of decisive help to get me in the Department of Foreign Languages and Literature (the DFLL) at the National Cheng Kung University (NCKU). One is Chinese and World Geography teacher, Wang Hungwen; another, Math, Wu Gongxun.

As Wang has taught Chinese and World Geography many years, he has an excellent command of this subject. During the class time, he didn't have any handouts edited by him. Every time, he came to teach always asking about the information from the one of the students who sat in the front row regarding what the geographical region it was he talked about in the previous session. Once told clearly, he turned around and drew the map on the blackboard for this teaching session. And then, based on the map, he began lecturing on and on without letup.

He demands that students should commit the geographical features of a region to memory and have them narrowed down, and written into one topic sentence which must be easy to remember. And then, based on that topic sentence, students can get not only the right answer but also the other information inferentially. For example: "the climate type determines the essence of agriculture, in another word, as you have subtropical climate, you'll have subtropical agriculture; the sort of mineral produced determines the type of industry. To solve the given question deductively and inductively step by step, you'll get the correct answer. In another word, students don't have to learn Geography by rote."

I was scared of Math. Therefore, once I got a chance, I would constantly ask Mr. Wu to tell me the secrets of ridding the fear of this terrible subject. He told me: "In the Math test for the B program students, there is always a Determinant appearing on the question sheet every year. If there is such a question, I guarantee that you can get 5 or 6 points on the Math test. If you try to straighten the "cause" and "effect" of a Determinant question out, it needs racking your brains. All you can do is to remember a simple formula, that is to add up all the rows of figures into a total and then, and to add up all the columns of figures into another total. At last, using the former total to detract the latter total or vice versa, you will get the right answer." As he didn't think his explanation satisfied me, he kept on elaborating the Math test as follows: "Every year, the Board of the JCEE gets the problem on the agenda to be discussed regarding whether the students whose math scores are zeroes can be admitted to universities or not. In the past, there were some cases concerning students who scored zeroes on Math being able to get admitted to the institutions of higher learning. Furthermore, the day for holding the JCEE is still some time away, if you come to the Math class as scheduled and get several Math exercise questions solved every day, you will find Math is an interesting subject." How did he know I had only the eighth grader's level of Math?

I worried about not only getting a big zero on Math that I could get admitted to university, but feeling doubt about whether I was able to be honorably discharged from the army.

However, in the twinkling of an eye, I realized what I had concerned about and doubted of was groundless. Since Mr. Wu said that the probability of a Determinant question presenting on the question sheet was very high, I didn't have to continue worrying about it, and since Li Pingbo said that the case for our discharging from the army had already been settled, it seemed that there was no reason for me to doubt of it. On no account, would the prospect of getting in a university be compared to sort of sleep talk by a fool in his dream.

I was also likened to "a dangling man" swinging between "success" and "failure." However, I had turned in the fee already and was aboard a vessel going towards the direction of university and the vessel was voyaging in the middle of its course. And there was no way for me to get off but to attend the JCEE.

The day for holding the JCEE was getting closer and closer. Besides weekdays, after office hours, I went to that After School Program, and so did I on Saturday mornings. Furthermore, as the examination day was just a few days away, we were all gearing up for that examination. And even on Saturday afternoons and whole Sundays, I went to classes, too. In another word, we would use the limited space of time in the hope that we might be able to go over all the key points of the test subjects, or the important contents of the textbooks that students had studied in the three-year program of a senior high.

I can still recall that as it was noontime when those Saturdays' morning classes were over, I went to New Park for the lunch break. I firstly got a piece of egg roll and a drink on Xuchang St. and then walked eastward. On the one hand, I was walking, on the other hand, I was eating and drinking. Upon my arrival, I finished my lunch.

Lying on a built-in bench in a pavilion, I quickly fell asleep. Having waked up from that nice nap, I felt I was in good spirits. As far as the eye could reach, I saw many young couples in "their own little world" doing "the touchy-feely" stuff. And I couldn't help thinking of my own situation in which I was stuck that I was not allowed to get married. Who had made such a lousy law that non-commissioned officers and private soldiers were not allowed to take a wife? By doing so, there would be no offspring continuing their family trees. And were there any justice and fairness under the heavens?

I had received two notices from the Ministry of Defense successively: the first one was to find out how many student soldiers from Shandong who wanted to be discharged from the army; the second one was trying to find out if there was anybody who wanted to participate in the 1960 JCEE. If there was, and then, how many? The former required us to fill out the form with name, service number, birthplace, age, the date and place of joinng the army, the title of the earliest unit, and the current rank; the latter, only the name was needed. From all the signs shown, we were about to be discharged from the army and our dreams would come true.

The servicemen permitted to take part in the JCEE for going to university are classified into two categories: one is those who are still in the active service at the time; another, the veterans in the military reserve force. The former is only permitted to take the tests getting in the programs related to the needs of the national defense industry. In another word, they were only allowed to take part in the tests for enrolling in the science and engineering programs; the latter is free of these lousy restrictions, and furthermore, they can enjoy the privilege of having the extra points added to what they have actually earned. (For this, I couldn't help giving another credit to the National Government for the veterans). In order to get this kind of privilege, we, especially, appealed to the Ministry of Defense to have a name list made for those who would like to participate in that year's JCEE, and simultaneously, sent a letter to the Ministry of Education requesting of them to inform the 1960's JCEE Board to let us take the exam first based on the veteran status, and later, when our Discharge Certificates were out, we would send them to the board to have the veteran status verified.

After going through several obstacles, the problem for entering our names for the JCEE was finally settled. I thought to myself that if there was no zero on Math, I should be able to get in one of the universities "easily."

On the night before the JCEE, I couldn't fall asleep, tossing and turning on the bed. Having counted thousands and thousands of black and white sheep, I couldn't sleep a wink. Despite the fact that I had made up my mind not to think of anything else, but to focus on the tests held tomorrow, it didn't work out that way. The events that I had gone through were compared to ocean waves overwhelmingly crashing on me: How I left the Chinese Mainland, how I was press-ganged into the army on the Penghu Islands by Generals Li Zhenqing and Han Fengyi, and how I was transferred to Taiwan. Once discharged from the army, if I had had money, I would have got into the business world and try to learn how to be a businessman. If I had had a wealthy relative living in Taiwan, I would have gone to him to seek help. There was no need for me who was going on 30 years old of age to go to university. Since I had none of these and there was only one way left for me to take, and that was to go to university to get a diploma that would qualify me to get a job so that I could survive in the society of this kind in the future.

As I was obssessed with the thoughts as the foregoing, not until the stroke of four or so, did I drop off. Overall, for the whole night, I got less than two hours' sleep. And once awaken, I was in a hurry to catch the bus heading to the examination site set at Shida Senior High affiliated to the National Taiwan Normal University.

After the first period, Chinese test, was over, I deeply regretted that I had been so reckless. Because I had misread the essence of the questions, having the whole sentences explained instead of the key words in Classical Chinese, for example: "*Shi rou zhe bi, bu neng yuan mou, or* those who are meat eaters are 'short-sighted' and cannot be compared to statemmen with vision." It is the right way for the examinees who explain the meaning of the hyphenated words, 'short-sighted,' not necessay to explain the eight characters, the whole thing. And I had all of the 10 subquestions under the first question explained by whole sentences, not by key words in the single quotation marks. If a professor marked the examination papers carefully, reading through the whole things, maybe, gave me some points based on the right parts of the answers. Otherwise, if he wanted to catch up with the pace of the progress done by other professors in marking examination papers, and saw the answers going off on a tangent, without doubt, he would give me a 0 on this 20-point question. Fortunately, I did quite well for the next two tests, otherwise I might quit the whole thing.

On the following morning, the first period was the Math test. When I got the question sheets, I was panic-stricken feeling my heart was pounding very fast, and having thumbed through the pages, I surprisingly saw there was a question, Determinant, there. And I was overjoyed at it, and within several minutes, got the answer. Henceforth, I sat on my seat keeping silent. At the time there was a regulation by the Board of the JCEE that examinees were not permitted to leave the classroom until the end of a period of 40 minutes. I sat through that time limit and turned in the examined papers quietly and left the classroom.

When I filled out the choice card in terms of university preferences, they were in the decreasing order of Taida (Taiwan University), Shida (Taiwan Normal University), Zhengda (Zheng Zhi University), and Chengda (Cheng Kung University). Namely, the Depatment of Foreign Languages and Literature of Taida is my first choice, the Department of English of Shida, second, the Department of English of Zhengda, third, and the Department of Foreign Languages and Literature of Chengda, fourth.

After taking the JCEE, I held a copy of the following day's newspaper with all the standard answers on for the test takers to check with. As the result of that check was quite satisfactory, I felt I might be able to get in one of these four institutions of higher learning. Based on my wishful thinking, the one I mostly wanted to get in was the Department of English at Shida because it provided students with public grants, and when graduated, one would be certainly assigned a teaching job at a junior or senior high school somewhere in Taiwan. This is called *tiefanwan*, or iron rice bowl meaning, you don't have to worry about your livelihood from now on.

By mid-July 1960, we, the group of student soldiers from Shandong was eventually notified to assemble at the Municipal 2nd Taichung

Senior High School waiting for going through the process of discharging from the army and the reinstatement of students' status. Because time was changed, I completely forgot the entire JCEE stuff.

Priot to the Provincial Yuanlin Experimental Secondary School (the school was firstly established at Magong City, Penghu Islands, and later relocated to Yuanlin township in Zhanghua County, and renamed as indicated) officially accepted us, The Special Teacher-training Program at Hualian Teacher-training College (STTP-HTTC) came to Taichung to give us a screening test.[63] This program was commissioned by Veterans' Association under Executive Yuan (executive branch). If we could pass the test, we would receive one year's teacher training education at HTTC. And furthermore, if we could pass all the compulsory and elective courses on offer in that program, we would be assigned to various elementary schools across the island and assume the elementary school teachers' posts. I thought to myself that being an elementary school teacher to educate the younger generation was a "holy" job. Without doubt, I could get a "footold" in the society, and earned a decent living. Therefore, I started learning *Zhuyin fuhao*, or Mandarin Phonetic Symbols, and read out loud "brief comments" or "editorials" on the newspapers in the hope that when interviewed, I could give them the answers in standard Chinese referring to Spoken Mandarin. Or when I wrote a composition, I could come up with a piece of good writing with the help of prepositions and conjunctions. In addition, Social Studies would be tested. Because I had just gone through the JCEE and what I had learned in that After School Program was still kept in my mind, I didn't have any problem to pass those subject tests. And to the best of my remembrance, there was no Math test.

When a name list for those who succeeded in passing the screening test was out, I saw my name on it. At the time I left Taichung City, I was given the Discharge Certificate on which there are some Chinese characters in the box for the reason to quit the army: "Based on the personnel management," that literally means this guy quit the army because the army had already been overstaffed. Besides the certificate, what I had got were: a set of mosquito net, a suit of plain clothes, a pair of black leather shoes, and a quilt. As to my lump sum for leaving the army, I was only given 940 yuan called "return fare" for going home.

This group of student soldiers, who had passed the screening test held by the STTP-HTTC, boarded the train firstly to Keelung Harbor, and then from there, we were shipped by a freighter to Hualian.

After we settled in Hualian County two weeks, a typhoon hit that area. The traffics by land, sea and air were completely disrupted. Naturally, there was no way to get newspapers. Furthermore, I was unable to get any news from the Board of the JCEE that was held accountable for releasing the results of the JCEE. The news that I got in a university was from a buddy who happened to listen to the radio and accidently got it, and when that news passed on to me from mouth to mouth, I was, by then, rather skeptical about it.

When the typhoon died down, newspapers hit the street. And I checked with the paper, and it was proved that my name was listed in the Department of Foreign Languages and Literature at Cheng Kung University. I was overjoyed at it, of course, because my dream of going to university finally came true. However, in the meantime, I was worried about what I had got was only a small amount of money called "return fare" given to me just for returning home (I have no home to return in Taiwan). How could it defray the expense to study in a university for four years to come?

Based on the saying: "Everything will work out in the end." I made a good use of that saying to cheer myself up.

Simultaneously, Wang Yuhuai with whom I had been in the same squad during the time we were in the 5th Company. He, who had graduated from the Department of Journalism at Fuxinggang Political Warfare Cadres Academy, was being stationed in Hualian County. I didn't know how he got the information of our arrival at that county. In one of the holiday weekends, he unexpectedly appeared before us.

With his leadership and with some of the former buddies from the same company, we firstly went to an eatery to "feast" and then to have a group picture taken under the pretext that "we want to celebrate this gathering at Hualian!" But when the picture was processed out, there was an amazing line inscribed down there. It reads: "Congratulations on Ma Chungliang's success in being admitted to Cheng Kung University." Having finished reading that line, I cried, my face drowned in tears.

I stayed in Hualian County for another week, and then hastily headed for the Provincial Yuanlin Experimental Secondary School. And right there, I would wait for the notice from the Board of the JCEE. When I signed up for taking part in the JCEE, a mailing address was required. But because at that time, I had not completely gone through the process of discharging from the army, therefore, I had no way to have *hukou.* or residence permit. And accordingly, there was no residential address to be used to fill out the address box on the application form except that Yuanlin was my mailing address.

Based on the specifications listed by Cheng Kung University for the tuition and miscellaneous fee, I, as a veteran, would be exempted from all of tuition, and enjoy another priviledge, a half miscellaneous fee. Aside from these two fees, there were many others that I needed to pay, for example: lodging, textbooks, uniforms, and food. Added up, if I hadn't had the cash money like the sum of 1,000 yuan or 800 yuan in hand, I wouldn't be able to get the registration done. But I made another way of calculation. If I didn't want to live in the on-campus dorm, and lived off campus and shared the rent with a fellow student, how much could I save? If I bought the secondhand textbooks, how much could I save? If I still wore what I had had on instead of having a suit of school uniform tailored, how much could I save? And if I didn't eat in the cafeteria on campus, and cooked by myself, how much could I save? calculating this way, I felt that I could deal with this financial "crisis" with the cash money in my pocket.

For the first-year students, registration was conducted on the upper floor of the general library located on the Shengli, victory campus. When my turn was due, I submitted my Discharge Certificate to a stocky colonel respectfully to be checked. By then, I sincerely hoped what my case could get approved. And once his chop was affixed on my registration form, I could move on to have all the privileges I deserved processed: no tuition and only a half miscellaneous fee. But he held my thing and took a long look at it, and then, said to me very rudely:

"In your case, the fees cannot be exempted! In your case, the fees cannot be exempted!"

I felt as if I had been struck by lightning, and my mind went blank. I became speechless.

"I have the legal paper, Discharge Certificate. Please tell me why can't I be exempted from those fees?"

"Because the box on your certificate in which the reason regarding your discharge is marked with "Quitting the army based on the personnel management, not marked with the word, disability."

"Please tell me, based on the provision regarding the exemption from the tuition and a half miscellaneous fee for the veterans, is there any difference between these two types of veterans, discharged due to personnel management and disablility?"

"As I said that you couldn't get exempted, that is it!" He was apparently exasperated by my retort. On the one hand, he returned my certificate to me, but on the other, he gave me a hint that I might go away without bothering him any more. Following what he had just said, he came up with such a mumble: "You are so young, why did you quit the army so early!"

No matter how I pleaded with him for reconsideration, he remained tight-lipped with a deadpan face.

Such a blow made me lose my head, and I didn't know what to do. At this juncture, there was an administrator, aged about 50, who got up from his seat, pulling me downstairs. He said: "It is not reasonable! You may go to the Headquarters of Tainan Regimental District for the

Reserve seeking help from Commander, Lt. General Shoin and asking him to issue you a sort of document on behalf of that organization. Anyone, who has served in the army 10 years and held legal Discharge Certificate, is eligible for enjoying the priviledges of exemption from tuition and the half of miscellaneous fee if he has passed the JCEE and been admitted to a university!"

After hearing my appeal, the officer in charge checked with everything against the provision regarding the fee exemption for the veterans who had got admitted to colleges or universities and said: "There is no such thing like the guy who has done to you!" He instantly issued a document with the official seal on, and signed by the commander asking me to register with Cheng Kung University, again. I handed it over to the same colonel directly who had turned me down before. Pointing at my nose, he was still quite arrogant and overbearing and said bluntly:

"This is not lawful! This is not lawful! Do you know this?" I could see that he had pent-up anger, cross-eyed and brow-tightened. But he held that document issued by the Tainan Regimental District Headquarters for the Reserve for a while, not knowing what to do with it. Finally, he became sullen but said: "I let it go this time for the sake of Lt. General Shoin. Next time, I cannot endorse your exemptions!"

He stamped my Registration Form with his chop. After that, I had nothing to worry. And based on the ground that everything was legal, I became driven to argue with him to vent my pent-up rage. But with consideration of firstly returning to the civilian life, I thought this was the first challenge. And anything I wanted to do must be in conformity to the noble virtue of patience. Therefore, I decided not to take any retaliatory action against him.

CHAPTER 21

UNIVERSITY DAYS

In the 1960s, Cheng Kung University was a provincially-funded university, not a nationally-funded one.

There were only two campuses: Cheng Kung (success) and Sheng Li (victory). As to colleges, there were only three: engineering, business, and science and liberal arts. And these three colleges were situated on the campus, Cheng Kung; the rest, such as library, students' dorms and cafeteria on the Sheng Li campus. In addition, on the Cheng Kung campus, there were a 400-yard stadium and four basketball courts. There was neither a sort of river flowing through the campus nor a sort of lake lying. The greatest features of the campus were: 1. Engineering Boulevard, 2. department buildings with the Japanese architectural style, and 3. lofty evergreen trees.

On the first day of school, we, the whole class of 66 freshman students of the DFLL from all the parts of Taiwan, rallied on the southernmost basketball court. Li Guangcheng, a Shandong man, who was from the Office of Military Training Program and assigned to our department to be responsible for students' safety and military education, lined us up. And as he saw me much older than other students, he hand-picked me as the class leader.

Li's appointment was not appropriate from my point of view because I had just been discharged from the army and didn't know anything about the "university culture." I would habitually lead the class by a set of rules practiced in the army. That I made a fool of myself was not a big deal, but that my leadership made some of my classmates furious with me about the way they had been led was the most embarrassing thing. Thanks to my prescience, I did the serving based on the saying: "Happiness comes with service to others."

After having lined us up on the Cheng Kung campus, he made us file in Cheng Kung Auditorium. Having seated ourselves, we waited for the orientation ceremony to start. That day, President Yan Zhenxing, Dean of Academic Affairs, Zhuang Jundi, Dean of Discipline, Ding Zuoshao and Dean of General Affairs, Liu Xianlin all delivered short speeches to us. But at present, as to what they talked about by then, I have been left no impression. The only thing that has still been embedded in my memory is the president's Mandarin tinged with the strong accent of Henan Province: "Cheng Kung University has made a lot of progress on many aspects in the recent years. And everybody has known these very well!" Afterwards, I related what the president had spoken to a junior student named Liu Zhaoxian at the Department of Industrial Management (He was also one of the "student soldiers" from Shandong, several years later, assuming the position as chief of the First Section in the Auditing Bureau in the National Government). He said that the president's cliche had been transformed into a sort of mockery to him with some of words added: "Cheng Kung University has made a lot of progress on many aspects in the recent years. And everybody has known these very well! Zhenxing's health is excellent, except that my neck is a little bit short!" Of course, these words should be spoken in Henan dialect, otherwise you didn't feel that funny.

At that time, we didn't have department building of our own. The DFLL was just the satellite of the Department of Physics in terms of education facilities. One classroom was borrowed from that department and divided into two rooms: one being the chairperson's office; another, staff members' office. And even our classrooms were borrowed from that Department, too. As that small and cramped space was thronged with too many students, we felt extremely uncomfortable. Fortunately, in front of our classrooms, there was a small yard growing flowers and plants with exuberant foliage for us to walk around and have chats during breaks between classes.

Located several yards away, south of our department or we may say, just behind the Administration Building is a small auditorium called *Gezhitang,* or Way to Knowledge which was built by the Japanese. It is of unique architectural distinction. Designed for multipurpose, for example, it can be used as auditorium for public gatherings, large classroom instruction, and site for holding different examinations for different classes at the same time if there is such a need.

Our department building was bounded on its north by the chemistry department building. And on its right-hand side on the second floor of that two-story building, there were more modernized classrooms with custom window curtains, spacious and comfortable. And a Chinese American instructor named Amy Lin taught us one short story written by Joseph Conrad, "The Witches' Inn" there.

Our chairperson is Prof. Fu Chongte who originally taught at the DFLL at the National Taiwan University. Though he was in his early fifties, not quite old, yet he was balding. With a pair of gold-rimmed spectacles on, he looked quite scholarly.

He taught us Freshman English. He is a super grammarian but he is especially good at the usages of past participles. As a result, when our mid-term and final exams were due, he always got sets of questions ready asking us to state the functions of past participles in sentences. Questions like these we went through were too many, and in turn, we dubbed him Mr. Past Participle, and simply called him Mr. PP.

Another trick for showing his attainments in the field of English grammar is to diagram sentences. It doesn't matter how long and how complicated a sentence is he can tear it apart drawing a diagram to illustrate grammatical functions with lines and curved lines, "This adjective modifies this noun; this adverb qualifies this adjective; still this adverb can be used to qualify the adverb that follows. All of their functions are tied up and dealt with meticulous care." In the textbook edited by him for the freshman English class, we often saw the sentences written by reputed writers present themselves in the forms of various diagrams.

Our Conversational English teacher is Father Callier. He is an American, heavyset. We frequently saw him come to our classes by motorcycle with his stomach jutting out. He was a chain smoker, so addicted to tobacco that he couldn't stand for a minute without a cigarette held between his lips. During the class time, on the one hand, he was lecturing, on the other, he was puffing. He was quite exultant and overjoyed as if he were a *Daluo shenxian*, or a celestial being. The most embarrassing time for him was that he forgot to bring enough packs of cigarettes for him to consume. Once his last cigarette was gone, he had to borrow cigarettes from the students who smoke. If unavailable, he had to put his fountain pen between his lips as a substitue. The textbook he used was the simplest one that I had ever studied. He laid the greatest emphasis on everyday English, every sentence counted!

Prof. Hu Hanjie is our Phonetics teacher. He had just come back from the United Kingdom of Great Britain and spoke British English fluently. He often enumerated pronunciation mistakes the Chinese students frequently committed by contrasting one word with another for example: mispronouncing "of" as "off"; "live" as "leave" and "world" as "word."

He had a set of valuable handouts for teaching Phonetics but when I got through this course, I deeply felt it was useful and practical. However, after having left school so many years, I forgot what I had learned from him. With his tall frame, neat features and a pair of sun glasses on, he looked so cool.

The courses of Modern History of China and History of the World are conducted by Prof. Wu Zhenzhi. Although she is from Zhejiang Province, she can speak Mandarin very well. She conducted the classes at her own pace. She was able to untangle the historical knots one by one by using two methods of reasoning, inductive and deductive. She especially paid much attention to students' pride and dignity. If some of the students failed in the middle term, she would secretly hand him or her a slip of paper warning him or her to work harder and be more careful about giving the answers to the questions when the final was due.

When I was in my freshman year, what troubled me the most was short of financial source. One classmate named Liu Guanghua was in the similar condition, and initially, he and I planned to co-organize an after-school program, and later, I found out that our efforts were in vain because there was a limited number of students to sign up for this progam. The total income we had made was only enough for one person's living expenses. If I was included, it wouldn't work. As a result, I withrew myself from that after-school program voluntarily. However, I had no other choice but to use the money left after registration economically. Sometimes I went to class with hunger pangs; at other times I went on a full stomach. I was struggling for not becoming a drop-out.

Zheng Zhendong, one of the military training instructors, run an after-school program in his own house at New Village 96, and became aware of my financial crisis opening a junior high English class for me to teach. And this way, I enabled myself to get through the hard time in the first semester of my freshman year.

When the second semester started, two literary friends of mine in the army, Wang Chuanpu and Guo Guangren, made special trips to Tainan to see me, and when they took leave of me, they gave me all the money they had had in their wallets: Guo Guangren gave me a sum that he had just cashed for a check paid for one piece of his prose work published in the newspaper; Wang Chuanpu, a certain amount of money that could afford me to pay for, approximately, a half month's food expense. Coming from the same county in Shandong, Zhang Chunsheng who was in the graduating class of 1954 at the ROC Military Academy, just by then, was stationed at Tainan Artillery Training Center providing me with 400 yuan. Zhou Tingkui and Wang Jinfang, who lived in

Hualian County, far away from me, mailed me checks respectively, too.

During my sophomore year, Mr. and Mrs. Caruther, who remain unforgettable, were from the British Isles and engaged in teaching at Tainan Theological Seminary on a full-time basis. When they were free, they liked teaching at the DFLL at NCKU on a part time basis: Mr. Caruther offered a course called the Outline of Western Literature in our class; his wife, Selected Reading of English and American Novels, in other classes. As the scope of the Outline of Western literature is too big, even in the definition of the word, "outline," no man can get it done within one or two semesters. Therefore, he had the whole book, *The Outline of Literature* by John Drinkwater edited into the tabular form and printed out as handouts. And he asked for us to study the book by referring to his handouts. And we found out that studying the textbook, to his way of thinking, benefitted us very much. He is an interesting man, and during the class time, he often made a lot of witty remarks that sent the whole class in a roar of laugher. As Tainan is in the region of tropical climate, woman who lives in such a climate is easy to get pregnant, and one day, he stepped into the classroom announcing: "My wife gave birth to a baby boy last night!"

Teaching us American Literature is Mrs. Eaton. Because she often pronounced the preposition "about" as "a butt," henceforth, we called her "Mrs. A Butt" mischievously. She taught us a plenty of poems by American poets but at present, I only remember the masterpiece of Annaba Lee by Edgar Allan Poe. Since she and her husband were missionaries having spread the gospel many years in Taiwan, they had considered Taiwan their first home country. Unfortunately, one winter, when they returned to America for Christmas and a great blizzard hit their hometown, her husband died of a stroke while shoveling snow in front of their door.

Even though with the great pressure of our homework in our sophomore year, I was the one who took the lead in setting up an "English Speech Club" in our class.

In our club, there is no charter, nor is there any verbal promise about how to run our club. Classmates can join as members at any time and withdraw likewise. The only requirement is that we go to our international teacher's home by bike-riding on Saturday evening to practice our conversational English. If any of the members is willing to chip in some money to buy refreshments and nonalcoholic beverages sharing with the rest of us, it is fine, otherwise we do not feel anything wrong or weird if there is no one to do that sort of thing.

Whenever we saw our international teachers standing at the doors to welcome us to their homes cheerfully, we felt as if we had been exposed to some of the Western culture already. Initially, we didn't have any topic, but just to ramble as we wished. That way, it didn't get what we wanted. Later, as we had some topics fixed in advance and got ourselves ready, our talks became sort of something meaningful and seemingly led us unto track. Furthermore, on the one hand, we felt our horizon had been broadened, on the other, we felt we had made much progress in our Spoken English.

This "English Speech Club" benefits me a great deal. And I feel it gets rid of my bashfulness while speaking English. Furthermore, I have developed a good habit of loving to express myself in English since then.

As I recall, we went to one of Chinese teachers' homes only once, Prof. Zhu Yaolong's, for this sort of activity. He encouraged us not to be afraid of making mistakes. The fluency of spoken English comes from constantly practicing.

At the beginning of my sophomore year, the Veteran's Association made an amendment to the provision of its financial assistance as follows: "Those who are discharged from the army based on the personnel management are included for financial aids." Three hundred and fifty yuan had been appropriated to each one of us per semester for funding parts of our living expenses. That reduced my financial stress a lot.

I met Mr. and Mrs. Anderson when I was a junior: the former conducted the course entitled: Biblical Literature; the latter, Greek Literature. They were from Great Britain, too and taught at Tainan Theological School. They were invited to teach two hours per week respectively at our department on a part-time basis.

Mr. Anderson, the image of godfather, is very straightforward in terms of daily dealings with his students and others. Though a missionary, he has a great sense of humor. His teaching materials are mostly from *The Old Testament: Genesis, Exodus, Joshua, Judges, Ruth, Samuel, Esther, Job*, and the four gospels of *The New Testament*. He said: "*The Old Testament* of the *Holy Bible* emphasizes commandments, and in another word, Israelites must obey the 10 Commandments; *the New Testament,* grace, namely, followers are saved due to the love of God. The Holy Bible is one of the sources from which the Western literature is derived, and very few accomplished writers are not influenced by it." In addition, he taught us the Bible based on logic and enabled us, even non-Christian students, to accept what he had elucidated. Furthermore, his teaching method interested students to study the Bible by themslves.

Mrs. Anderson is an extremely charming lady. Her eloquence is amazing. Because she has expressive eyes and expressive mouth, she is able to get the Trojan War in *Iliad* vividly depicted to the full. Once, she asked us such a subtle question: "In the Trojan War, there are two great heroes, Achilles and Hector. Which one do you like the most, the offensive hero, Achilles or the defensive hero, Hector?" We chorused our answer, "Hector!" She said: "She prefers the latter to the former, too: Achilles is too overbearing and Hector is unassuming. But Hector is a tragic hero, and historically speaking, a tragic hero can evoke more sympathy than any other type of hero. People shed tears for him."

By then, Shakespeare was an elective course but we felt that one, who studied at the DFLL without taking this course, was not like the student of the DFLL. As a result, this course was elective in name but compulsory in reality. Each one of us had that thing, fat and heavy, 37 plays in total. And we carried in our armpits walking back and forth on the campus and looking like sort of students who were truly fond of Shakespeare. In fact, of the 37 plays Shakespeare wrote, we only studied three plays from the beginning to the end: *As you Like It*, *Hamlet*, and *Merchant of Venice*. Aside from these three, we studied only the best parts of *Macbeth*, *King Lear*, *Othello*, and *Romeo and Juliet*, not in the same token of studying the foregoing. The rest of 30 other plays we didn't tap at all, and even cannot commit the titles of the plays to memory.

At that time, the one who offered the course was a senior professor, Zhao Mo, at the department. The approach he conducted the course was teaching the whole thing by textual reading, word by word and sentence by sentence. In another word, he interpreted the verse lines by referring to the footnotes listed below, and tirelessly led us through the most difficult and dark parts of "the tunnel" of English grammar. If he found out that the students were still trapped in the daze state, he started all over again. He had such a wonderful voice, sounding as loudly as the bell rings. During the break, we often saw his face drowned in a sweat and he wiped it off with his handkerchief.

By then, the elective courses at the DFLL were under our chairperson's control. If he found out that the courses offered by Mr. A and Mr. B are very helpful to students, he would have those elective courses changed into the ones that students had to take even though they were nominally listed as elective ones. For that reason, some of the elective courses, if without chairman's support, could result in a sort of situation that no students wanted to sign up for them. On the second semester of my junior year, I was seemingly driven by a mysterious force, not clearly knowing what I was really doing, having taken an elective course, Introduction to Western Philosophy. Accordingly, I became a "disciple of Prof. Feng Weiren's."

Since there were only three students taking this course, it

conformed to the real "mode of a small class" in name and in realty. As time went by, Prof. Feng became aware of my story that I was a veteran having had no close relatives to financially support me in Taiwan, and it went without saying, my life was anything but pleasant. Accordingly, he helped me get a scholarship from Southern Taiwan Compass Club. Though the sum is not big, it helps me a lot.

At that time, the members of the club were Americans in majority. And they were technicians stationed in Taiwan doing different advisory jobs. Besides holding lunchens or dinners regularly, they often conducted various sorts of charity activities, one being the awarding of scholarships to students who were impoverished by varying reasons while studying at the different levels of school. When the Chinese New Year Festival was in the corner, the club held a party and invited all the recipients to attend, of course, including me. As a result, I prepared a "Thank-you" speech, rich in the contents and good in the style, to deliver to them. But there are several sentences polished by Prof. Feng.

When I was in my senior year, Mr. Daniel Beeby taught us Western Drama. Even to this day, I still can recall the look when he taught the play: *An Enemy of the People* by Henrik Ibsen. He was indignant at the way those ignorant people acted, and in the meantime, was sympathtic with them. Mr. Harris is our Public Speech instructor. We were mesmerized by his standard British English which is very pleasing to the ear regardless of the contents of the course.

The course of History of English Literature is conducted by Feng Juenlai. His teaching methodology is the one unmatched by no one else's. He had the whole thing of *English Literature* by Dr. Guy E. Smith transformed into the question forms based on the passages, paragraphs and even chapters. In another word, to locate answers from wherever they are in the textbook is his teaching methodology. If you can answer all the questions listed by him, there will not be any problem for you to grasp the whole thing of the History of English Literature. Truly, the way, the questions that he has made and the answers we have got, is very effective in terms of teaching and learning. And it deepens our knowledge and understanding of the History of English literature.

Mr. Feng was then capped with snow white hair, not a colored one found, his frame being angular and thin. And senility rendered his looks much old for his real age. One of my classmates told me secretly: "Mr. Feng bears a resemblance to a withered tree fully exuding the smell of a piece of rotten wood. However, there was something special about his eyes. They register wisdom." We were really worrying that he would collapse while he was lecturing due to frailty.

He is a native of Jiangsu Province, speaking Mandarin tinged with Jiangsu accent. What he had lectured was not understandable. Therefore, he went on his own way; we, on ours when we were sitting on our seats and trying to locate the answers to the questions that he gave us by referring to the textbook.

In addition, he likes making roll-call. At one time, he mispronounced a girl student's name, Huang Shuxia as Huang Douya, or sounding that way in Mandarin. And that sent the whole class guffawing.

Originally, I lived in the 3rd Dorm on the Shengli campus. But after having lived there one school year, I felt that I was constantly annoyed by the noise made by roommates (there are 8 beds in one room.) Therefore, Zheng Jizhong, my classmate, and I rented a room in a remodeled house located on Lane 8, Daxue Rd. for leasing to students only. It was a furnished room with two beds, one desk and two chairs. Jizhong and I had the similar background. Apart from paying for food, clothing, rents, and used textbooks, the university students' necessaries, we couldn't afford anything else. We usually went to classes by riding our old and wobbling bicycles. Poor as we were, we tried to have fun the way the poor could. While on our way to classes, on the one hand, we were pedaling, on the other, we were whistling.

At the time there were two biggest events taking place both in Taiwan and abroad.

On November 21, 1963, President of the United States, John F. Kennedy was assassinated in Dallas, Texas, and the entire world got shocked. The most absurd thing was that the alleged suspect, Lee Harvey Oswald, who had been caught by the police and shortly after, before everyone, with maximum-security escort, was gunned down by a guy named Jack Ruby. Such a dramatic happening made us feel that the U.S.A. was unpredictable.

Around 8 p.m. January 18, 1964, when Jizhong and I sat on our chairs facing each other at our desk and preparing for the final exam of the History of English Literature held the following morning, suddenly, we felt the ceiling overhead and the floor beneath our feet were shaking. We immediately realized that it was nothing but an earthquake. Initially, we didn't care much, but within a matter of seconds, the ever-increasing power was felt. Hastily, we hunkered down under the desk for safety. When it was gone, we came out of our hideout, and looked at each other unblinkingly, truly understanding the essence of a friend in need is a friend indeed. That quake was a 6.1 one on the Richter scale figures of earthquake magnitude. Its epicenter was in Baihe township, Tainan County. There were 106 people reported killed, 650 others injured.[64]

The building of the Department of Chinese Literature was adjacent to that of ours, and I often saw an old skinny lady with an oversized coat on walking through the hallway in front of our classroom every day. As days went by, I came to know that she was a septuagenarian, one of the giants in the field of literature in the May 4 Renaissances Movement of China. Her name is Su Hsulin.

When I was a freshman student, our Three Principles of People teacher was Chen Zhenwu. Though Prof. Chen was dumpy, he could engage every part of his body, especially, *dantian*, or the lower part of abdomen, to get his high pitch voice out as if *Shengzhen wuwa*, or his loud voice could penetrate through the roof and made the tiles of our classroom building shake. I saw Prof. Su, from the corner of my eye, who was walking through the hallway with her head down. Seemingly, she got shocked by such a loud voice. She stopped walking, firstly listening to it carefully, secondly shaking her head repeatedly, thirdly covering her mouth with one of her hands, and finally setting off smilingly.

Prof. Su is one of crusaders against Communism and Lu Xun, a left-wing writer, in the Chinese Mainland. And her frequently walking through the hallway of our department building becomes one of the most memorable scenes now when I recall my undergraduate program years at NCKU.

CHAPTER 22

NANTOU SECONDARY SCHOOL

Besides me, another two classmates possessing veteran status are Xu Zhaolin and Miao Lizhong. Some years later, Zhaolin assumed the office of the Deputy Director of the Foreign Trade Bureau affiliated to the Ministry of Economy, and more than a decade later, Lizhong was promoted to Associate Professor at the DFLL at NCKU. Though we, three of us, were ten years older than our other classmates, we didn't fall behind in academic performances.

In June 1964 when the flowers of Delonix Regia, or the flowering plants, were in full blossom like flames and the loudspeakers were blaring forth Auld Lang Syne on the campus, some male students, who went home, would wait for the draft notice to do the mandatory services in the army; some female students, who had got admissions to graduate school programs, would get ready to further their studies in American universities; and still others, who were overseas students, would pack up everything and return to their overseas residences. Since three of us had done the military service already, we were exempted from that kind of stuff. Furthermore, amid three of us, Xu Zhaolin who, before our graduation, had found a job already, and only Miao Lizhong and I worried about whether we could land jobs after leaving the NCKU campus or not.

Based on my own mental leaning, I thought the job that suited me most was teaching. Accordingly, I worked very hard toward this direction.

At the time there were two persons who would like to help me find a teaching job: one was Zhang Zhixing, a senior student at the

Department of Mechanical Engineering; another, Prof. Liu Xianlin, also Dean of General Affairs, with whom I took the course of Political Science in my freshman year. Zhang said that he had a close friend who worked as the Head of Purchase and Maintenance Section at the Provincial Nantou Secondary School. And he could write a letter for me to explore the possibility. Prof. Liu recommended me a teaching job at Da Cun Junior High in Zhanghua County.

Both had the same sort of opinion, indicating that if I wasn't so picky about the location, willingly keeping away from the cities and townships along the north-south rail line in the western part of the island, that I wanted to be a teacher in the rural area was without question. By then, I thought to myself that getting a teaching job to be settled was my first priority. For a guy like me, there were not many choices left.

Firstly, I went to see the principal of Nantou Secondary School, Sun Hungzhang, for an interview. At that time, in Taiwan, there was not such an education policy stipulating that senior high was funded and run by the province; junior high, by the county. Nantou was a "comprehensive secondary school," the junior high and senior high programs combined. Its campus is great and spacious, classrooms on a horseshoe shape bend. There is a big stadium outside. Judged from its size and others, the school looks magnificent.

Sun interviewed me in his office. After the exchange of pleasantries, he asked me to have a seat. And then he abruptly tossed out a question like this:

"We know you served in the army. Please tell me how many years you have been in." On the one hand, he sized me up, on the other, he thumbed through my personal information.

"I have been in the army 11 years." After I answered him the question, I immediately noticed that there was a sort of hesitation appearing on his face.

"We have an English teacher who has tendered his resignation to me recently. However, he changed his mind yesterday, and wants to retract his resignation saying that he would like continuing to teach here. How is that we will keep your resume in the file, and if there is an opening arising, we will hire you?"

Without doubt, I was rejected not bluntly but the way of a polite saying. If there had been no opening, how could you ask me to travel such a long way from Tainan to this county city, Nantou, for an interview? I realized that the sticking point was attributed to my "veteran status." By then, I knew that doubtedness had taken its place in his mind and I didn't lack that sort of wisdom to understand what he thought: "Firstly, you take the JCEE on the veteran status, and can your academic performances be on a par with those who are "regular" students? Secondly, can your English be good enough to teach our students?" (At that time Nantou was the best secondary school in the whole county). For the time being, I found our conversation was unable to continue, and I had nothing to do but to rise, and got ready to leave. When I was accompanied walking to the door, suddenly, an inspiration struck me that there was a copy of transcript in my trouser back pocket. And I fished it out and handed it to him:

"Here I have just had this copy of transcript for the second semester in my senior year which is used to apply to the Veterans' Association for sort of scholarship. There is a provision stipulating that those veteran students in universities, who have got an average over 80 points of academic performances on a one-hundred scale in each semester, can get 200 yuan as "incentive money."

He held that copy closer to his glasses and looked at every subject very carefully with its grade listed below. And I noticed that that copy of transcript caused a change in his facial muscle. And then he stopped me and intended me to go back to retake the seat. In the meantime, he said to the director of General Affairs, Mr. Ye, who stood beside him:

"Mr. Ye, Get the director of the Personnel Office here!"

In a little while, the director came running to the office. Sun introduced him to me on the one hand, on the other, said to him:

"Right now issue a contract to Mr. Ma, and we offer him a teaching job and let him teach elementary and advanced English in our junior high and senior high programs." This way, I got my first contract in my life.

After having left Nantou, I was heading Da Cun Junior High for another interview.

Da Cun Junior High is a typical of school in terms of the rural area in Taiwan. I should use four Chinese characters, *pu shi wu hua,* or the definitions of simplicity and practicability to describe it.

The principal is a very lovely and down-to-earth person. Hardly had he finished exchanging a few words with me when he bluntly asked me to clarify my marital status. When he knew that I still remained single, he said he would act as a go-between to introduce a decent girl to me if I would like to sign the contract he offered. He further indicated that before I came for interview, he had already made the decision to hire me because Prof. Liu Xianlin had been his superior before, and he trusted him completely. I told him that his straightness in this dealing was greatly appreciated.

On my way back to Tainan, I stayed at Yuanlin for one or two hours visiting my classmate, Yen Yunpeng. Some decades later, she became the proprietor of the *Commonwealth Magazine*. Having not finished a listen to my entire story about landing a teaching job, she immediately jumped on her bicycle to the Provincial Yuanlin Experimental Secondary School to give a try for me. As expected, there was no job opening for an English-teaching post. Clearly, the teaching job openings in the schools located in the little bit bigger cities or townships along the rail line from Taipei to Kaohsiung were all filled in 1964. Though I didn't get the job on the location I liked, what Yen Yunpeng has done for me is still kept in my mind.

After having thought about the pros and cons of both schools over and over, I carried my simple luggage to Nantou County and reported to the school.

Upon moving into the sole dorm set for the unmarried faculty, I discovered that I didn't have the feeling of being solitary. There were two colleagues who were also from the Shandong schools in exile: Qu Liheng and Dong Jinyue. The former was one of the teachers but not in the same school of mine in the old years; the latter, a fellow student in the same token. Now Qu taught Chinese in the senior high program; Dong, History, in the junior high. Besides these two men from the same province, there was another teacher in the same nature, Ma Xianxing. According to his account, during the time when the majority of students were illegaly drafted into the army on the Penghu Islands, he was 12 or 13 years old, extremely short for his age, and thus, made a narrow escape from the disaster of being press-ganged into the army.

The Provincial Nantou Secondary School was deemed as a "hide-away place" in which there were many well-known "giants," metaphorically depicted as *canglong wohu*, or coiled dragons and crouched tigers. Among them, there were two figures surnamed Deng and Sun who outshone others. The former commanded tens of thousands of crack troops as commaner of a division; the latter, Sun, once the chief of one of the counties in Mainland China which is about hundreds of Chinese li in circumference. Their stories became "a barrel of laughs" making us feel cool and "slaking our thirst in the heatwaves." Even having listened to the stories of theirs one hundred times, we would never get tired of them.

One of the funniest events that had happened to Deng was told like this: it was said that in the early 1940s, there was an encounter between his men and the Japanese force on the border line between Henan and Hubei provinces. In the daytime, his men and Japanese troops fought tooth and nail, neither side won this encounter battle; at night, both sides, in the pitch-dark night, tried to get each other, but no breakthrough. And they got into a deadlock. At last, both sides backed down a little and redeployed their troops to get ready for another round of life and death fight.

One day, when Deng's men got to a township, and had the division headquarters settled, his adjutant was busy trying to get the commander's wife to keep him company. But out of "mistakes," he snatched a bride to him as a substitute. And that poor girl's head was still covered with a piece of red veil. Consequently, the girl became the new Mrs. Deng. And at last, they retreated to Taiwan together and settled down in this school, living happily and depending on each other.

Having been the county chief in Xunhe Province in the Chinese Mainland, Sun acted as Cao Mengte, a witty hero in the Three Kingdoms Era or *Romance of Three Kingdoms*. With his broad back like tiger's, waist line like bear's, bushy eyebrows and huge eyes, he walked on the campus with his hands behind, intertwinted. While walking, he acted out in a way that firstly he got his left foot on the ground to the direction of 9 a.m.; then, his right foot, 3 p.m. Seemingly, steps of this kind are tantamount to those of an actor who played the role of Cao Zhengxiang (prime minister Cao) in Peking opera.

Though he spent years studying the Three Principles of the People, Constitution of the Republic of China, and the Doctrines by our founding Father, Dr. Sun Yat-sen, he became a laughing stock in grading examination papers. One of the stories was told like this: he graded papers not based on the answers, right or wrong, but on the number of words put on the papers, meaning the more words a student wrote on, the more points, he would get. So, students knew this secret of getting higher points and consequently, put more, more, more irrelevant words on the papers to suit his fancy.

Once when the final was due, one of the students got a question sheet. And of the questions, there was one puzzling him, and he didn't know how to deal with it. and suddenly, an inspiration struck him that he put the lyrics of the theme song from the movie, *Liang Shanbo and Zhu Yintai*, or Romeo and Juliet as the answer. As Sun saw that the answer sheet was filled full with words, not caring about what the student put on, he simply twirled his pen and gave him 95 points based on the 100-point scale.

When I began teaching at Nantou, I was assigned to teach two English classes by the Office of Academic Affairs: one class in the junior high program; another, in the senior high. Owing to the favorable feedback to my teaching and on the following school year, I was assigned to teach all senior high classes. Of them, one class is of gifted students. Overall, of all these classes, the deepest impression left on me was the 3rd Class students in the 2nd year of senior high program. They were all male students, though their academic performances were a little bit different between each other, they were all nice and highly motivated students.

Teaching the students in the junior high program in this school, one needed a lot of patience. In another word, if the students didn't get what I had taught, I had to repeat the same stuff, once, twice, or thrice. After

On February 30, 1966, this photo was taken with the third class of Nantou senior high in their second year. By then I was their classroom teacher.

that, if there were still some students unable to catch up with others, I had to conduct an individualized program to help them.

In the middle of the second semester of that school year, there was an incredible event that happened to me.

One day when the lunch break was on, there was a guy from the Section of Purchases and Maintenance coming to inform me that "You have a visitor, and he was waiting at the entrance!" And as I was wondering who that guy might be, I saw a man, aged 40 odd years old, come up to me. And he held my hand firmly:

"I am from the Ling County, the same place as you are. And I am the Deputy Commander, the Coast-patrolling Headquarters of Taiwan. I travel to Nantou because I am invited to attend a meeting held by the Provincial Government. As it is near Nantou, I come to see you. My name is Hou Jahju."

I had never heard of such a man whose name was Hou Jahju from Ling County in Taiwan, but from his behavior and the way he was talking, it seemed to me that he was not a bad guy. Therefore, I asked him to go to my roughly furnished room in the dorm for the unmarried faculty for a chat. After having ourselves seated, he began telling me how many people from Ling County in Taiwan. He told me that in Kaohsiung City, we had Cao Zefang, in Taichung City, Xia Shuyuan, the sole representative elected from Ling County into the National Assembly, and in Taipei City, Zheng Daoshu. Having finished counting the people from Ling County, he got up pretending to leave:

"My chauffeur is waiting for me out there, and I have to leave now. Later, if I have another opportunity, I'll be back to see you again!"

"Well, as you can see, lunch time is due. And it is on me. How is that?"

He didn't say "yes" nor "no." Subsequently, we walked shoulder to shoulder to a restaurant. While I was ordering the dishes, out of one of his breast pockets, he took a cigar and held it between his lips. On the one hand, he was puffing, on the other, he gave me a sweeping gaze from my head to my toe.

Aside from that I ordered three dishes and one big bowl of soup, I got a bottle of Shaoxing wine. His talk was not cliché-ridden. It seemed to me that he was a man who had been well-educated. After three rounds of drinks, he loosened his tongue, beginning to talk big. But as I noticed, when he came to the "real stuff," he immediately held what he wanted to say. When he said, "Goodbye" to me, he repeatedly encouraged me to work hard so that one day, I would become an honor of our home county, Ling. But unexpectedly, when I returned and was passing the entrance of the school, A prompt delivery mail was handed over to me by the doorman. Having opened it, I found that the note had been written by Cao Zefang (I usually call him Uncle Cao) who lived in the city of Kaohsiung. Its contents are as follows: "Recently, there is a guy named Ho Jahju claiming that he is a Ling County man but actually, a fraud telling a lot of lies to get ill-gotten gains everywhere. I have fallen a victim to his fraud once. If you see this guy, please rush yourself to the police station!" At this juncture, I realized that I had really been defrauded. Fortunately, I felt that he didn't get much out of me except for a meal I shared with him.

Shortly after, I read an announcement published on the supplementary edition affiliated to the *Taiwan Shin Sheng Daily News* (*the Newborn*) that they would like to have some short essays about "The True Story of Being Defrauded." I was stimulated by a strong urge and wrote a 500-word essay entitled: "The Deputy Commander Who Comes from the Same County as I Do." In about a week after I mailed it out, it was published.

Another interesting episode is so funny that even to this day, whenever I think of it, I cannot help bursting with laughter. That is that the *Shengxue lu*, or exam pass rate, was not low in terms of the Nantou Senior High Program students' enrolling in colleges and universities that school year. In order to make the school's fruits of this kind known to the public, the Office of Academic Affairs got out a special issue of publication to promote the school. But it was a pity that the proofreading work was not done correctly and made a big irrevocable mistake as such: "In our school, for this school year, there are 33 students who have passed the JCEE getting in colleges and universities. Instead, it is mistakenly printed as 33 students who have failed." Because in the Chinese language, the two characters *qu* (取pass) and *bai* (敗fail) have the similar appearances. The guy, who was held responsible for the proofreading work of this special issue of publication, should be severely spanked.

During the time I stayed at Nantou for one and a half years, there was someone who liked to act as an intermediary trying to introduce girls to me so that I could change my marital status from single to married. However, due to many a factor, I almost got there but finally failed. Though there was a girl student who had taken a shine to me wishing me to stay at Nantou, yet after thinking about the insurmountable age gap, I couldn't live up to her expectations—continuing to stay at Nantou Secondary School. I quit the school and responded to the call of my alma mater to assume an assistant post at NCKU.

CHAPTER 23

EATING AND DRINKING CLUB

In the fall of 1965, Tian Tingfu, who, at that time, was a teaching assistant at the DFLL, (later, dean of general affairs at NCKU,) wrote me a letter indicating that Wu Renmin, dean of the College of Science and Liberal Arts, needed an administrative assistant. And Dean Wu sought the help from Fu Chong-te, chairperson of the DFLL, to get such an assistant who must be a graduate from the DFLL.

For the college, the duties of an administrative assistant involve doing routine tasks but he has to be employed under the name of the DFLL. Maybe, considering that there are some tasks that have to do with English. Furthermore, it is stipulated that if in the future, this "extra-pair-of-hands" is not needed and if there is a teaching assistant opening arising in the DFLL, this guy will be able to have the opportunity of getting that post.

At that time, I initially thought to myself that I had just settled down, and sticking to this teaching job was better than going anywhere else. Moreover, the colleagues and the students of Nantou Secondary School treated me very well, and I enjoyed the happiness of being respected. I also thought of the reality that I was alone in Taiwan. That I was able to get settled in Nantou Provincial Secondary School was something more than expected. What a high-flying life goal did I dare to pursue?

But later when I calmed down, I thought that if I missed such an opportunity, there wouldn't be another one coming. An assistant of today would be a professor of tomorrow in the university. There is a saying that reads: "Man struggles upwards; water flows downwards." This is a long-standing principle from the Chinese ancient time to the present day. Why did I want to adopt a "counter-trend" action? Furthermore, in the university, I might have many academic opportunities and research links. And every day, I could learn new stuff.

With that enticement dangling in front of me, I began considering this "windfall" seriously and made up my mind that I would quit Nantou next January at the end of the January of the 1966, also the end of the first semester of the school year.

Both my colleagues and students, especially, those students, who were in Class 3 in the 2nd year of the senior high program, hated to see me leave. But as they thought that there might be a career with a brighter future ahead of me, they had no choice but to let me go.

Back to NCKU, I moved into a "temporary dorm" renovated from one of students' dorms for unmarried faculty and staff members. Among the roommates were my classmates Zheng Jizhong—later, professor of the Chinese Language program affiliated with the Department of English at San Francisco State University; Lian Wenxiong—later, Associate Professor at the DFLL at NCKU; and Zhang Shunan—later, Deputy Director in the Foreign Trade Bureau connected with the Ministry of Economic Affairs. The first two guys, who had long been recognized as outstanding students and, after the graduation and mandatory military service of theirs, were employed as teaching assistants by our chairperson, Fu Chong-te. The third one had just found a job in Asia Airlines. For the time being, he couldn't find a good room for rent. Therefore, he hoped he could temporarily live with us for a few days.

At that time, the Office of the Dean of College of Science and Liberal Arts was situated on the second floor in the Chemistry Department Building. And it was within walking distance, only 5 minutes needed. Everything went better than I thought.

Dean Wu received higher education in the U.S. in his earlier years, having a Master's degree in the field of Physics. After teaching a lot of years at NCKU, he became a senior professor at the Department of

Physics.

He is studious. When free, he always picked up a book to read. However, he was aged, often seen sitting in the sofa, thumbing through few pages, and dropping off with his head down. And his book slipped his hand and fell unto the floor.

He worked the way as an American does. If I could get my job done during the office hours, the free time was totally at my own disposal. He neither assigned me any extra work to do nor found fault with the work that I had done.

He had another teaching assistant from the Department of Physics to help him. In case, he was out of town, this assistant would teach the course of Freshman Physics as a substitute. This assistant's routines included reviewing the students' homework and grading mid-term and final examination papers. His name is Sun Zhongguang.

As to the paperwork, he had another assistant named Zhuo Xiuyan, the then instructor from the Department of Chinese Literature to help him.

After I worked in his office a year, a teaching assistant opening became available at the DFLL. And since then, I became a teaching assistant in name and in reality. Accordingly, I was qualified to move into the dorm located at Dongning Rd. which was set up specifically for the faculty and staff. Its official title is the NCKU Single Faculty's and Staff Members' Dorm.

At that time, the DFFL had 6 teaching assistants on staff. And their major works involved providing services for those who were associate professors, full professors and international teachers. Each one of us was assigned to support three to four of them. Our services included doing the students' homework correcting, supervising tests, grading mid-term and final examination papers, getting grades on grade reports, and working as liaisons between the personnel office and international teachers, and checking with the cashiers for their pays based on the number of hours they had taught.

We were also assigned routine tasks: scheduling, doing the paperworks, counselling students, inventoring and managing the properties, etc.

Aside from the foregoing, I had once acted as a "feeler" for our chairperson, running here and there and exploring the possibnility of that were there any international teachers, (the majority of them were pastors of denominations or nuns of Catholic churches) who, having lived somewhere in the Tainan area, would like to teach at our department on a part-time basis? The best candidate, of course, was the person who was a master's degree holder with English and American literatures as his or her major.

For teaching assistants, the greatest pressure comes from promotion. Having met the three-year services requirement for qualifying a teaching assistant to be promoted to instructorship is only one of them. The rest involves moral conduct, services and papers. The first three requirements are much easier to meet; the last one, producing the high quality of papers, is the hardest. For that reason, our chairperson spared us several hours per week to sit in classes to sharpen our academic calibers.

To me, getting promoted might be a crucial thing, but getting married was more critical because I couldn't remain single for the rest of my life. For that reason, I rekindled the idea of getting married.

I was 36 years old, now. Old as I was, I had little money deposited in my bank account. In that case, who would like to tie the knot with a "poor guy" like me?

However, I was not going to downgrade myself. Even though, people targeted nothing else but money in the society, how many of them were able to grab an opportunity as I was, being a teaching assistant in the institution of higher learning today? If I was highly motivated and willed myself to get instructorship, there would be a day for me to climb up the academic mobility ladder to the rung of it. And only then would I be able to dismantle the inflexibility of the office hours from 8 a.m. to 4 p.m. set for only teaching assistants.

My classmate, Ren Shiyong, later, dean of the College of Liberal Arts at NCKU, who taught English somewhere in Pingdong County, wanted to pay a visit to his family in Taipei. And on the way back home, he made a stop at Tainan and came to see us in the department. Knowing of my marital status, he acted as an intermediary introducing a Taipei girl to me. Her name is Wang Paolien.

Having gone through various frustrations, two years later, I happily tied the knot with this girl on May 4, 1968, and the wedding ceremony was held in Nanhua Hotel, a rather big one, on Minzu Rd., or People's Road in downtown Tainan. And on the early morning, around 6 a.m., March 16, 1969, she gave birth to a baby boy, in the hospital called Chongai on Zhongshan Rd., and according to the genealogy book of mine I could recall, I named him Taohung.

In the late 1960s, a teaching assistant could only make around 1,200 yuan per month. That salary "to keep the ball rolling" for two persons' essentials of living was barely enough. As a newborn added, only the cost of milk powder made my income unable to make ends meet, let alone other costs.

The most unacceptable thing was the criteria for promotion, all the openings having been filled at that time.

Curriculum offerings and class-size are among the determinants of the department teaching force. In another word, the total number of professors, associate professors, instructors, and teaching assistants needed is written in black and white, "one pit," "one radish." By then, all "pits" were occupied. If there was no one getting to be promoted to associate professor, how could an instructor get advanced? And in the same token, if there was no instructor getting to be advanced, how could a teaching assistant get promoted? Even if there was a "pit" for an instructor arising in the department, it must follow the first come, first served rule to determine which teaching assistant got the priority for promotion. If the one who was nominated to be promoted was rejected, most reasons due to the quality of the paper submitted, he still had the second chance to apply. By so doing, there was no way to figure out when my turn was due. To what year and to what month should I have to wait in this kind of situation?

At the time I was 39, and I couldn't wait any longer. After consulting with my wife, I made up my mind to go to the U.S. to get my Master degree. In the winter of 1968, I passed TOFEL, and based on the evaluation of my own academic performances, began requesting application forms from three American universities. In those days, how many Social Science and Humanities majors could get scholarships? If one could get a tuition waiver, one was considered the luckiest.

Consequently, all three universities to which I sent application forms accepted me.

I decided to go to the University of Oregon to study Curriculum and Instructions. The reasons are: firstly, it is "easier to get the degree from the field of education," because in this field, the English vocabulary needed "is limited;" secondly, I was quite old then, almost 40, and furthermore, I had a family in tow, thus, the degree should be gotten, the earlier, the better; and thirdly, the University of Oregon gave me a tuition waiver, demanding US$1,400 for one year's living expenses, the lowest as far as I knew. If I had this amount of money, I would be able on my way to the University of Oregon.

Even though in the year of 1969, the amount of US$1,400 was not a big one as thought, but at that time, to me there was no way to raise such a sum. However, thanks to the members of "the Eating and Drinking Club," the so-called "wine and meat friends" who offered their timely financial help to me.

The so-called "Eating and Drinking Club" was an informal organization, mainly consisting of those who lived in the Unmarried Faculty's and Staff Members' Dorm on Dongning Rd., with the main purpose of occasionally enjoying food and booze outside.

Initially, we gathered together, seeking the pleasure of eating and a couple of drinks, and later, all of us became the "outlaws" in *Water Margin*, toasting one another with large gulps of the hottest stuff served out with big bowls and wolfing down bigger chunks of meat. Furthermore, if we didn't want to go out boozing, we just forgot it. However, once we gathered together starting to drink, what we drank was nothing else but *Gaoliang* made from sorghum, hot stuff, or Daqu in the same nature.

We didn't have the rule about how often we gathered together for this kind of binge drinking, nor did we have any regular spot in which we intended to gather together. To surrender ourselves to the pleasure of eating and drinking completely depended upon a whim. Members were from the Department of Mechanical Engineering of the College of Engineering in the majority. There were also several of them from the Department of Physics at the College of Science. And only two members were from the College of Liberal Arts: Ms. Xu Xiaoyun nicknamed *xiaoya*, or little girl, from the Chinese Department, and me from the DFLL.

Most of these "meat and wine friends" thought that the post of teaching assistant was only a "springboard" and once they got scholarships from graduate schools abroad, they quit and left without any hesitation. When I got admission to the University of Oregon, these buddies had already got scholarships in their hands and would be on their ways. When they heard of my financial difficulty, they offered what they could, helping me out of their own accord. In general, each one of them lent me US$100. But there is always an exception that one of them lent US$600 to me. These buddies were Liu Hanlie, Wang Weiqiang, Huang Zhihung nicknamed Yellow Cow, and Huang Zhiyuen, Yellow Fish.

Another biggest factor that emboldened me to go abroad was due to Paolien's family. Hardly had her parents heard the news that I wanted to further my studies in America when they immediately gave their endorsements and furthermore, said that during the period of my absence from Taiwan, Paolien and Taohung could move into their home on Taiyuan Rd., Taipei. Their proposal gave me peace of mind while I was going to study in the U.S. How lucky was I who had such kind of father-in-law and mother-in-law with such a "tacit understanding?"

The Veterans' Association under the Executive Yuan (executive branch) has a provision for the veterans who want to advance their studies abroad. It is stipulated that those who have got admissions to the universities abroad are provided with one-way air fare. I should give a credit to the National Government again, and it was a big financial help to me at that time.

The buddies, who resided in the Unmarried Faculty's and Staff Members' Dorm on Dongning Rd in those days and enjoyed eating bigger chunks of meat and drinking hot stuff with bowls, are scattered all over the world. Some of them have had great accomplishments in the field of engineering in the U.S., for example, Liu Hanlie and Wang Weiqiang. And they have settled down on the East coast, Washington D. C. and New Jersey. Huang Zhihung (Yellow Cow) died young. Huang Zhiyuan (Yellow Fish) who was the first one returning to NCKU and contributing what he had learned in the U.S. to our Alma Mater. During the period of from 1978-81, he was the chairman of the Department of Chemistry.

In the fall of 1998, I was invited to join the tourist group organized by the NCKU Alumni Association and paid visits to the alumni in the U.S. In Washington D. C, I met Liu Hanlie, and mentioned the loan stuff when I embarked on the trip for my advanced studies in the U.S. And he grabbed one of my hands and shaked it firmly, while covering my mouth with another, meaning, "don't mention it."

CHAPTER 24

FIRST TRIP TO THE U.S.

I can still recall the scene, 43 years ago, on September 15, 1969 when I left Taiwan. That day, there was mist hanging over Taipei City.

As the time was not up for Northwest Airlines to process the passengers, I was queuing in the hall of departure in Taipei Songshan Airport. As I saw Paolien with a big tummy, her second pregnancy, and a six months old son, Taohung, in her arms, accompanying me in line and occasionally giving me a strained smile to see me off, I was really unable to bear the situation I had got stuck in.

Besides my mother-in-law and two sisters-in-law, Baoxia and Baohua, who put a wreath around my neck, and waited quietly in the hall, unexpectedly, one of my best friends, Wang Chuwanpu, who lived in the Nangang area of Taipei, rushed to the airport in time, and hurriedly had some pictures taken. And those pictures are considered the most valuables that I have ever had in my life.

Before we went abroad for furthering our studies, the International Cultural Exchange Bureau connected with the Ministry of Education had held a one-day "Study-Abroad Program" for us. It was conducted by a "young scholar" who had just finished his advanced studies in the U.S. and returned to Taiwan. Included in this program are: table manners, cultural shocks, know-how for taking courses, library ordinances, and housing problems such as living on-campus or off-campus, students' insurances, and how to handle car accident. He explained everything in detail and held a Q & A session to clarify some confusions in our mind. Of these various things mentioned, the opportunity of getting a part-time job interested me the most.

We flew Boeing 737. And it was a flight scheduled for only the students who went to the U.S. for furthering their studies that year.

After having got on the plane in Taipei Songshan Airport, we felt as if we had already arrived in the U.S., because all the stewardesses were blondes with blue eyes and when we turned to them and had eye contacts, they grinned at us, the shining white teeth broad shown, and giving us friendly smiles. We were a little bit shy, but to wave them hello. The plane landed in Narita Airport for a two-hour stopover in Japan. And hardly had we finished touring a few of duty-free stores in that airport when we had to rush to the departure gate for boarding.

Shortly after, on board, we enjoyed the first Western-style food.

Once the dish on the tray was laid on the folding table, I thought that I had to use what I had learned from the "Study-Abroad Program." Firstly, spreading the paper towel on my lap, secondly, squeezing the lemon juice on the steak, knife in my right hand, fork in my left, I cut the steak into small pieces like the shape of cube and dipped them into the A 1 sauce and finally, put them one piece after another into my mouth. And while chewing, I was on the alert keeping my mouth closed, not letting any smacking sound out.

I looked sideways at my neighbor cutting his steak into three or four pieces, putting them between the bun like sandwich, biting off a large piece of it with his teeth, and completely ignoring the way of taking the steak we had learned. In the meantime, he winked at me and then, said: "Any way of taking this will be all right as long as you can put it into your mouth!"

After several hours' sound sleep, the plane was approaching Seattle.

As the plane was ready to land, it bumped into the most severe turbulence. And the fuselage rose and fell violently. And before long, there was the retching sound letting out in the cabin, and I saw a student, who was hunchbacked, sitting to my right but one row before me and vomiting. And worse, he had shortness of breath falling into coma.

The stewardesses masked him up with the built-in oxygen installation, further, performing cardiopulmonary resuscitation on him. And to this day, this is the only CPR operation that has ever been seen by me in person on the airplane since then.

Worse, heavy mist blanketed the entire Seattle Airport when this inbound plane was about to land. And the visibility was very low. After the plane was circling several times, the captain announced that there was no way to touch down. And he had no choice but to pilot this jumbo jet toward Portland Airport in the state of Oregon.

Although the captain landed the Boeing 737 there safely, we were not permitted to get off the plane because at that time, the airport had no immigration and border protection establishments. Therefore, we had to wait until the mist dissipated in Seattle. Only at that time, could we get back to Seattle Airport in the same plane.

Having gone through the Customs and finished claiming my baggage, I headed to the Greyhound Bus Station.

Between the airport and the bus station, there was a bridge shaped like an arch. Though my canvas drawingstring bag was equipped with wheels at the bottom, yet encountering a flight of terrace stairs, I found that the wheels lost their functions. I was stuck in a difficult condition of getting myself to one stair first, then lifting up my bag with both of my hands to the stair on which I stood. This way, I went through the whole thing. When I reached the top of the bridge, I was drenched with sweat. I thought to myself: "Isn't this the first trial on the way to get Buddhist Sutras described in *Journey to the West*?"

After having got the ticket and fixed the baggage in the "baggage compartment" of the bus, I inserted coins into the slit of a vending machine and got a cup of hot coffee. On the one hand, I enjoyed the drink, and on the other, loitered outside the station.

When it was around 7 p.m., I got on the bus and was on my way to Eugene, Oregon. Usually, it won't get dark until 9 p.m. on the West coast in the month of September. At this time, the sun stood very low in the west, casting its rays on the red, yellow and purple leaves of maple trees on either side of the mountainous declivity of the highway, and making me feel as if the greyhound bus had been running through the paintings by famous watercolorists.

It takes about seven and a half hours from Seattle to Eugene by Greyhound Bus.

When the bus finally got to Eugene, it was around 2 a.m. Additionally, as I was a guy as *Alice in Wonderland*, where could I find a hotel which was still open at this hour? Under the circumstances, I had to brave myself to call Mr. Peach, one of the international students' advisers in the university by inserting coins into the pay phone installed in the station. Thanks to him who said that he would pick me up in the deep of the night at the bus terminal, and for the time being, installed me to stay in a sort of the hotel like the hotel run by YMCA on Xuchang St. Taipei. And he said: "Throughout the whole city of Eugene, you can't find any other hotel cheaper than this one. They charge you the going rate of three dollars a night."

When the school started, in order to sharpen my spoken English, I moved in the dorm, Carson Hall, for graduate students. The building stood four stories high: the lower two for male students, the upper two for female students. Besides there was a TV room in the basement, each floor was provided with a house master or supervisor, the posts assumed by senior students. Up to the present moment, I can recall my supervisor's looks. Though young, he wore thick sideburns similar to Walt Whitman's (the author of *Leaves of Grass*.) His name is Joe.

Chinese students are great at English grammar, reading and writing but bad at listening and speaking. Without having sat in classroom half a year or a year, no one can sit there comfortably.

There was one of the students whose family name is Li coming from Taiwan and studying Journalism. After attending classes for some time, he was bothered by his poor listening ability. One day, he dragged me down into the basement sobbing out the story of his being unable to go on, and decided to give up. I told him: "Studying Journalism is not easy for there is a large vocabulary involved, including the rarest ones. And Journalism is a subject beyond our imagination, no words can depict the scope of it. And to anyone who is from a non-English speaking country like Taiwan, being unable to understand the instructors' teachings is natural. Don't panic." Furthermore, I advised him to keep on attending classes as scheduled, and progress would be made as time went by.

I also told him that in an American university, applying for transferring to another department or to another graduate school program was an easy thing. Among the numerous departments or graduate school programs, he could find the one that was suitable to him. Finally, I consoled him by saying: "Keep going the way you are doing now for some time, and later, if you find you are still unable to deal with it, certainly, you can take the thing you have talked about with me into consideration, again."

At last, he got himself ready for the unbearable embarrassment of that kind when he would face his parents back home in Taiwan, packing up all he had had and heading home.

In Carson Hall, living on the third and fourth floors were female students. By then, this kind of arrangement was "a brand-new idea" to the students from Taiwan, causing a lot of curiosity. As male and female students lived in the same dorm building, the outcome would be that there might be many pairings arising. It was rumored at that time that American girls applying for graduate school programs didn't intend to seek expertise but to find a life-long spouse.

Ronald Hendricks, my roommate, is handsome majoring in Architecture. It didn't take him long to get a girlfriend. Another graduate student named Mary in the Phd program of English is good-looking with exceptional personality traits. And she had a boyfriend by her side without taking much time. That they socialized themselves with each other didn't mean that they would end up being wedded in the church but to make friends with the opposite sex first. Everyone has "a bottom-line" in his or her mind, possessing the absolute freedom of getting whether a life-long spouse or not.

Mary is a good girl. One afternoon, she saw me sit alone in the lobby coming up to strike up a conversation with me and saying that there would be a beer party held at the upcoming weekend. And she hoped that I could attend to experience what a beer party in America really was. Driven by curiosity, I immediately promised as told.

Once in the beer hut, I became aware of the fact that only drinking wouldn't suffice, and dancing was a must. I was reserved by nature. Though dancing is one of the basics in social activity, I haven't learned it, let alone experienced it. Accordingly, I made up my mind only to drink, not to dance. However, with a pitcher of cool beer down, I couldn't help surrendering myself to going down on the floor and dancing to the music among them.

As Mary knew that my wife had given birth to a baby girl, she asked for the address of ours in Taipei. Two weeks later, Paolien wrote me a letter saying, "There is a girl named Mary sending me two suits of baby clothes. If you see her on the campus, you must thank her for what she has done for us!" And when I saw Mary and did what I was expected, Mary was just grinning, making a gesture with opened palms as if having said: "it is not a big deal!"

At the beginning of the 1970s, the Vietnam War was raging. The Anti-war demonstration ran rampant throughout the country. The University of Oregon was no exception. On the campus, there was a sit-in demonstration going on. And it was conducted in the president's office.

President Richard M. Nixon, reelected less than two years, emphasized his policy repeatedly on the air, "The Vietnam War should be Vietnamized!" However, this policy didn't stop the bloodshed tragedy taking place in Kent State University. The eye-catching close-up shot of a girl, who leaned over to a male student gunned down by the national guards, was on the front pages of major newspapers and televised by the big three networks on the following day. Accordingly, it brought the nation-wide demonstration to the acme of the Anti-Vietnam war. President Nixon suffered insomnia that night, walking back and forth on the White House lawn. And this newsreel footage was broadcast on the big three TV networks without letup.

During the Vietnam War period, streaking became a fad in the U.S.

One afternoon, while it was drizzling unrelentingly, there suddenly appeared a bunch of students on the campus. They rallied on the lawn, east of Carson Hall and held a streaking activity. They stripped themselves naked. And against the rain, they went in single-file beginning to run from the starting line, running and keeping running. And when they got to a landmark, they prostrated themselves with their limbs outstretched and bellies against the lawn, sliding all the way down and making the rainwater pooled in the lawn splash. They yelled and hooted, on the one hand, and on the other, they burst into peals of laugher, looking extremely excited.

From my room on the second floor, I caught the sight fully of all the kinds of their weird behaviors and felt that the whole thing was unbelievable. I asked my roommate a question: "America has had enough freedom already, is it necessary to further show their little birds in this way?"

The university of Oregon adopted quarter system by then. Namely, there were four terms in accordance to the four seasons in a school year. And roughly, one term has 10 weeks. The majority of students enrolled in the fall, winter, and spring terms taking a break in summer. However, some of the departments or graduate school programs wanted to meet some students' special needs and offered courses in summer, too.

In the graduate school program, term paper was the major way for assessing students' academic performances. Certainly, some professors liked to give two tests, midterms and finals. The advantages of the quarter system are: No. 1 the length of time is shortened but it enables students to concentrate on their studies to the effect that within a short span of time, they can get bigger improvements, in Chinese we call it "Half the work with double results." and No. 2 the contents of the varing textbooks can be "condensed" in such a way, the best kept, while the outmoded, removed.

A 10-week term passes as fast as "a horse's galloping." There is a kind of feeling, the term to start is seemingly the term to end. Once professors gave out the list of reference books, I had to rush myself to the library and located the books quickly, otherwise somebody else would grab them before me. And it would be harder to wrap a good term paper up in time.

In the first quarter, I took three courses. Unless coming across the unique terms related to the big events in the history of American education, and the special terms for education bills, I found that there were not many other difficult vocabularies in the textbooks. Even if coming across some of them with hard pronunciations, and because of the increased chances of reading and hearing these vocabularies day by day, I found out they were eventually learned by heart. At the end of that semester, two As and one B were on my Grade Report.

Among a bunch of professors in the university, the one I admired and respected the most was Prof. Hugh B. Wood. He had a lot of life experience possessing the best qualifications of an expert in education. Since he had once been invited by the Educational, Scientific, and Cultural Organization in the United Nations as an education consultant to Bhutan, Nepal, and India, he understood the education issues in those developing countries. For that reason, he could often create the kind of education theory which could be used as the universal model, namely, a "one-size-fits-all" approach.

He had at a time taken us to pay a visit to a vocational school in which there were not any tests held. Whether students could do the job or not was the key, for example, the skills for repairing car, television, radio, and all sorts of other electrical appliances. If a student could get the job done, he could graduate from the school; otherwise, he had to be kept in school to be a repeater practicing and practicing until he was able to master his specific pursuit. There was no time limit for graduation, nor were there any other tests held for the courses like humanity studies and social science.

In the summer of 1970, I followed other Taiwanese students to Reno—the Biggest Little City in the World in Nevada to get a summer job. In the casino connected with Holiday Inn, I held a dustpan in my left hand, a broom in my right, picking up the trash around the slot machines. Aside from my regular pay, I often picked up some coins of quarters, dimes, and nickels strewn on the floor. After I got off the day shift, I went on another job, washing dishes in the kitchen of Silver Spur Casino. Two and a half months' labors enabled me to earn the living expenses for the next quarter of that school year.

In the autumn of 1970, in order to experience off-campus life, I decided to rent a room nearby the school. Owing to a Taiwanese student's recommendation, I moved in Mrs. Mobley's house.

Mrs. Mobley's house was a two-story building, wooden-framed. On the second floor there were two rooms for rent, and in the courtyard, there was one room, a renovation of a storeroom. In addition, there was a kitchen down the basement where all the cooking utensils were obtainable. There were several Datong brand rice cookers left there by the Taiwanese students who had graduated from UO.

Mrs. Mobley was very picky going her own way in terms of renting out her rooms, totally based on races. She didn't rent her rooms to the whites and blacks nor Mexicans and Puerto Ricans. She only rented them to the students from Asia, her most favorite prospective tenants, Chinese. She said that the Chinese students who were affable and quiet, most of the time, studying hard and getting things done without making fuss. And most important of all, they seldom held parties, not to mention getting drunk and making scenes.

Every Monday morning, she took advantage of the time when we had gone to classes to clean our rooms. Several weeks later, she found that there was no need for her to clean mine. All she did was to get the sheet straight on the bed. There was one time that she asked me how I could all times keep the things in order, and the windows and desks squeaky clean. And I answered her by saying that: "I have been in the Chinese Nationalists Army for eleven years in Taiwan and the habit of keeping a room tidy and clean has gotten into my bones."

Somebody says: "For the elderly, America is deemed as the grave." This saying cannot be applicable to Mrs. Mobley.

She busied herself working all day: at a time, she was in her "Green House" providing plants with fertilizers and watering them; at the other, worked in her backyard pruning the apple trees and spraying pesticide on them. Again, at a time, she raked the dead leaves off from the turfs; at the other, cleaned the trash on the sidewalk in front of her house.

One of her routines that I had observed was to frequently call or write to her son or daughters who lived somewhere else in Oregon. When she had nothing to do, she sat in her rocking chair, rocking back and forth, and at the same time, with her cat on her lap, talking to it.

She and her husband are of Irish stock. Ten years ago, Mr. Mobley suffered a stroke and passed away. During his lifetime, he worked in the lumbering industry, and with her, started this family. She bore him three children, one son and two daughters, and all of them got married and set up their own families respectively.

She didn't agree to intermarriage. She said that with different cultural backgrounds, customs and habits, and language barriers, there wouldn't be a happy marriage.

I described once to her what I saw somewhere on the street a young man and a young girl hug each other and do the French-kissing as a kind of cultural shock. And she thought for a while and retorted me by asking: "In China as well as in Taiwan, don't you, Chinese, do the same sort of thing privately as this couple of young folks did in public?"

CHAPTER 25

WORKING DAYS
IN SAN FRANCISCO

At the end of spring quarter in 1971, and also on the same day when UO conferred Master's degree on me, I initially planned to pack up and go back to Taiwan for family reunion. But when I thought of how to clear myself from the debt, I immediately fell into the state of hesitancy. Furthermore, in March, the timing for returning to Taiwan is not right because all colleges and universities hire people either before the beginning of the school year or after the end of the first semester. Is there any reason for them to hire people in the middle of a semester? Accordingly, I decided to go to San Francisco getting sort of work and making some money to pay the debts that I owed my buddies when I flew out of Taiwan in 1969. As for the other problems, I had to leave them to the future to be solved.

Using the same old ruse to travel from Seattle to Eugene, I took the Greyhound Bus to San Francisco.

Around the area adjacent to Chinatown San Francisco, I rented a one-bed room on the street called Pine. After turning in the first month's rent and deposit, I had the amount of cash money in my wallet only for two weeks' living expenses.

At that time, there were two ways to find a job in San Francisco: No. 1 was to read the classified ads in the newspaper; No. 2 was to seek help from the employment agency. In order to solve this urgent problem, aside from registering with one employment agency, I bought two types of newspapers, Chinese and English, searching through the classified columns of help-wanted ads. If I came across the job openings deemed more than likely to get, I drew circles around them by pen, and then, made calls one by one. But as a couple of days elapsed, I didn't get anything. As I was in the state of *zou kun chou cheng*, or be walled in by my own worries, suddenly inspiration struck me: "Goodness me! haven't I served in the Chinese Nationalists Army for 11 years? Why shouldn't I try security companies?"

From the ads of the *San Francisco Chronicle*, I got the telephone number of a security company, and unexpectedly, having made just one call, I got a positive answer. The Pinkerton Security hired me.

This security company conducted its operations by phone. And following the instruction on the telephone, I went to one of the hospitals taking up a patrol job, and I was assigned the evening shift, from 4 p.m. to 12 p.m. In addition, I was assigned a mission to escort the nurses who got off at 12 p.m. to their dormitory located on the opposite side of the street.

The first day I got on the job and found out that this area had security challenges. John White, who worked day shift, told me that if I ran into some drunkards and drug addicts, under no circumstances, did I show weakness in self-defense. Sometimes, pressing a long-handled flashlight hitched on the belt or showing one of the postures from the Chinese Martial Arts was effective to deter them. (John believes that every Chinese knows Chinese Kung Fu.)

One night, I didn't meet with any drunkard but a drug addict. He was hysterical, two eyes bloodshot. He spoke incoherently, but to try to speak to me, and from his long soliloquy, I made out only one word that was: "Hi, how could you get this easy job?"

Every Pinkerton man wore a sort of policeman's uniform with a pin badge over the left chest of the uniform. At night, a long-handled flashlight was carried and often mistaken for a baton if it was not closely checked. As he saw me with livid looks ignoring him, he went away lifelessly.

Every night, I met with different cases, and every night, I had my heart in my mouth. For that reason, after working for a while, I decided to quit, and simultaneously calculating if I couldn't find a new job right away, the balance on my checking and saving accounts would ensure that I wouldn't go hungry. However, when I called my boss whom I had never met in person and reported to him about my attempted resignation, the answer I got was: "You don't have to quit, and I will transfer you to San Francis Hotel!"

The hotel is situated on the opposite side of Union Square in downtown San Francisco. And this is the busiest area of commercial activities, accessible by all kinds of vehicles. It was not far away from my residence on Pine St., and a round trip, getting on and off work even if on foot, took no more than 30 minutes.

I was assigned to work at a checkpoint located in the basement watching the employee clock in and out and keeping an eye on if there was any outsider sneaking in the hotel or if there was any employee who, when getting off, walked out with hotel's property (shop lifting). I was assigned the graveyard shift. And though this shift I worked was the opposite of the day shift, yet to me, working at night was nothing. What I needed was to get the sleeping time in the night changed into the daytime, and there was no problem for me to adjust myself to the change of sleeping time.

To avoid falling asleep during the quietest hours in the deep of the night, I bought many "masterpieces" of the world literature to read from the used-book bookstore, for example: *The Flowers Drum Song* by Li Jinyang, *The Good Earth* by Pearl S. Buck, *Tess of the d'Urbervilles* by Thomas Hardy, *Jane Eyre* by Charlotte Bronte, *The Inn of the Sixth Happiness* by Alan Burgess, and *Red Star over China* by Edgar Snow.

I wrote out two essays about what I had observed and heard about San Francisco: one is entitled: "The Setting Sun in San Francisco"; another, "The American Concept of Jobs." I contributed them to the *Chinese Literature and Arts Magazine Monthly*. When I received two free copies of that magazine, a note was enclosed in one of them indicating that Yin Xueman, the chief editor, intended me to start a "column" in the magazine and asked me to write a series of reports about the U.S.A. The column is entitled: "America through a Chinese Eyes." It was pitiful, at that time, that I didn't have the willpower to keep it going. I didn't live up to his expectations.

The room on Pine Street was a very good one but I had to turn in US$40 each month for rent, and if telephone, water and gas bills were added up to, I could deposit only few of dollars in my checking or saving account monthly. And if I went on like this without doing anything else about it, I really didn't know when I could rid myself of my debts.

One day, when I was sauntering along one of the streets in Chinatown, I ran into Professor Feng Weiren with whom I took a course called Western Philosophy, back my undergraduate years at NCKU. "Though the sky overhead looks so unlimited; the earth beneath our feet looks so vast, and human beings are tiny creatures living between them, yet it is a small world indeed. And there is still a chance for "long-lost friends" to meet each other despite wherever they are!" It was unbelievable. In the past, I knew that his wife, Qiao Aili, a German national, son and daughter and he had emigrated to America, but by then, I had no idea in which state they lived.

Prof. Feng indicated to me that after becoming an immigrant in the U.S., originally, he would like to apply to the colleges or universities in California for a teaching job planning to offer courses related to oriental philosophy—his dissertation is on Laozi when he studied in Germany. However, hope has been disappointed. Though lady luck befell him several times, eventually, it slipped away from him. Afterwards, he wanted to use his unique, self-created style of Chinese landscape painting in the hope that he could blaze a trail for making a living. However, though exhibits were held and all his paintings were lowly priced, yet there were few buyers. What made him so frustrated was his wife, Qiao Aili, who couldn't tolerate his "slovenliness" and "pedantry" any longer and booted him out of his own home. Any time, he thought of this, he was filled with fury that he couldn't get himself under control.

The dialect, Cantonese, is helpful. He finally got a job in the Chinese Chamber of Commerce as a secretary, otherwise he would become a homeless person and live on the streets.

He rented a room on the second floor in the same building where he worked. It provided him with a place to sleep in the night. As I saw the room was big enough for a desk and two beds, thus, I proposed voluntarily that both of us should split the rent so that we could save a little bit in terms of economy. And furthermore, he had someone to keep him company. He thought it would do. As a result, Prof. Feng became my roommate for some time, not by a "predetermined plan" but by chance and I, for that reason, was able to make the money-saving stuff more efficiently. Without much time spent, I disburdened myself of the debt.

Chinatown San Francisco was and is still regarded as the best one in the U.S., expremely prosperous. It is said that it is attributed to some of its earlier Chinese immigrants who were able to pick out this place, auspicious from the view of *fengshui*, or wind and water—Chinese geomancy.

Where there are the Chinese, there is nothing short of *luwei tian*, or braised shops, and in front of the shop, hanging on the metal rod is freshly roasted ducks, Chinese herbal medicine stores, kungfu schools, antique and jewelry shops, galleries, fortune tellers' stalls, and newspapers stands. There are restaurants, big enough for holding wedding ceremonies, and eateries noted for their mouth-watering delicious foods, too. The biggest joys I could get here were: getting the big bowl of beef noodle and reading Chinese Newspapers like the *Xing Dao Daily News*. Best of all, I could watch martial arts action films.

Broadway Avenue is located at one stone's throw away. There is a big difference between it and Chinatown in cultural atmosphere. When all the lights were on, and in order to experience how hot erotic modeling was by myself, I walked back and forth several times on that avenue. I couldn't recall who that romantic poet was but such a remark of his: "You either get in sitting seeing the show or turn your head around and go away!" The avenue was filled with the most bizarre stuff: There was a guy standing in front of the theater house touting loudly the business; another on the sidewalk amid the crowds shouted: "Sex is nothing!" "Repent! Repent! "The wages of sin are death."[65] "Come and believe in God," and "I am the way, truth, life, no one can come to our heavenly Father but me."[66]

Sometimes, I took the cable car going down to Fisherman's Wharf and Pier 39 for pleasure cruises. And while on board, I was watching the seagulls soaring overhead above the the ongoing ship. And the sea lions were seen lying on the rafts and basking, their nostrials held widely open to breathe. Their lazinesses look funny.

Half a year later, Zheng Jizhong, a Library Science major, graduated from the graduate school program at UO and made his appearance in San Francisco. He had already got a job offer from the San Francisco State University Library. Before he went on, he still had some time at his disposal. Therefore, he decided to apply to San Francis Hotel for being a security guard to join me. Having been hired by the hotel, he was assigned evening shift from 4 p.m. to 12 p.m. And I worked grave yard from 12 p.m. to 8 a.m. In a large country like the United States of America, chance mattered and brought us together and worked together: "The relationship of brotherhood having been established at NCKU was once again renewed at the particular time like this, and at a particular place like this."

I kept on working as security guard until the summer of 1972. And at that time, I got a job offer in Taiwan. And I packed everything up I had and headed to the place where I had come from.

Li Yunshan, is also one of my classmates at DFLL at NCKU. Later she changed her given name from Yunshan to Lande. She bore Zheng Jizhong a second baby boy named Jiaxuan who was just turning one month old. As both of them were working, they didn't think they were able to take care of two kids. Taking the opportunity of my going back to Taiwan, they asked me to do them a favor—taking Jiaxuan back to his grandparents to rear. I held Jiaxua, one-month old baby boy, close to my chest when I got on China Airlines flight, and he, after crying a while, slept through the whole journey in my arms to Taipei.

CHAPTER 26

THE TAIPEI COLLEGE OF BUSINESS

Jiaxuan and I arrived in Taipei Songshan Airport safely. Once out of the international arrival lobby, I felt there was a blast of hot air hitting my face, and I felt a little bit hot-headed immediately.

That day, there were two sets of families coming to meet us: leading along by holding my two little kids' hands and coming up to meet me was my wife, Paolien; another, Jizhong's parents showed up for picking up their beloved grandson.

As I handed Jiaxuan and his stuff including dampers, pacifiers, and canned milk over to this old couple, they thanked me repeatedly. And we exchanged our telephone numbers.

Having got on the yellow cab, I got the opportunity to talk with Paolien. Firstly, I discovered that my son, Tao, was energetic and active. And he was very conversational, trying to communicate with me in Taiwanese with the help of the body language. Secondly, I noticed that my daughter, Hungling, whose both arms were covered with a layer of white-colored ointment because she was suffering a sort of sweat rash. Sitting on the rear seat, she was struck dumb by my presence, most of the time, keeping quiet.

As far as the eye could reach through the windows, I felt that Taipei remained the same as it had been. The lofty palm trees on either side of the street still swayed their fronds gracefully in the faint breeze. However, there were lots of propaganda slogans here and there proclaiming: "*Zhuang jing zi quang*; *chu bian bu jing*," or "United, and make our country stronger and stronger from within; when the country is faced with crisis from without, do not panic." Hot and humid as it was in the month of June, there was a bone-chilling flow in my spine. Was it true that Taiwan became a sort of "orphan," diplomatically isolated from the international community?

After Taiwan's withdrawal from the U.N. in 1971, there were many graduate students who would rather take the odd jobs in America than return to serve their own country back home. I was one of the students who went against the dominant trend at the time when Taiwan's situation was unstable.

Not until I reported to the National Central Library situated on Nanhai Rd. Taipei, did I know that the head librarian appointed me one of the chief editors. After having worked for two weeks, I felt that this sort of sedentary job, verifying data, editing and rewriting didn't fit in my personality. I was longing for a teaching job as I had done at Nantou Secondary School before. During the class time, not only could I enjoy the freedom of assuming an air of self-conceit and writing something on the blackboard, but I could enjoy the freedom of walking around on the platform. Working in the library, desk-bound, I couldn't have the freedom of that kind. Furthermore, when having class to go, I would go to teach; when having no class, I made use of the time to prepare myself; and this kind of life would never be deprived by anyone else. Even if under the rule of an imperious emperor, he couldn't interfere with a commoner's work. Wasn't it cool to live my life that way?

Zheng Jizhong's uncle named Wang Xianhua who was teaching at the Taipei College of Business came to visit me one day, and said: "The president of the College, Wu Shihan, would like to offer you an English-teaching job. Think about it. Take it or not!"

To me, there was no need to think about it, and I immediately grabbed this opportunity following him to see the president. On the same day, I signed a contract with the college.

Moving in my father's-in-law home on Taiyuan Rd. for a temporary stay was the tactic of expedience. But living there forever in an extended family like that was not what I wanted.

At that time, the shock of Taiwan's withdrawal from the U.N. was still keenly felt. People were panicky. The U. S. dollar against the New Taiwanese yuan rose again and again in the black market. And during the hottest moment, the exchange rate was US$1 to NT$45. Though the amount of American dollars that I had taken back was not big enough to buy a single house desired, yet making the first down payment for an apartment was more than enough if I wanted to buy that kind of dwelling. Furthermore, when the housing market was in the downswing, I immediately took action to make an offer with the company for one apartment located on the 4th section, Zhongqing N. Rd. The project was under construction, and it would be delivered to us one year later.

The Office of the Third Section at the Veteran's Association, charged with the responsibilities to help veterans find jobs and go to colleges or vocational schools, scheduled a time for me to see Minister Zhao Juyu. In the meeting, besides he lavished praises on me for patriotism by citing two verse lines which read: *"Ji feng zhi jing cao; ban dang swhi zhong chen,* or "Sturdy grass withstands a strong wind and a loyal official can be found during unrest."[67] Other than that, he would like to have me on the teaching staff at the Huaxia College of Technology established by him. But after weighing the advantages and disadvantages of teaching in these two types of school, public or private, I decided to stay at the Taipei College of Business.

At the time the students that I was teaching at the TCB were in the five-year-junior-college-system (In this system, in the first three years, they are the equivalents of senior high students, and in the last two years, they are the equivalents of freshman and sophomore students in a four-year college or university). Moreover, they were the best of the best coming from various junior high schools in Taipei. They were job-oriented students who would prefer enrolling in the junior college of this kind to get practical skills such as: accounting, statistics, booking, banking, commodity money, international trade, and business administration to going to four-year university for academic studies.

They were the smartest students that I had ever taught. When I explained something to them, they were quick on their uptake.

I also taught at a privately-funded junior college on a part-time basis. Without teaching long, I learned of how hard to run the privately-funded college like this one. Students were the source of financing to keep the ball rolling. As a result, honstly speaking, the school couldn't be too demanding nor "letting all go" in "students' academic performances." And they had to strike a balance between these two polar extremes. If too demanding, more than 80 percent of students could be flunked out, and where did the school's source of financing come from? Conversely, if every course had become a pipe one and every student could pass, the school would be notorious for the sake of a profit-making undertaking.

After the holding of the Joint Junior College Entrance Examination, teachers from different fields and from different schools gathered together in an auditorium to grade examination papers, and I was one of them to grade English. Because of the oppressive heat, worse, the air-conditioners acting weird, off and on, we were feeling hotheaded. It seemed that we were likened to those air-conditioners, off and on, getting several papers marked, and then standing up to walk around. And simultaneously, we wiped the sweat off with our handkerchiefs. At this moment, a funny answer to a question in the History and Geography section spread through the auditorium and "cooled us off." This is a question regarding Geography of the World: "Please specify the differences between North Korea and South Korea in their geographic locations, produces and climates. One of the students wrote the answers as follows:

1. Location: the differences between both two countries are: South Korea is south of North Korea while North Korea is north of South Korea. South Korea faces southward; North Korea, northward.

2. Produces: South Korea has some of produces North Korea

doesn't have, while North Korea has some of produces South Korea doesn't have.

3. Climates: it is not hot but very cold in North Korea; it is not cold but very hot in South Korea.

These answers are really in the scope of truism, not necessarily to be told, and no relevant to the answers of the questions at all. Despite the fact that these students' academic performanes are far under the average, I still want to lavish some praises on them who want to enroll at the private colleges of this kind. Our country needs all kinds of young "talents." Someday, in the future when they will graduate and step into the society, doubtlessly, there will be openings to them in all trades. To say the least, if we can hold this type of students in the school letting teachers lead them and books spark their spiritual enlightenment as a Chinese saying goes: *chunfeng huayu*, or having the spring wind pick up some of water vapor and finally getting it changed into rain, they will be in more advantageous positions in school than be left out roaming on the streets. If they are on the streets with nothing to do, they are "goofing up," including fighting, etc. From this point of view, keeping them in school is the better strategy.

In fact, to me, there is no difference at all between these two types of school, public or private, in terms of management and administration, for example: while teaching, I often noticed that there was an administrator from Office of Academic Affairs standing outside to check with the attendance rate.

In these two types of junior colleges, there are two men worthy of recalling: one is President Wu Shihan of TCB; another, a historian, the son of a renowned navy officer named Li Zhun in the late era of the Qing dynasty. However, I can remember his last name, Li; his first name, forgotten.

President Wu Shihan is really a fatherlike figure helping and caring about the well-being of the junior faculty in his capacity as the president of the college. He understands that young scholars lay much emphasis on pride and dignity. If they have something that bothers them, they are reluctant to speak out. Thus, quite often, before they take any actions, the president has already grasped what their problems are and voluntarily helped them. In addition, he knows both sides of human nature, dark and bright. If one committs a mistake, he will save one's face in public. His catchphrase is: "There is nothing there. If you can get it straight, you will be okay!"

When I met Professor Li, he was over 90 years old. He could see and hear very well, capable of moving around by himself. Having almost lived through one century, two dynasties, he, himself, could be regarded as a volume of the living history of the Qing Dynasty and the Republic of China. Of course, he has had many legends and real stories to tell.

He studied in Germany and married a German woman. Right now, when his glorious years had been gone, he found himself dwelling in Mt. Yangming and living by himself. He said that he had self-educated himself into the condition of "facing death as if he were returning home." He came out aiming to get some fresh air, and teaching little ones was the way he entertained himself during his twilight years.

After having taught English to the students like those who were in their senior high program two years, I didn't think that this was what I wanted. What I really longed for was to do something greater than this teaching job. Therefore, I was inclined to throw myself into the unkown again. But how could I achieve this vaguely-conceived life goal? Eventually, I decided to return to the U.S. to get my doctoral degree.

CHAPTER 27

SECOND TRIP TO THE U.S.

In the fall of 1974, I got on the trip to America again for my doctorate. But this time, I went to Southern Illinois University located at Carbondale in the southern part of Illinois. The reason for choosing that school was that it had the Department of Higher Education.

One week before departure, I went to the Shezi area in western Taipei to bid farewell to Dr. Wang Runen, one of my closest friends, who ran a clinic there. Upon hearing my story, he didn't ask whether I needed any financial aid or not but to generously hand me a stack of money out of his coffer, "This is it, take it with you and use it whatever it is needed!" And it seemed as if there were a tacit understanding between him and me. How many friends of this kind does one have in one's lifetime?

By then, Carbondale was a university city with its population of around 30,000, and among them, the student population accounted for two-thirds. In the first year, I was struggling for my doctoral studies alone. In the second year, I asked Paolien and my two children to join me, the whole family standing together to "beat the odds."

In the previous year when I was by myself, I rented a room off campus in a boarding house. After Paolien and my children got to Carbondale, I shared the rent of a two-story single house with a newly-engaged couple, the male student whose surname is Xie. They lived upstairs; we, a family of four, on the flat.

Paolien and I taught Taohung and Hungling the "modern" English alphabet, 26 letters. When they had learned them by heart, we sent them to schools which were quite different in terms of the learning environment, Taohung enrolling in the first grade in an elementary school; Hungling, a preschool program.

I also told Taohung and Hungling to abide by a simple rule, following the teacher's teaching. In whatever the way the teacher taught, and so did they learn. At this point, that they didn't understand what the teacher's teaching didn't matter. The most crucial thing was that they should concentrate on listening and paying attention to what the teacher was doing. Taohung went to a school called Thomson Elementary while Hungling, Kindergarten called Spring Kindergarten. Both of them were situated in our neighborhood, and they were near and easy to reach.

Later, we moved in the married dorm for graduate students, firstly, Southern Hills Apartment, and then Evergreen Terrace. Accordingly, Taohung and Hungling were transferred to United Points Elementary. And the school provided bus services for picking them up in the morning and dropping them off in the evening. Furthermore, free lunches were supplied, and so were children's readers.

They spent seven and a half hours in the school from 8:30 a.m. to 4 p.m. When the school was over, the yellow bus would be seen in our compound. And we saw these little kids get off the bus looking like as if they were little cheerful birds. After chirping a little while, they returned to their own nests.

Carbondale is located far away from metropolises. And by then, there was a few of Chinese living there. For that reason, the practice of sending children to learn Mandarin on Saturday to the after-school program was never heard of. Children are quite curious, and at that time, there was a fad called "sleepover" flourishing: "You sleep one night in my home, and I sleep one night in yours."

I was granted a full scholarship, US$500 per month. After paying 150 for the rent, utilities and telephone bills and daily necessities, there was not much left. To eke out our livlihood, Paolien following other international students' wives went to work as seamstress in a clothing factory. After she got off, she immediately went on another part-time job in Mrs. King's Grill.

When I had no car, it took me 40 minutes to go to school on foot. And later, when our financial condition was getting better and better, I bought a used Dodge car priced at US$800 driving instead of walking.

In one of winter days, there was a heavy snow falling. Because I didn't get any news from the radio that classes were cancelled due to the bad weather, I insisted on going to my supervisor's class scheduled that day. I was extremely frustrated by my old car. And though I made an all-out effort trying to start it, it didn't work out as expected. Having no choice, I had to get there in the snow afoot.

With the falling snowflakes on me and the newly-fallen snow on the road, on the one hand, I kept walking, on the other, I was thinking of those old snowy years in my hometown, Jinan, Shandong Province. I couldn't help asking myself the following questions: "Is that snow-capped family house of ours still there? Don't my family members still live in that house now? And how are the playmates in my childhood with whom I got into fierce snowball fights going?" I, with all these questions in my mind, was accompanied by the snow all the way to the campus. And as the snow and reminiscenes got into a tangle, there was no way for me to slip back from memory. As a result, I had a strong urge to write something. Later, I jotted down what was on my mind in the form of a short story tinged with the shade of "stream-of-consciousness." It is entitled: "Walking in the Snow" and it got published in the *New Literature and Arts Magazine*.

At that time, the so-called Department of Higher Education was only established in a few of American universities. And in their previous existances, these universities were usually teacher-training colleges, expanded later as universities. And Southern Illinois University is one of them.

Amidst professors, Dr. John E. King, the then chairman of the Department, is the one I admire and respect the most. Having been the dean of a college before, he is not only an experienced university administrator but also well-connected. And especially, he is broad-minded treating his colleagues, who even are opinionated about running the department, with respect. In another word, he exercises patience to deal with them. To international students, he does his utmost to look after them, giving them the kind of help at the right moment.

In the middle of 1975, the state of Illnois had slashed higher education funding. And in turn, the number of students in the university to get full scholarship was decreasing. As he knew that I had a family in tow, he did his utmost to get a full scholarship for me. To express my gratitude, I wrote an article in Chinese entitled: "Professor King" and had it run on the supplement affiliated with the *World Journal*.

My supervisor is Prof. Paul Morrill, who is my unforgettable mentor. Originally, he was a senior professor in the English Department. Later, he was summoned to be the president of a college. When the term of that work expired, he was invited back by Prof. John E. King to offer a course, College Teachers and College Teaching, in the Higher Education Department. He has an excellent command of the English language having produced a plenty of high-quality papers. Even in his twilight years, he still hung on there coming up with a novel that attracted the attention of one of reputable publishing houses to get it published. This was not easy at all.

When he got the news about his eldest son who had received a military draft notice letter to fight the Vietnam war from the drafting board, he flew into a rage and yelled: "Why do I send a healthy son to that remote country to get killed? And I have nothing to do with that country, don't I?" He encouraged him to be a draft dodger fleeing the U.S. to Europe by way of Canada.

He polished my dissertation, word by word, sentence by sentence, patiently without grudging me for that writing. When one better-written paragraph met his eves, he never missed the opportunity to praise me, "Jim (my English name), you wrote this paragraph very well!"

He had been to Taiwan before, and this island country left a positive impression on him. The deepest impression left on him was one of his travelling experiences obtained from the Taiwan railway services. By then, the Taiwan Railway policy provided passengers with free tea. The guy carried a large metal kettle with one hand and glasses with tea bags in with another, pouring the hot water from the air accurately and dexterously into the glass with the exact quantity of water without any spilling. He asked: "How long has this guy practiced to get this extraordinary skill?"

For a Phd student who studies education and wants to wrap up his dissertation, there are two ways for him to take: No. 1 is finding untapped resources or mistakes committed by former researchers by tracing back to the sources from a large number of books. Having found them, he has to have them supplemented or rectified by the way of *Pang zheng bo yin* or the way of being well documented. The findings will be used for future reference or enable the readers to understand the truth. This is called historical type of research of education. No. 2 is developing the hypothesis, making a type of questionnaire and selecting the subjects. And then, when the returned questionnaires are validated, the student can use educational statistics of T-test, F-ratio, or K-square to analyze the data to prove whether his hypotheses in the questionnaire are okay or not. The last step is to provide the findings for the institution or organization concerned and the prospective researcher for future reference if they are going to do the same sort of research. This is called the analytic type of research of education.

Dr. Loren B. Jung is a specialist in analytic research. And he helped a lot of students wrap up their dissertations in the department. As he saw that I had difficulty getting my dissertation done, he suggested to me that I should endeavor to find a topic in the last school that I had taught in Taiwan. Because I had taught at the TCB two years, I was sort of familiar with commercial education. Accordingly, I finally selected a topic entitled: *The Commercial Education in the Republic of China: An Evaluative Study*. I wrote out the first part of it regarding the historic setting, of course, with my supervisor's polishing, and finished the second part of it with Professor Jung's hand in regarding the analyzing.

As my conscience dictates, the hardest part in a doctoral program is whether one can come up with a dissertation of originality. With a wide range of American education, it is not easy for a Chinese student to get out something really meaningful, especially in English. Having crossed out a lot of more than likely topics, finally, I couldn't help returning to the field related to Chinese education in Taiwan in which I had long been involved. However, at present, whenever I think of that hardbound copy of my dissertation, I feel ashamed of it even though I did my best. Here is the conclusion for wrapping up my dissertation, and I may say that I have only learned the methodology of how to do it.

In the late 1970s, the Carter Administration became impatient and wanted to establish diplomatic ties with the Chinese Communist regime. And there was an eerie atmosphere spreading through the Chinese students' groups on the campus, one group agreeing to the left-wing politics claimed: "It's a big joke that the PROC that has occupied the entire China with such a large population and such a huge territory but is unrecognized by the United States," while another group, of course, "the staunch but foolish loyalists from Taiwan," claimed: "Even though the Republic of China withdrew to Taiwan, the Penghu Islands, Kinmen (Quemoy), and Matsu, she has not been completely annihilated by the Chinese Communists Army. Spiritually, she is still the legitimate government that stands for China!"

No matter what the reason was, the United States for her own interests had decided to switch her diplomatic links from Taiwan to the Chinese Mainland. And this was an irrevocable decision. For that matter, I wrote President Carter a letter to protest his unilateral act. It availed me nothing except that I had done my part to support the National Government in Taiwan.

The conflict between these two groups didn't develop into the situation of a showdown, but in fact, the tension was mounting and mounting almost to the situation of *Jian ba nu zhang*, or the sword being drawn and the arrow on the bow being tautly pulled. There was one time they invited a scholar in from the Chinese Mainland to give a talk, and the topic and the contents of that talk have long been forgotten, but that he confused the English word, concubine, with the word, cucumber, was inexcusible. He said, "Qin Shi Huang has a lot of cucumers instead of concubines," became a laughing stock. Even to this day, that funny thing has still been kept in my mind.

In 1978, I successfully passed the oral examination of my doctorate. When my supervisor made the announcement to me, I shed tears of joy. To others, the degree was not of that significance, but to me, the degree stood not only for my all-out efforts but for the sufferings and hardships my whole family had gone through with me.

At the time I graduated, there was no job offer for me back home in Taiwan. I applied to the department for getting on a three-month post-doc program so as to have more time for readying myself to return to Taiwan. Simultaneously, I didn't forget my hobby—writing. I wrote five essaies and had the first two, "If I were an International Student Again" and "Getting Haircut in America" published in the supplementary edition connected with the *World Journal*; the last three, "Ms. Glenne's Story," "Flying East," and "Professor Feng," in the *New Literature and Arts Magazine*.

When the time was ripe, I, accompanied by my wife and two children, returned to Taiwan by way of Hawaii.

CHAPTER 28

RETURN TO NCKU AGAIN

When Southern Illinois University officially conferred doctorate on me, I attempted to apply to junior college for a teaching job in the city of Taipei. The reasons why I chose the school located in Taipei were: firstly, in the past, I had taught at the Taipei College of Business for two years and got used to the city's living environment, and secondly, Taipei is also Paolien's hometown and her parents and siblings lived on Taiyuen Road. She could see them any time, taking good care of them or being taken care of if needed. The main reason was that I was quite aware of the degree that I had earned. It was the doctor of education. If going back to the DFLL at NCKU, I didn't know whether my degree and my specialization fitted in with the criteria set by the department or not.

However, my former colleagues, Tian Tingfu, Zhang Farun, and Miao Lizhong at NCKU, thought that because I had had the degree, teaching in a comprehensive university like this one was "perfectly justified." Prof. Fu Chong-te, former chairman of the department, also thought positively that though my advanced study was in education, yet it was not irrelevant to English. English education is a kind of education, a part of general education, and improving one's English is one's lifelong business. Based on this point of view, there was no conflict between my EdD and my going back to serve the department from which I had graduated.

By then, the Ministry of Education was promoting a project entitled: "The Massive Project for Recruiting Overseas Scholars." A newly minted Phd holder would be paid by associate professor salary, and in addition, he could get the living quarters allowance of 6,000 yuan per month for a period of two years.

As this biggest housing problem got resolved, I didn't care about anything else and therefore, I made a decision to return to NCKU.

By the end of December 1978, I started packing up the "valuables." And I packed those items I could carry and disposed of all other items I coundn't by either discarding or selling them. My used Dodge car that had served me back and forth between my home and the school for three years was sold to my neighbor who had just moved in at the price of US$200, while the Brother Manual Typewriter I had used three years, US$30 to a student from India.

Because the start of the second semester was one and a half months away, and in between, there was a Chinese New Year Festival to be celebrated, we decided to accept Li Changgeng's invitation by way of Hawaii when returning to Taiwan. For that reason, we were able to leave some footprints on Waikiki Beach. Simultaneously, we broadened our knowledge by watching the graceful and slow-motion Hula dance. Even to this very day, as I recall those days in Hawaii, I am deeply grateful to Li and his wife, Yuhuan, for their cordial friendship and hospitality

At the beginning of February 1979, we got to Tainan.

At that time, Prof. Zheng Zhongxin was at the helm of the DFLL at NCKU. He was no one else but the one who, professor at NCU, was on loan to NCKU to be acting dean of the College of Liberal Arts by our former president Ni Chao. By chance, he was asked to do another university administrator work as acting chairman of the DFLL. Having consulted with him, I finally had the courses that I was going to teach scheduled temporarily: Newspaper English, Freshman English, and Writing. The first course to be offered was due to my proposal; the other two out of his idea.

Newspaper English suggested by me is based on two reasons:

Number one is that the course of Newspaper English or Journalistic English is a practical one in nature. A piece of well-written English news always consists of the most frequently used words. Grammatically speaking, declarative or simple sentences are commomly used in English news writing, easy to read and easy to grasp, not like the sentences written by novelists whose writings are full of compound, and even compound and complex sentences. When we read those sentences, we have to spend a lot of time and energy to do the analyzing. Furthermore, the contents of the Newspaper English course are unlimitted. When we have read English newspapers long enough, we are able not only to get something new but those specific words and technological terms from a variety of trades and fields spontanuously. Certainly, we can get the secrets of translation. No. 2 is due to Zhu Yaolong's influence. Zhu, though teaching at the DFLL at NCKU on a part-time basis, he is extremely popular with students. Originally, he is the editor-in-chief in the *Chinese Daily News* having produced a plenty of good essays and had them published by the pseudonym of Zhu Yuenon. He also has them published in book form entitled: *Holidays in Europe*. And it turns out to be the best book of his all. He is a knowledgeable and experienced person. During the class time, he often told some of the "inside stories" that had happened in the press. And for that reason, our horizons were greatly broadened by simply lending him our ears. In addition, the students who had signed up for the course of Newspaper English, might be able to blaze a new trail in landing jobs after graduation. With this one course taken, some of us might have created our careers in the newspaper agency and culture centers. Having gone through the curriculum offerings of the DFLL in that school year, I found out that there was no such course on offer. I recommended myself to teach the course and got this course back as an elective one on the list.

The course was open to senior students. My teaching method is to utilize the current news published on English newspapers in Taiwan as the teaching materials (most of the clippings are from the *China Post*.) I explain the headline, lead paragraph, body of the news, and conclusion if there is any. I selected two textbooks: One is *Newspaper English* edited by senior professor named Li Jianying who taught at the Department of Journalism at Cheng Chi University, another is *The Professional Journalist, 4th Edition,* by Prof. John Hohenberg.

The course of Freshman English is the English continuation of senior high, the toughest for any teacher to teach. The reasons are listed as follows:

1. The number of the freshman students in the English class was too big.
2. All the freshman students admitted to different departments had different levels of English ability.
3. The textbook edited by the DFLL was not able to meet the needs of all the freshman students from various departments of the university.

I also used the textbook edited by the DFLL. However, the lessons that I singled out to teach were largely based on students' interest. Interesting students to learn English, as I thought, was the most important of all, interest first, others secondary. If there were not enough lessons of this kind in the textbook, I would like to use some of the features with human interest from the English newspapers issued in Taiwan to fill the gap.

The English writing course was one of the courses that caused headaches for teachers who were assigned to teach.

In the 1980s, the DFLL was the first choice for B category students who wanted to study humanities. In all the universities, the maximum number of enrollees in one class around 60. Even though the English writing class was divided into two groups, each group still had 30 students. And if I assigned each one of them to hand in one piece of writing per week, there were 30 pieces to be polished. Who could have this sort of energy and endurance to do the job of this kind? Furthermore, students' writing skills were not good as expected, and they often came up with a lot of "English sentences" with the Chinese way of thinking. To correct them was not an easy job. If I wanted to get their stuff completely done grammatically or idiomatically, I had to rewrite them piece by piece. Where did the competencies come from in me?

Having corrected tens and tens of their writings, I compelled them to use *The Advanced Learner's Dictionary of Current English* edited by A. S. Hornby. The greatest advantage of this dictionary is that there are 25 verb patterns exemplified. If a student has run into the "bottleneck" of not knowing how to use a verb, he can look it up through this dictionary and the problem will be immediately solved, or he just put that verb in a sentence according to the pattern as tabulated. And the sentence is written this way can be guaranteed right. I am of my opinion that anyone who can manipulate the verb well, has a good command of the English language.

This was the way I taught the writing course a year.

When the second semester of that school year was to be close to an end, acting chair Zheng ran into a problem while doing the scheduling for the next school year. One day, in the hallway on the second floor of our department building located on the Guangfu campus, I met him accidently. At first, he muttered to himself, and in a second, bluntly told me that he had not got a right person in hand to teach the course, English Literature, and asked me to take such a tough job even if I felt disinclined. His proposal made me speechless but I only responded to him by having him try other more eligibles than I one more time.

My Master's degree is in education, and so is my doctorate. But during my undergraduate program years, my major was English, and I took many compulsory and elective courses related to English, American and World literatures: History of English Literature, Shakespeare, Greek and Biblical Literatures, the Outline of Western Literature, Western Dramas, Selected Readings of English and American Novels, and American Literature. Furthermore, when I studied in the U.S., once free, I tried to read some of the books related to English and American literature. Having weighed the whole thing in my mind, I didn't think that I was a layman in the field. Consequently, I had the idea of "overstepping my bounds," and decided to accept the challenge because my assumption was that I was placed on to deal with an "emergency case" instead of the case that "a dove takes a magpie's nest."

By then, for the course, the textbook commonly used by various universities throughout Taiwan was the fourth edition of *The Norton Anthology of English Literature*. Even up to this day, I still can recall what I selected to teach: *Beowulf, The Wanderer, Sir Gawain and the Green Knight, Piers the Plowman, The Canterbury Tales, Dr. Faustus, Pilgrim's Progress, Songs of Innocence and of Experience, The Rime of Ancient Mariner*, "Ode to the West Wind," "The Secret Sharer," *The Importance of Being Earnest, Dubliners, A Portrait of the Artist as a Young Man*, and *Mrs. Warren's Profession, etc*. I totally emphasized textual reading, seldom mentioning criticisms from a bunch of critics. In another word, paying much more attention to student's initially felt responses was my teaching method.

I was of my opinion that if a student enabled himself strenuously to reach the level of having grasped the texts, he was thought great in his academic growth. If he could understand the historical settings of those masterpieces and familiarized himself with the authors' biographical sketches, I was of my opinion that he had been in the stages of the morpholization from caterpillar to butterfly.

In order to get the general idea of English literature, I reread *English Literature—Its History and Its Significance for the Life of the English-speaking People* by William J. Long.

The textbook, *A Handbook of American Literature* by Martin Day, is one of the most admirable literary critical works that I have ever read. Especially, I like his analyses about the twentieth century novelist, Ernest Hemingway. They rekindled my passion to reread his novels, and in consequence, I, in sophomore class, offered a course entitled: Selected Readings of American Novels. Nominally the course was titled as such, but in fact, I just concentrated on teaching Hemingway' works. I also taught the students one short story, "Of Mice and Men" by John

Steinbeck.

After having taught Hemingway's four major works, there was a strong urge to write something about them. One day, I felt there was nothing I could do to dampen that kind of strong impulse, feeling that it was on its way to me and the work entitled, "A Tentative Analysis: *For Whom the Bell Tolls*," around 5,000 words, was produced in accordance with the time as wished. I sent it to *The Literature and Arts Magazine Monthly,* and got published. The editor, Yu Yunping, praised me as such: "The article is well-written but with many scholarly strokes in it. If the language had been changed into a little bit of colloquialism, it would have been much better."[68]

One thing in my mind made me feel uncomfortable, and even to this day, it still rankles in my mind whenever I think of it. That was when I made that decision to return to my Alma Meter, I was promised to be given by verbal promise the chairmanship of the DFLL by the then president, Dr. Wang Weinong. But he didn't stand by what he had said. When Zheng Zhongxin's term as acting chairman was terminated, the announcement made by the president to replace him was not me but Lu Naizheng. Lu is a senior professor and a real gentleman in our department with wonderful personality traits. He is well-read, too. And based on these qualifications, there wouldn't be any grievances and complaints against this appointment. However, as the president of a university, Wang should stay by his word.

There was one time that I had an opportunity to be with President Wang alone. I bluntly asked him: "What was really going on there?" And he beat around the bush, not telling me what was on his mind but indicating that I would still have the opportunity to get that post in the near or distant future.

The president's sudden death, at the age of 44, the prime time of his life, made all faculty and staff members as well as students in the university feel grief-stricken and sorry for the loss of him. On the day scheduled for the funeral service, the then President Jiang Jingguo of the ROC, putting off all his important work he was doing, showed up and caused a big sensation on the NCKU campus. After he personally paid his tribute in the service and bowed to the body on the bier behind the curtain, he left. And we followed suit and did the same thing. When I bowed to the body, I saw that Wang's face was shrunk, but remained peaceful as if he had been in a profound sleep, I murmured a prayer to it: "Mr. President, as for the matter of appointing me chairman, it comes to an end. I wish you on the road to another world have a safe journey!"

That I was able to return to NCKU was due to all the faculty and staff members at the DFLL who were willing to accept me, and especially, I was grateful to Tian Tingfu for his all-out efforts to get me back in the DFLL, again.

Prof. Xiong Xuehong, who was my mentor as well as my friend, was extremely kind and nice to me. He thought that "I am the first graduate with Phd. from the DFLL at NCKU and return to my Alma Mater to teach."

In a month after officially reporting to the university, I was scheduled to give a talk, open to all the students of the university through Prof. Xiong. The topic was "Pursuing Studies in the U.S.A." And he wanted me to talk about nothing else but what I had gone through in that country, and how I had felt during my stay there as an international student. An A & Q session was followed. And within my knowledge, I gave all the best answers to those who wanted to further their studies in the U.S.

CHAPTER 29

HEADING THE DEPARTMENT OF FOREIGN LANGUAGES AND LITERATURE

Following the death of President Wang Weinong, the presidency was taken over by Dr. Xia Hanmin. Of course, the top university administrators had to be shuffled. And after that, the university was moving in a new era.

President Xia is a hard-working man. Having assumed office, he immediately mapped out a plan for the development of NCKU. His first prioriety was a huge project — getting a college of medicine and NCKU hospital established. Aside from the fact he vigorously led a team to work on the blueprint, simultaneously, he launched a campaign reguesting of the city mayor, the county chief, the legislator, and the council man and woman to find opportune time to tell the authorities that the college of medicine and the hospital were really needed in the Tainan area. Therefore, in 1981, the College of Medicine of NCKU and its hospital got approved, and furthermore, the whole thing was listed as one of the 14 major economic construction projects in the country.

Prof. Wu Zhenzhi was appointed dean of the College of Liberal Arts. With her, I had taken two courses during my freshman year: Chinese Modern History and Wold History.

Prof. Wu is a devout Christian, demonstrating her personal traists: she is not only modest but careful not to do anything pell-mell. As long as you see her smiling face, a wave of warmth comes over you. Therefore, the numerous controversial issues in the college got melted by her iconic image of this kind. Involuntarily, all of us reached a consensus on that the college must have been in the state of stability in which we were able to pursue our own academic growth. The most regrettable thing was that because of her church work, and at the end of her first 3-year term, she made up her mind to quit.

In the year of 1983, President Xia appointed Prof. Yu Dacheng as dean of the College of Liberal Arts. Dean Yu is a follower of Taoism running the college by the philosophy of "governing by noninterference." He is a witty and talented man, being able to execute the Chinese brush writings done by Liu Gongquan, to the best. What we were concerned about him the most was that he had gone through a heart surgery, having one of his malfunctioned heart membranes replaced by a hog's one as a substitute. If getting a little bit excited, he would feel terribly uncomfortable.

There was one time that he hosted a talk given by a professor from other university, and after presenting the guest to the audience, he seated himself on one of the chairs in the front row and enjoyed listening. He strained his ears keeping on listening and listening, and suddenly, he slumped down to the floor and passed out. This incident made the talk have to be stopped temporarily, and he was hurriedly rushed to the ICU in the Base Hospital 804 which was fortunately located on the opposite of the Guangfu campus. Because of the timely help of first aid available, his life was saved. Afterwards, I paid him a visit at his sickbed and saw him sleep like a log on his side inside the mosquito net with his upper part of body slightly arched and his legs bent up as if he were a baby boy.

In the summer of 1983, our chairman, Mr. Lu's application to one of American universities for advanced studies for one year was approved, and he recommended me to be the acting chair. After assessing the "goings-on" in our department and thinking of the status of my being an acting chair, I thought following suit was my best strategy, having no guts to make an inch of change of any kind. And I didn't get myself bogged down in terms of the administrative work of the department that year.

In 1985, shortly before the beginning of the summer break, I got a call from the office of the president asking me to see the president. After taking a seat in the office, without further ado, I was told by President Xia: "The DFLL is yours!"

He hoped that besides doing the routine duties and the developing for the department, I could do as much as I could to improve the students' English-listening and -speaking skills for all the students of the university. In addition to the feeling that the appointment came unexpectedly, I didn't say anything to pretend modesty. Instead, I was delighted to accept the challenge.

By then, following the dictates of conscience, I could say that there was a little bit of friction existing in our department. However, as I recalled when I studied in Southern Illinois University, my supervisor had mentioned the word "friction" to me once. He said that if there was no friction in the department, there wouldn't be any progress. I thought to myself that if I was broad-minded considering all the others' grievances good-natured, all the disputes in the department might be resolved or alleviated. And if I could abide by a guiding principle practiced by the Chinese: "When I have disagreement with anyone else, I want to focus on the essence of the disagreement, not on the person who stands up." By so doing, any disputes of this kind in the department would go off without a hitch.

The so-called big "accomplishments" I had done for the department when I was in office could be listed as follows:

1. FINDING A WAY FOR THE TEACHING ASSISTANTS TO BE PROMOTED

The work for the chair to do in the DFLL is no end. In another word, no matter to what level you bring the department to, there is always a room for improvement. To elaborate further, I cannot keep the department running in place. Getting the department better and better is the proper way. The first problem I had noticed was about our teaching assistants.

At the time there was a huge difference among the College of Liberal Arts, the College of Science, and the College of Engineering regarding the teaching assistants. An assistant, who was once employed by the CLA, considered the school his home, working hard in the hope that one day, he would be able to get promoted to instructorship. And that way, he could get rigid of the office hours schedule off the hook. But an assistant, who was hired by the CS or CE, considered his job a springboard only. Once he got an admission to a graduate school program with scholarship or fellowship abroad (mostly an American university), he would immediately quit. Three or four years later, he would be able to have earned his doctorate. By then, if returning to his alma mater, he would be employed as associate professor. In another word, he could skip three ranks to the highest but one. How couldn't he be admired?

The most unfair rule in the CLA was that though the teaching assistant was regarded as "faculty," yet he was mistreated as such: he couldn't get the real opportunity of applying for advanced studies abroad and taking a leave of absence without pay. Seeing this, I made a suggestion to President Xia in the hope that the teaching assistant in the DFLL should be treated as the member equivalent to the instructor, who, going abroad for advancing his or her studies, could have the right to take a leave of absence without pay. President Xia is the type of person who would like discussing problems with his subordinates and listening to people to get good advices. As a result, there were three teaching assistants in the DFLL who went abroad to get their masters' degrees. Of them, one did quite well and later, was able to scale up to the top echelon, chairmanship of the department.

2. HOSTING THE SECOND ANNUAL CONFERENCE OF ENGLISH AND AMERICAN LITERATURE, R.O.C."

By the end of 1985, I was invited to attend "The First Annual Conference of English and American Literature, R.O.C." hosted by the National Chung Hsin University located in Taichung. At the end of that conference, the chairperson, Zeng Xuanyi, asked me whether the DFLL at NCKU would like to host the next conference? My reaction at the time was that the key point for hosting a conference lay in the availability of financial resources. If the financial resources were not obtainable for holding such an academic activity, how could I do it? Based on this assumption, I gave him an indefinite answer, "Once back to my school, I will report it to my boss. And if I can get the financial support, I will certainly like to do as proposed. Otherwise, there is no way for me to hold a conference like this one." Upon returning, I reported it to President Xia right away. And he said to me that he fully supported me. Furthermore, he said that "If we don't want a conference to be held at NCKU, we just forget it, otherwise, the scope of it should be enlarged. Aside from inviting home scholars and specialists in the field to attend the conference, we will also invite overseas scholars from Hong Kong, Singapore, and America to come to NCKU to attend such a conference. All the expenses including the round-trip air fare, board, and lodging will be defrayed by NCKU."

With this promise, I became extremely excited, and instantly gave Zeng a call saying that the Second Annual Conference of English and American Literature would be hosted by NCKU. Moreover, on the phone, I was seeking his advice about how to host the conference of this kind, and the dos and don'ts of doing the preparing.

In the past, I read an article by Prof. C. C. Hsia that had been published on the supplementary edition affiliated with a newspaper in

Taiwan. In it, he heaped a lot of praises on Dr. Chuang Hsincheng's solid academic background including his powerful writing style, sophisticated language, and wonderful personality traits. I was deeply moved. Henceforth, I got Dr. Chuang's address via the editor. And surprisingly, I got his big "Yes" in his immediate reply.

The second one that I got is Dr. Zhou Yingxiong at the Chinese University of Hong Kong where he was teaching as visiting professor. He gets his Phd. in the field of comparative literature from the University of California at San Diego. He specializes in modern literature and literary theory. What he has cumulatively attained in the field of English and American Literature cannot be ignored. In addition, he speaks English very fluently, and his voice is very pleasing to the ear.

After making the call for papers via mail to all the Departments of Foreign Languages and Literature in all the universities throughout Taiwan, we received a tremendous amount of feedback, and at intervals, collected 23 papers. Having classified them according to the genre, we had the conference with parallel sessions, moderators, and commentators fixed. The only drawback was that by then, we were still at the stage of learning how to hold this sort of conference. And participants were more encouraged than anything else. Therefore, the papers having come in by mail were not put through the process of reviewing. As a result, there was a phenomenon shown, a mix of good and bad papers together.

To express the feeling of mine about the academic activity of this kind and to promote our first academic conference, I especially wrote a short essay entitled: *Jianshu bujianlin di chouchang*, or "An Indefinable Sadness Comes over Me When I Can't See the Wood for the Trees." And it was published on the supplementary edition connected with the *United Daily News* on the same day of our conference.

The Second Annual Conference of English and American Literature, R.O.C. was officially under way on November 14, 1987.[69]

The last item but one on our conference program is, especially, designed for a panel discussion. And I wanted to make it different from the previous one by having a topic chosen in advance: "The Writing Skills in Western Literature and Their Transferability." I have often heard that novelists who are capable of writing fictions may not know literary theories, while literary theorists who know many approaches to literature may not be able to write novels. Oh heck! What are some of the writing skills in the Western literature worthy of being learned by us, the Chinese writers? And what are some of their skills that can be considered worthless through the Chinese writers' eyes? I didn't have the answers to these questions by then. I was simply tossing out such a topic on a whim letting "scholars and specialists in the field" think about it and talk about it.

The audience packed the auditorium for the panel discussion session. No single seat remained unoccupied. Furthermore, owing to these scholars or specialists who were the best of the best in the field, what the opinions they voiced were not "mediocre" but real stuff. Accordingly, the whole auditorium was fully shrouded in the academic atmosphere. There had never been such a grand conference ever held by the CLA at NCKU before. And it also served as a dose of "stimulant" that was injected into the DFLL.

After the conference, following the example of "The First Annual Conference of English and American Literature, R.O.C." hosted by NCHU, I did the editing by getting the 23 conference papers into a book form, and designed the book cover with thick *wenye quxi,* or thick literary style. The color of the initial coat is beige, or a pale sandy fawn color superposed with several English and American writers' portraits. Owing to the proper chromatic printing, the whole book cover of this collection of papers looks quite elegant and chic giving off a strong love of literature originated in the West.

I wrote a piece of about 800-word preface describing the whole story of holding such a conference by NCKU and handed the whole thing over to Bookman Books LTD. Taipei, Taiwan for publishing. The man in charge of the bookstore is Mr. Su Zhenglong whose guiding principle of managing his business is nothing else but honesty. What he intends to do is not only to earn a decent living but to promote the English education of Taiwan. He is a guy with unusual broad-mindedness. He promised not only to have the reported number of copies of this book printed but to strike off more copies to be distributed to all the departments of foreign languages and literature for future reference.

By then, out of his own pocket, he generously donated 20,000 yuan to the DFLL at NCKU. That was a big sum.

President Xia was extremely happy and considered the conference successful. Making an exception for the chair of an academic unit and his team in the NCKU Merit and Recognition System, he had all of us awarded, commendations or merits, by issuing official documents. The Executive Order or the message serial number of the Official Document is (77) NCKU 0105.[70] And the contents are as follows:

Ma Chungliang: one merit, for the record.

"The DFLL of this university hosted the Second Annual Conference of English and American Literature, R.O.C. on November 14-15, 1987. Aside from playing the lead role of organizing the conference, Mr. Ma had a well-thought-out plan mapped out, inviting overseas scholars to deliver papers, compiling the conference papers into book form, seeking the help of reputable scholars or specialists as commentators, and fixing a great specific panel discussion. And he won all particiants' thumbs-up from the field as well as from others. These contributions he made will redound to the fame of this university. Therefore, he should be given one merit as a sort of encouragement."

Huang Yingfu: one merit, for the record.

"Mr. Huang helped make a master plan of supporting the general affairs for the 2nd Annual Conference of English and American Literature, R.O.C. During the conference time, he was in charge of a variety of odd jobs, for example: booking the railway tickets and being held responsible for accommadations of the participants, etc. What he had done made every participant feel at home. He was efficient having got all his jobs done excellently. He should be recompensed one merit in recognition of his services."

Liu Kailing: one commendation, for the record.

"Ms. Liu was the secretary of the 2nd Annual Conference of English and American Literature, R.O.C. in the planning committee. She was held responsible for getting all the materials related to this conference ready including disseminating and filing. She also readied herself to support those who needed extra hands. She was always patient and grudging no one. Accordingly, she should be rewarded one commendation as a sort of 'patting on the back.'"

Lu Huiyang: two commendations, for the record.

"Ms. Lu was the secretary general of the 2nd Annual Conference of English and American Literature, R.O.C. serving as a link to deal with the correspondence from the home and international participants and fielding the stream of phone calls. And she was the proof-reader for editing the conference book. Furthermore, she was held accountable for releasing news to the press and doing the receptionist's work for our honorable guests. She did an excellent job. Therefore, she ought to be awarded two commendations in recognition of her services."

Lu Hunghui: two commendations, for the record.

"Mr. Lu did the budgeting work for the 2nd Annual Conference of English and American Literature, R.O.C. And he also had all the conference rooms reserved, not only properly cleaned but also properly decorated. He did a variety of services, too. No grumbling and no groaning. Therefore, he ought to be given two commendations for his contributions."

Though the conference was considered "successful," yet much to my regret, an episode had taken place, and its subsequent development remained unknown to nobody but me.

As is customary, the opening of a conference includes: No. 1 the head of the home institution should deliver a welcome speech to participants and audience. No. 2 one or more than two guest speakers ought to be asked to speak something congratulatory to the home institution and supportive words to the participants. Along this line, I, firstly, ask President Xia to give a welcome speech, because he is the incumbent president of the host university; secondly, I ask Professor Zhu Limin, former dean of the College of Liberal Arts at the National Taiwan University, to say something encouraging because he is the founder of the Association of English and American Literature. When President Xia addressed the audience and in addition to saying, "Welcome to the NCKU" to those honorable guests, he also expressed his gratitude to those home, overseas scholars and specialists who had braved their travel fatigues to get here and attend the conference for delivering their papers.

Unexpectedly, when the former Dean Zhu gave that speech, he spoke with acid sarcasm as such: "Visiting monks do the chanting better!" or "the grass is aways greener on the other side of the fence." With this out, the audience first got dumbfounded, and then looked confused. They questioned in their minds why Dean Zhu on this occasion addressed the audience by using such a bitter word!

However, I immediately sensed that Zhu is the founder of the association of English and American Literature and senior professor in the field. And because of his seniority, he shouldn't be sidelined. In another word, I ought to invite him to be the keynote speaker instead of Chuang Hsincheng from New York and Zhou Yingxiong from Hong Kong as "ice breakers." From this "incident," I can surely say that experience matters a lot! Nevertheless, this is neither my fault nor my negligence. Because inviting overseas scholars to be keynote speakers is not my idea, I just followed my superior's order. In another word, blaming me was not fair.

During the break, a senior professor named Li Junqing from Su Zhou University came up to me and repeatedly flayed him for saying such an inappropriate word on such an occasion.

However, Prof. Zhu is a senior professor, experienced and sophisticated, and a few days later, I received a postcard from him with such words on, "When I am addressing the audience in the conference, the rhetoric that I used is not of propriety. Would you like to forgive me?" I thought to myself that this "thing" had become outdated already. Keeping the postcard was of no significance. And therefore, I disposed of it immediately.

3. GETTING MORE BOOKS FOR OUR DEPARTMENT LIBRARY.

As well known, NCKU is noted for its College of Engineering. It was rumored for a long time that the school authorities had had a bias against the College of Liberal Arts. But based on my own observations, this was not true. And at least, when President Xia was in office, he had done many things to improve the College of Liberal Arts, for example, making a plan for constructing a new college building based on the blueprint of the Ministry of Education Building in Taipei was one of them.

One morning, President Xia suddenly dropped in the Department for sort of inspection. At the time, aside from the general library, each college had its own library; each department, its own, too. Accompanied by me after his inspecting other facilities and equipment, he finally stepped into our department library. As he saw a few of books stacking disorderly on the shelves, he blurted out something that I will never forget for the rest of my life even though to this day, "As I see that you are a man who can get the thing done, therefore, besides the budget for books and equipment that has been dealt out this fiscal year, the university will additionally appropriate two million yuan to your department to buy books. And I hope that you can get the requisition form filled out at the earliest date as possible!" This was a piece of good news, indeed, and I immediately asked my colleagues to work on what books they needed, and simultaneously asked for the helps from the deputies of Western books to mail us their catalogs so that after getting the books selected, we could order them.

4. HELPING EDIT THE *COLLEGE ENGLISH READER.*

The work for editing the *College English Reader* for freshman students gave all the chairpersons of the Departments of Foreign Languages and Literature a headache in the universities throughout Taiwan. No matter how hard the chairpersons worked, naturally, the "Reader" edited couldn't meet the needs of the students from different departments of the universities.

At that time and on principle, the DFLL at NCKU revised the *College English Reader*, every two years but sometimes, every three or four years, as necessity dictated. By so doing, the department was able to get the newest and best essays in the "Reader" in time, and to get rid of those essays that had become outmoded.

Every time when we tried to renew our *College English Reader*, we would set up an editing committee. Firstly, the committee let members pick essays from what they had read, and secondly, had the potentials duplicated and distributed to each member of the committee to review. And finally, whether a recommended essay would be accepted and compiled into the "Reader" or not totally depended upon the decision of the committee members in the meeting (usually by tallying up the votes). Unfortunately, among the members of the committee, there were always heated arguments arising. In the committee established when I was in office, there were two members whose opinions about one recommended essay were so different that they argued fiercely and endlessly. And the loudest voices they used brought the committee meeting to an early adjournment. Further, a sort of resentment was nursed, and they hated each other beautifully. Additionally, the teaching issue got involved. This American instructor deliberately questioned his opponent viciously: "It is even hard for an American like me, to understand *Faerie Queen*. How can you take the material of this kind to teach students?"

Since some of the committee members were busy teaching, researching and doing the student counselling services, they couldn't hand in the assignments to them on time, for example, the "biographical sketches of the authors," the "introductions to the essays," and "footnotes." And repeat notice letters sent to them were of no avail. If our *College English Reader* dragged on like this kind of progress, there would be a severe impact on the time of publication. Finally, the guy, who chaired the editing committee, turned in the draft of the newly edited *College English Reader* to the chairpman of the department to be resolved. It went without saying that the chairman had to do the "clean-up job."

Despite the fact that there were numerous arguments and difficulties to get the *College English Reader* out, historically speaking, our *College English Reader* published by Bookman Books LTD that year, was undoubtedly the best one the DFLL at NCKU had ever got. The preface written by Dr. John Scott hits the nail on the head based on the contents of the *College English Reader*.

To improve the teaching quality when I was in office, I invited Prof. Peter E. Firchow of the Department of English and his wife, Prof. Evelyn S. Firchow of the Department of German from the University of Minnesota to NCKU as visiting professors. The former offered the course, English Literature; the latter, Advanced German.

For preparing to set up our Master's degree program for the department, I got Prof. Yang Chenying of Taipei in. In a flash, it seemed that the DFLL readied itself as if it were an eagle that flapped its wings starting to fly.

CHAPTER 30

RECRUITING ESL TEACHERS IN THE U.S.A.

Aside from the fact that President Xia supported the academic activities held by the DFLL, he also launched another unprecedented venture by sending me to the U.S. immediately to recruit three native English speakers whose majors must be in the field of ESL, to improve all the students' English-speaking and -listening skills at NCKU. The time limit for this mission was only one month. And the three openings for these three teaching jobs were provided by the university on a temporary basis.

When I was following this order to get my visa, and in the meantime, I felt that I couldn't agree with him any more.

I thought to my myself that the best way to do this was putting these three employed native English speakers on the staff in the language center under the CLA. And these three guys would do nothing else but to conduct the English speaking and listening course for all the students of the university. And the course should be listed as one of compulsory courses in the curriculum offerings.

The next way to do this is that we must have this plan mapped out half a year earlier and gradually contact the ESL programs affiliated to the Departments of English in American universities. Simultaneously, we have to ask them to get the recruitment information, for example, qualifications, salary, housing, and free roundtrip airfare out and let them post on their bulletin boards. If there is anyone who is interested in teaching in Taiwan, he can contact the DFLL at NCKU directly.

Worst is the way with this short notice. As there might be a large number of qualified candidates in the U.S., where should I turn to and find the right ones that fit us? Even if I had been a superman with *san tou liu bi*, or three heads and six arms, I might not be able to get this "mission impossible" done as expected.

Although there was no clear picture of how to do this job in my mind, an order was an order, and "I don't have the guts to defy it." Anyway, I calmed down to get two things done before embarking on "The 10,000-mile recruiting journey" to the U.S.

Number one is that I asked the Youth Commission under the Executive Yuan in Taipei to get the ESL teachers recruitment information published in its English journal issued for overseas Chinese and foreigners. (At that time, there was no internet access).

Number two is that I wrote an "all-purpose" letter of recruitment in English and made many duplicate copies. I signed a batch of them and sent out by airmail to various universities in America. In addition, I carried dozens of copies with me in case they might be needed while traveling around America.

In such a hurry, I made a decision to go to four places in the U.S.: San Francisco, New York, Minnesota and Hawaii to give a try.

THE FIRST LEG: SAN FRANCISCO:

San Francisco is one of my most favorite cities in the U.S. It is neither bitterly cold in winter nor extremely hot in summer. Moreover, there is a life-long friend, Zheng Jizhong, living there. By then, he worked as a librarian in the oriental section in the San Francisco State University library, and in the meantime, as a professor on a part-time basis, teaching Chinese classics and modern literature in the Chinese Language Program connected with the Department of English. Thinking of having this opportunity to renew our camaraderie, I felt extremely happy. I thought to myself that if I was lucky enough, I could get the three teachers here in one go, and then, the rest of the journey could be at ease: eating, drinking, and having fun as a tourist to cruise America.

After having got to San Francisco, with the knowledge of the city I had got in the early 1970s, I could easily check in the hotel I had stayed ten years before. On the following morning, I took the city bus heading for San Francisco State University. Walking on the campus with patches of lawn, I watched students be in a hurry. With their heads down, necks in, books carried in their armpits and full of energy, they were shuffling back and forth hastily as if they had been heading somewhere, labs and classrooms. And I felt as if I had been back to my graduate school years on the campus when I furthered my studies in the U.S.

There was a squirrel ahead of me, seemingly, leading the way. And I saw it arch its back, raise its forelegs, firstly, check surroundings with its eyes, then, listen to any sound from all directions and finally, sprang forward with the lifting of its forelegs and the pushing of its hind ones, one jump after another to the base of a tree. It climbed up the tree by a circuitous route and vanished into the thick foliage. Everything remained tranquil and peaceful. Behind this grove of the trees, the building of the English Department is located.

Upon entering the building, I walked to the bulletin board to see if there was my duplicate copy there. Lifting my eyes up, searching for my stuff from the left to the right and from the top to the bottom, and though having seen a variety of public notices there, yet I didn't see the letter mailed by me on it. In the beginning, I had a strong urge to see the chairperson in his office but as I thought to myself that there was no appointment made with him in advance, and rushing myself to see him would be an inappropriate and reckless act. Consequently, I took a duplicate copy out of my briefcase and nailed it on the bulletin board with my current telephone number added. And then, I returned to my hotel immediately.

In the evening, I went to Jizhong's home for dinner according to the time we had fixed on the phone. Since we had not seen each other many years, I felt that the wheel of the time had left some "gullies" on his face, the hair around his temples turning white. He is a man of integrity speaking his mind. In addition, as he has steeped in Chinese classics for long time, and even when engaged in small talk, he chats with you with a faint air of dignity and pride shown by Chinese literati. Because San Francisco is one of the important seaports for entering America, his home becomes the link for the writers and celebrities from China, Hong Kong, and Taiwan. He often picks them up at the airport when they arrive and drops them off at the airport when they depart. People of this kind as I know include: Shen Tusingwen, Shao Jun, Shao Hung from the Mainland and Chi Pongyuan from Taiwan.

In the course of the dinner, we talked about Prof. Xu Jieyu who had been killed by a catastrophic flooding. And we sighed deep sighs for his wretched death.

Prof. Xu came to the U.S. for advanced studies in the 1940s. At the time the Anti-Japanese War was boiling in China. Having been in the U.S., firstly, he studied Journalism, then, switched to the field of literature and finally, settled down with a teaching job in San Francisco State University. By chance, he married a French American woman. He could speak American English with fluency. Superficially, he had long been assimilated into the mainstream of American society, but on the contrary, still flowing in his blood vessels was nothing else but the blood of the Chinese People. And his longing for his hometown was still perceptive. In the daytime, he lived in a different culture; at night, brooding over the future that he would be the ghost in this foreign land. How couldn't he feel sad? Therefore, he called upon the Zhengs as a habitue. Having got several tumblers of his favorite wine down, he sang Anti-Japanese songs and recited the poems of the Tang dynasty and the Ci poems of the Sung dynasty to banish the bad thoughts in his mind. And at present, I can still recall the scene when he recited that five-character quatrain entitled: "A Suggestion to Liu Shijiu" written by Bai Juyi: "Newly brewed is the rice wine with green foam, and there stands a red-colored clay stove with fire ablazing, and as there is the highest percentage of snowing at dusk, would you like to be my guest having a drink with me?"

He and Li Jinyang, a writer, were the international students of the same times in the U.S. Their English proficiency was next to none, and each one of them had big ambition trying to come up with an English novel to kick the door open in the U.S. literary world. The agreement they have made is that anyone, who, being able to get a novel firstly published and recognized, will treat the other "a roast chicken." Consequently, Li Jinyang greatly surprised the readers at one blow by *The Flower Drum Song*. Moreover, the novel was adapted to a play and staged, having charmed the large number of audiences throughout America. Prof. Xu said: "Li Jinyang has not fulfilled his pledge yet, and he still owes me a roast chicken there."

One year, there was a terrible downpour in the San Francisco area. Torrential rain caused a serious damage on the mountain area. And not only Prof. Xu's house located on the declivity of the mountain was swept down but he, himself, was killed, his body being washed down to the Pacific Ocean. When retrieved, it was full of bruises and wounds. He really died an ugly death.

He has written a small book entitled: *Gu Guo Xing*, or Our China Trip, and has it published not for the commom readers but for himself and his inner circle of friends to read. The title of the book is a pun alluding to: (the italics are mine, *on the one hand, the word "gu" means "old" referring to a trip to his home country, but on the other, the word "gu" means "death" referring to his home country that has long been dead.* Jizhong said that "the purpose of his writing this small book in English is purely to relieve his pent-up fury on account of his having been detained in the Shanghai detention center."

On the following morning, I got a phone call from an American who firstly, spoke English with me, and then, tried Mandarin as communication tool, indicating that he was very much interested in teaching the course, English-listening and -speaking, in Taiwan as announced, and hoping that I could see him as soon as possible.

His Chinese name is Ma Ming. As to his English name, I have forgotten. When we met, his first word is: "I am easy-going but disciplined," meaning that though easy to get along with, he has his own principles to live by. Deeply impressed on me is his English pronunciation and properly wording. Besides he has an expressive face filled with great enthusiasm. He is not only a grad with the master's degree but a Mandarin speaker. At that time, I thought to myself that I was lucky to have him, "This is the best candidate that I dream of."

When everything got settled, I suddenly became conscious of his marital status, single. He is tall, of slim build, and handsome. If he appeared on our campus, there would be "the romance between teacher and student" taking place. If that happened, it might break up the taboo practiced in our school. Hardly did I get this "cryptic message" to this theme in our conversation when he expressed clearly that he had spent some of his years in Chinatown San Francisco and learnd of some of Chinese culture: "The hare won't gnaw the grass nearby, will it? I don't want to fall in love with anyone, that's it, period. Otherwise, I will court a girl off campus like the movie actress Ms. Chen Chong!"

THE SECOND LEG: NEW YORK

A week later, the dream of getting all the three ESL teachers at one sweep in San Francisco came to an end. I had no choice but to head the second leg, New York, I had scheduled on my itinerary.

That night, when I reached the La Guardia Airport, our plane was caught in the heavy rain, and the visibility was very low. Accordingly, the captain announced that the aircraft had to stay in the air for 15 minutes or so, and then to try to land.

The airplane circled and circled trying to land, and as it was coming in close to the runway, its nose was pulled up with the wings outstetched. Not until the rain was slackened, did the aircraft touch down on a landing strip.

Having sat in a yellow cab, I gazed into New York through the windows. With *Wan jia ding huan,* or with the lights shining out of ten thousand homes, the city of New York was in the drizzling rain which was raining vertically downward. And it also seemed as if the city of New York had been shrouded in a thin mist, possessing the image of the faint moonlight.

On the following day, I used the same old trick to go to the Department of English at New York City University, trying to check my recruiting letter by going to the bulletin board: "Is there my duplicate copy there?"

Disappointed, I nailed a copy on it out of my briefcase as I did in San Francisco. I dreamed again if I could get the two ESL teachers with masters' degrees here, I might or might not go on the next two stops, Minnesota and Hawaii. All depended upon something instinctly driven. But the thing didn't work out the way as I wished. I didn't get any phone call at all.

Out of desperation, I looked up through the New York Yellow Pages Directory and found out some organization like Teachers' Union and made a call requesting of them to get the "English teacher-recruiting information" spread. This action I took was proved effective. And there were applicants calling me successively and asking for all the details. Among them, two applicants are a young couple.

By then, New York was at the end of winter and in the beginning of spring. It was bone-chilling. when I was waiting for this young couple to come for interview in the restaurant connected with the hotel, I felt there was a wave of warmth surging in me. And ocassionally, I said my prayers, and prayed to God: "Please let me have two right persons! Please let me have two right persons!" Otherwise, in such a large number of people, when was this anxiety of mine in the ESL teacher-hunting business to be ended?

They came at the time as set. At a glance, I felt that they were a good couple: male, good-looking and tall; female, pretty and charming. Both, at the age of around 30, spoke excellent American English which is pleasing to the ear. When they spoke, they spoke in soft tones, plus the right body language. And that reflected the good education they had received. Most importantly, they were masters' degrees holders from the English Department.

I told them bluntly that the salary in a nationally-funded university in Taiwan is not as high as expected from an American's perspective, but there are many side benefits. And based on two instructors' income, they could live a pretty good life in Taiwan. Furthermore, for them, teaching English-listening and -speaking classes is "as easy as the action of raising one's hand and thrusting one's leg." After listening to the whole thing that I had told them, they, with smiling faces, indicated that they had strong interest and decided to give a try in Taiwan.

I was very happy to have this sort of outcome for this interview. Because of a sudden decision, I said to them that I wanted to treat them a lunch. During "feasting," I became aware of a tiny part of their married life. Though they had been married many years, they were unable to have babies. I told them that Taiwan is located on the belt of subtropical region, and as far as I know, lots of foreign couples, unable to get babies for many years, can have them when teaching in Taiwan. At the time they wanted to quit and return to their home countries, the U.S. or somewhere else, one babby added. Upon hearing this, they couldn't help smiling but make no comment.

Up to now, I finally got the "mission impossible" of recruiting three ESL teachers done. But the appointments made for interviewing others had to go on. Perhaps, I was of the opinion that "The young couple interviewed are the ideal ones." I felt that though the following interviewees were with higher degrees, yet they were rather old. If they had been hired, there might be a generation gap between them and our students. From this point of view, I turned all of them down without hesitation.

THE THIRD LEG: MINNESOTA.

Prof. Peter Firchow and his adorable wife, Prof. Evelyn Firchow taught at the University of Minnesota. At the time I was acting chair of the DFLL at NCKU, I invited them to our department as visiting professors for one year. Having returned to their home institution, the University of Minnesota, the former taught English Literature and Literary Criticism in the English Department; the latter, Advanced German and Linguistics in the German. Peter has an excellent command of three languages, German, Spanish, and English; Evelyn two languages, German and English. The most valuable thing of their personality traits is that they like to make friends with all walks of life. When staying in Taiwan, they made a friend with a man who sold pastry made of ingredients of flour, cooking oil and green onion on their food cart on the street. They called the products, "Chinese Pizza!"

Because I had already got the three ESL teachers, I flew from New York to Minneapolis with nothing important to do but to visit old friends.

When I got to Minneapolis, it was snowing heavily, and the wind was cutting and getting into the marrows of my bones. Peter said: "Only the toughest people can survive this abominable weather." And by then, one of my colleagues, Associate Prof. Cao Dingren of our department, a grad from the Phd. program of the Department of Journalism at this university, happened to be here paying a visit to her Alma Mater. Accordingly, she was invited as a guest in the Ferchows, and three of us, each held a large mug of beer in hand, and we reclined sluggishly on the sofa and enjoyed the warmest friendship in the snowstorm weather.

Peter admired and respected the English novelist and critic named Aldous L. Huxley. As to the American novelists, he was reserved. I said to him that the number of novels that I had read in terms of English and American writers was limited. Honestly speaking, I had only read Ernest

Hemingway's works. He said that he liked his first novel *The Sun Also Rises* the most and considered it the best among his whole things. But to me, his novelette *The Old Man and the Sea* is the best and worthy of being recommended.

He has some biases against the DFLL at NCKU, "No. 1: the class is too large, out of control. And when marking examination papers, a teacher finds it difficult to mark the papers properly and give each student a fair grade as he deserves. No. 2: there are some 'moles' from the KMT having disguised themselves as students in his class. For that reason, many of the students, who are 'obedient,' have to look up to these 'moles' if they want to hold any activity." I agreed with him on his first point; absolutely disagreed with him on the second one, telling him that it was unbelievable!

He took me to tour the university library, bookstore, and the Department of English. When the cloudy sky cleared up, he took me to tour the neighborhood by car, and looking out through the front and side and back windows, we appreciated the scenery with snow everywhere.

Having stayed in Peter's home four or five days, I flew United Airlines to Los Angles. Originally, I planned to go through the whole thing as scheduled, the fourth stop—Hawaii, but due to the "mission impossible" that had been completed, and by then, I became mentally and physically exhausted. And I had no choice but to make a change on my itinerary. I flew China Airlines to return to Taiwan. It was 10 days earlier than scheduled on the itinerary

CHAPTER 31

ACTING DEAN OF THE COLLEGE OF LIBERAL ARTS

Throughout the traveling experience in my life by air, there was nothing comparable to that China Airlines flight from Los Angles to Taoyuan International Airport in terms of its low level of flight seat consumption rate. There was only a few of passengers taking that Boeing 747. I thought to myself that this was so cool that I could sleep through a 13-hour flight comfortably to Taiwan.

Human beings are animals, too, sometimes, becoming so "cheap." When you are faced with a full house of passengers, you wedge yourself into the seat. And the fellow travelers' elbows on either side of your seat, almost touch your arms, and with the feeling of being stifled, you can still hold your breath in deep concentration and drop off. Now, look, enabling myself to lie down there and with my head on a pad, I could not fall asleep no matter how hard I tried. Human beings are really "cheap," aren't they?

With the sound of *susu susu,* or slight rustling during the flight, my thought was simply racing. It could be compared to a videotaped autobiography of my life played in reverse from the present to the not-too-distant past to the far distant past: "How did I return to NCKU? How did I get on the two trips to the U.S. for advanced studies? How did I get into the undergraduate program of a university to get education? How did I get discharged from the army? How did I go through that experience of life and death? How was I pressganged into the army on the Penghu Islands? How did I run into those rough trails and survive by taking herbal plants as food in the eastern part of Fujian Province?

How did I go to see my immediate uncle at Longyou County? How did I study in that dilapidated dorm at the Jinan First United Secondary School at Changannzen? How did I sell shoes to have gone through those hard days in Qingtao? How did I leave my hometown? Is my father still in Jinan now? And how were my older sister, Zhonglan, and younger brother, Zhongxin?"

In reality, I was perplexed by two questions: "Am I the guy who can handle both the administrative work and the research work simultaneously? Am I really a guy of the highest caliber to do these two jobs equally well? In addition to that the three new recruits I have got can be used to sharpen the whole university students' English-listening and-speaking skills, how can the DFLL, itself, get their help, too?"

With these questions in my mind, the airplane was approaching Taiwan. I was not only unsleepy but super excited. Around 10:30 p.m., I checked out of the customs. Upon getting on Union Bus, I felt the bus flew like a dart directly to Tainan. On the early morning, around 3 a.m., I got to the doormat of my home.

After having returned to the office the following day, I immediately reported to President Xia the fruits that I had got in the U.S. And I assured him that once the fall semester of the new school year started, the entire school would have a new façade of the English-learning environment. After listening to what I had done on my mission to the U.S., he lavished some praises on me.

In those days, seemingly, I was a little bit euphoric. While walking on campus, I felt as if the bottom parts of my shoes had been equipped with springs. And I was bouncing, not walking. Shortly after, I received a letter from the couple recruited in New York saying that they had found jobs in that city already, unable to keep the promise they had made. The maxim by Laotse: "What one calls calamity may often give rise to fortune; what one considers fortune may often end with disaster. Who knows what the outcome would be? How can there be an absolute right answer?" or another simpler way of saying this, "No weal comes without woe." Lao-tzu's words turn out to be true as he predicated 2,508 years ago. No kidding at all.

Thanks to what I had done before my leaving for the U.S.—getting the information about the ESL teacher recruitment publicized via the English journal issued by the Youth Commission, Executive Yuan, and the duplicate copies of my letter sent out, right now, I saw the greatest returns on those actions as unexpected. Some application letters came in. Of the applicants, there were three Phd holders in the field of English and American literature and one Master's degree holder in the field of ESL. Dr. John Scott and his wife were the most ideal candidates completely meeting the requirements that we had set. I immediately wrote back asking them to report to our school one month in advance before our fall semester started.

Another two are true scholars named Bertrand Mathieu and Richard de Canio. They are graduates from esteemed universities in the U.S. having had a lot of papers and books published. The former was residing in Paris; the latter, in Seattle.

At that time, one of our associate professors, Cao Dingren, still stayed at the University of Minnesota, and likely returned to Taiwan shortly. And I asked her to fly back to Taiwan by way of Seattle, interviewing Richard de Canio on behalf of me. The outcome of that interview was: "Richard is a distinguished scholar of English and American literature, but a real naïve man." The implication of this remark was: "He is probably a person who is hard to get along with." But after I had closely reviewed his three recommendation letters by his former professors, I felt that he would abide by all the regulations of our department.

I hired both to come to NCKU to teach based on a 2-year contract out of a specific project, "The Massive Project for Recruiting Overseas Scholars." And their being hired was only by chance, not by plan, but it could be regarded as "a windfall" in "The Recruiting Story of 10,000 Miles of Mine to the U.S."

In the year of 1988, President Xia' successful career was getting one level higher—he was appointed the director of the National Science Foundation. The presidency of NCKU was taken up by the former dean of the College of Engineering, Dr. Maa ZheRu.

At this time, there was the most difficult issue arising in our college, that was that the Graduate Institute of History and Linguistics was cofounded by the Departments of Chinese Literature and History, and they were at loggerheads over which department was in charge of this institute.

In 1985, when the institute was in the process of applying to the Ministry of Education, the school authorities mobilized all the resources from both departments for its establishment, and divided it into two parts: The Department of Chinese Literature was held responsible for linguistics program; the Department of History, history. However, as a Chinese saying goes: "Two fierce tigers cannot live in one mountain," and with the days gone by, there must be disagreements arising between them.

As Prof. Yu Dacheng had finished his first term as dean of the College of Liberal Arts at NCKU, he wanted to be on a convalescence leave in Taipei. Since the summer of 1985, Prof. Huang Yunwu wore two hats, dean of the College of Liberal Arts and director of the Graduate Institute of History and Linguistics. To be the dean was easy; the director, very difficult.

Up to 1988, the two departments had reached an impasse about the objectives and curriculum offerings. Because Dean Huang is a Chinese major, it was very hard for him not to be doubted of taking the side with the Chinese Department. In fact, at that time he had signed the contract of deanship. And worse, the start of the new school year was a month away. As he was a very smart guy, he would be fully aware of what would be ahead of him if he kept going as the director of the institue. And his mental suffering would be inevitable and endless. Therefore, he got them unravled once for all by *kuai dao zhan luan ma*, or cutting the knot of hemp ropes with a sharp knife at one go, returning the two signed contracts back to school. Furthermore, he made up his mind to leave NCKU.

As it occurred suddenly, the newly inaugurated President, Maa JerRu, was immediately thrown into confusion, not knowing what to do. I met his wife, Dr. Young Youwei, a senior professor in the Deparment of Physics, in the NCKU Bank (Undergraduate Intership Program), on the Cheng Kung campus. And she said: "The thing is really troubling him!"

President Maa lives up to his first name that was given. He is philosophically-oriented and well-read. In addition to that, he is big-hearted and modest. Every day, he went on and off his work by bicycl. If he saw a professor or a staff member he knew walk on the campus, he didn't do anything else but to get off his bicycle and accompany him to walk for a while. By so doing, there was no factional infighting in the school. If there was, he would make it stop. Even to this day, after his presidency has been terminated for more than 20 years, he is still remembered and repeatedly praised by all the faculty and staff members for two things that he did while in office:

Number one: on the eve of the Chinese New Year, he carried presents to the gatehouses of the respective campuses and distributed them to the security officers who couldn't toast their loved ones in their New-Year's eve dinners.

Number two: prior to the Chinese New Year, he spared some time to pay visits to those retired professors who were the oldest.

Prof. Yu Xiwu, with whom I took a course entitled, English Grammar and Rhetoric, in my freshman year, was over ninety years old, suffering from a variety of ailments for years. Despite being deaf and wobbly on his legs, he booked a dinner to treat President Maa at Ambassador Hotel on Dongxing Road, and invited us to that dinner party to help entertain the guest of honor. While in the course of that dinner, Prof. Yu frequently gave nods as signals asking us to try the dishes and drinks on the table. Throughout the whole dinner, he said only one word: "I greatly appreciate President Maa's way of treating people!"

By the end of August of the same year, President Maa sent a one-year contract to me asking me to be the acting dean of the College of Liberal Arts. The reason for such an appointment was understandable: I belonged to neither the Chinese Department nor the History Department. I was an outsider standing on the middle ground between two departments. I belonged to the DFLL. And there was no reason for me to side with one department more than with another. Furthermore, I am an acting dean in nature, "smaller in terms of target, let alone the target of attacks.

By then, I had completed the first three years' term as chairperson of the DFFL and knew the ropes better in administration. It didn't matter what kind of meetings, large or small, I attended them all: *yi ji zhu guan hui yi*, or the top level meeting including president, dean of academic affairs, dean of students' affairs, dean of general affairs, and deans of all colleges; *xiao wu hui yi*, or the university assembly: aside from the foregoing, chairpersons, representatives elected from colleges and departments; *xing zheng hui yi*, or the administration meeting related to the policy about how to run the university; and *jiao wu hui yi*, or the meeting held by the Office of Academic Affairs mostly for discussing the teaching and research stuff, and the problems of students'academic performances, etc. As to the meetings held in the College of Liberal Arts that needed me to play the host role and the meetings held for continuing education in our Language Center, I do not remember I missed anyone of them. I thought to myself that right now, I was the man who was working as both chairman and dean at the same time, and though the workload was heavy, yet I thought this stage might be the pinnacle of my career. Therefore, I often warned myself not to "play with the fire": I should do my best to keep what I had got, and avoided being unseated by my rivals. Furthermore, I should adopt self-reliance and self-protection strategy. Under no circumstances, did I allow myself to commit any "misplay" while in both offices. If there had been one, I would fall out as if having been thrown into a bottomless abyss, never having another chance to be reinstated.

Here was an example to explain how I was not bogged down by "a kind of tempting" even as it was considered so small:

Though I wore two hats at the time as chairman of the department and dean of the college, I only got one "command pay." However, as the college has it that as dean of the college, one has also to be the head of language center. Because of this, I, sometimes, get some extra money, though the amount is very small but legal, for example, the balance left by running the continuing education program in the summer break is usually shared by all of us.

After the close of all the classes in summer, 1989, and based on the name list submitted by the language center, the balance had been evened up and was given out to the workers involved. But one mistake was made. That was one share belonging to the man, secretary of the office of the College of Literary Arts, was left out. This made the man in charge of the whole thing feel restless and unware of how to fix it. During the hottest spell of weather, people came in and helped run the program. And once they had got their shares and put them into their own pockets, who would like to take out the money that had been dealt out, even "a tiny part" of it? Consequently, the problem remained unsolved, and the situation became an embarrassing one for all of them. When I walked into the office by myself with my briefcase and knew what had happened, I, immediately, without one second's hesitation, had my share which had already been sealed in an envelope and laid on my desk, handed over to the person in charge and forwarded to the secretary. I didn't want anything so trivial as an obstacle in the way. This doing by me made everybody happy!

At that time, there were two comprehensive universities located in southern Taiwan: NCKU and NSYSU (National Sun Yat-Sen

University). Prof. Yu Guangzhong was the founding dean of the College of Liberal Arts at NSYS. Under him, there was a lot of outstanding young scholars. And he thought he might make some contributions by combining the human resources from these two universities to do something. He first made a start and then proposed that "An Annual Literature Conference—Southern Taiwan" might be held to boost literary studies in the College of Liberal Arts. This way, the College of Liberal Arts might be more driven than ever. As well known, Prof. Yu is a real scholar conversant in Western and Chinese literatures, especially with unique insights of English and American literature. When free from teaching, he engages in poetry- and prose-writing, famous for his writing "skills," poetry with "his left hand"; prose, "his right hand." Because his big name appeared on the posters on our campus for the conference, that year's conference held at NCKU was extremely successful.

One more thing which is probably worthy of mentioning here is that in 1990, professor of Columbia University, C. T. Hsia was invited to come to our school to give a talk. His topic is Chinese modern literature, and I played the host role.

On 10/15/1990, Professor of Columbia University, C. T. Hsia was invited to come to our school to give a talk.

In 1998, I hosted "An Academic Exchange Conference — Southern Taiwan". I was standing, Presient Ma and Professor Yu Guanzhong are to my right.

CHAPTER 32

DEAN OF DISCIPLINE

Following the dictates of conscience, of the three deans, academic affairs, discipline, and general affairs in terms of their duties, I think that relatively speaking, the second one's duty is lighter than the other two deans'. Of course, this refers to the "heyday of peace." If there is a stream of student protests taking place frequently on the campus, life is more difficult for dean of discipline than for dean of academic affairs and dean of general affairs.

In the school year of 1989, students, who, on all the campuses of the universities in Taiwan, made themselves ready for launching protests. And the situation could be compared to a Chinese saying: "The wind comes before the storm."

As it is customery, after the Joint College Entrance Examination is over, the summer vacation is under way. The school has it that all the administrators are required to work half a day only. One day, around 10 a.m., President Maa JerRu, firstly, gave me a ring telling me that he wanted me to wait for him in my office. And then, he cycled down to see me, and once stepping over the threshold of the door, he bluntly asked me to take up the deanship of discipline. My visceral feeling to this appointment was that I didn't have that sort of ability to do a big job like that. I got myself estimated that heading a department was in my element. If asked to do the job as dean of discipline to deal with more than 20,000 students, I couldn't do it. And even if I wanted to do, I presumed that it was beyond my capacity.

But when I saw the president sweat all over and heard him call me: "We are brothers," I immediately changed my mind and asked him to give me a few days to think about it. The outcome of that long brooding over the appointment was certainly that I was moved by those four words, "We are blood bothers." Accordingly, I decided to *ba dao xiang zhu*, or draw a sword and render help.

To me, student protests on the campus are not that terrifying. The most fearful thing is that we don't know how to defuse the tense moments of protests as they are about to explode. The homework for me to reduce student protests is trying to dig out the causes of them based on the political climate and then, going along with them, manipulating them to our advantage. In another word, letting the protests dissolve by "inherent changes" and never rubbing student protests in the wrong way.

In the 1990s, under the impact of the changing of the political climate in Taiwan, students on the campuses began acting weirdly and presumptuously demanded reforms for this and that. And the then President Li Denghui of the ROC, being great at political tactics, appointed the military strong man, General Hao Bocun, Prime Minister of Executive Yuan, but *in fact, to strip his military power* (my italics and this is also common knowledge throughout Taiwan), and for this reason, seemingly, added the fuel to the flames. In consequence, coming out from the university campuses across this island country was the slogan: "Firmly oppose military man who has been appointed the premier of the newly reshuffled cabinet!"

The studens on the NCKU campus casted the first stone demanding that "the right for running Sheng Li Cafeteria should be handed over to the students by the school authorities due to mismanagement." NCKU is noted for the stringent rule over the students' academic performances. Though working hard, days and nights, they might not ensure whether they could pass the courses taken or not. Did they really have any extra energy and time to shoulder such a heavy responsibility for operating the cafeteria? Even if they did, young and impetuous as they were, how long could they hold on, probably "a 5-minute period of enthusiasm." If the right to run the cafeteria was handed over to them, they might be compared to "unmotivated soldiers," in the middle of a combat discarding their guns and helmets and deserting as generally surmised. In case, Sheng Li Cafeteria couldn't be operated as usual, and the students couldn't be provided with proper meals, who was held accountable for this?

However, to launch a student protest must have a pretext. And that the students were furious with Sheng Li Cafeteria at what the poor food that they had been provided was nothing else but reasonable. And that became "the tipping point" to detonate the explosion of the protests on our campus. But from my point of view, if there had not been the Sheng Li Cafeteria issue, the students would have looked for another issue "to challenge the school authorities."

Once in office, I proposed that the school and the students should co-organize "NCKU Student Dining Services Committee." When we worked on the charter for the committee, we stipulated that there was a certain number of representatives of students, faculty and staff, nutritionists, and executive secretary included. Though it was "NCKU Student Dining Services Committee" in name, yet in reality, the cafeteria was operated by the faculty and staff members and secretary as well as students. And the secretary was usually the guy who was doing the counseling work related to the students' campus life under the office of dean of discipline. This way, each party yielded a little bit on the ground, reached "a compromise" and ended this wave of protest due to the food issue at Sheng Li Cafeteria.

In the same token, I also proposed that "Student Dormitory Committee" should be set up. Henceforth, the students' opinions about bed assignments, dormitory fee and on campus housing regulations were included. In addition, a new rule for charging those who wished to live on the campus during the summer and winter vacations was made so that the school was able to keep track of the students of this kind.

At that time, the Student Government Association was on the NCKU campus for years. In the past, this organization went begging.

But with the changing of the political climate, suddenly, campaigning for the president of the SGA got fired up.

Nothing having been done yet, the student, who, campaigning for the president of SGA with his aides, came to the office of the president of NCKU. Sitting cross-legged and swollen headed, he requested the president to clarify the status of the president of the SGA in the school. The most incredible thing was that he demanded the president of the university to give him an office and appropriated certain percentage of fund for the administration and management of the SGA. Furthermore, he thought that in a democratic society, the presidency of the SGA equaled that of the university.

The charter of the Student Government Association should be modified if it was outdated. However, we could not accept the "monkeying" he had demonstrated. In order to get a workable SGA, Huang Huanchien, the incumbent director of the Section of the Student Counseling Services (also a military training instructor) and I, myself, participated in the meetings held by the students for revisions. If it made sense, we would let it go in terms of anything amendable. However, under one condition, anything in black and white and published by the Ministry of Education and the university couldn't be compromised at all.

When the election of the president of the SGA was being held, flags and banners were flying everywhere looking as if the campus suddenly became a hustling place. But the majority of students had little interest in this kind of activity. Quite often, the number of the students who had showed up to cast their ballots was less than one-tenth of the student population of NCKU. So, the president, who got elected this way, was lacking something, in another word, whom did he stand for? And another election should be held again. Nevertheless, in order to get the president of the SGA elected successfully once for all, the election threshold had to be lowered.

But the president, who got elected by this low number of voters, often represented one force, and they could cause troubles on campus not only wearing face masks to stage sit-ins but also calling upon "the masses" to parade under the pretense of opposing the military man's interference in politics.

The students wanted to apply for holding a parade. If disapproved, we would be faced with strong backlash. If approved, the campus would be flooded by the sound of slogans. Therefore, I had to adopt a flexible measure: when there were not classes going on, such as the lunch break or in the late afternoon when the school was over, they would be allowed to hold a parade and get their voices heard. The routes must have been carefully mapped out and clearly staked. And furthermore, there must have been teachers as guides keeping it in order. Overall, we couldn't afford to let their "monkey business" get out of control. Though this "tricky ruse" was dangerous, it defused a crisis from the protest.

At the time the 1st KMT Youth Branch affiliated with the Southern Taiwan's KMT Youth Headquarters had been on the NCKU campus for years. During the times of authoritarianism, there was nothing wrong in terms of its legitimacy, legality, and operation on the campus. And no man had guts to say "No." However, in the 1990s, the KMT's authoritarianism went crumbled, and the KMT on the university campus became a symbol, the ear of a deaf man, being inactive and off-the-hinges. Furthermore, holding meetings so-called "small groups" for the KMT "cell members" became a matter of formality, and the cadres' meetings on the NCKU campus were held in the same token, too.

The dignified 1st KMT Youth Branch office on the campus in the past became an undignified one now. Though it was nominally staffed by "volunteers," yet actually, they were selected from a variety of sections under the office of the dean of discipline working in the KMT office. At the time the persistent outcry, "KMT gets out of the campus!" flooded the whole school, and the office couldn't bear the brunt of pressure giving in and backing to a secluded place to recuperate, not to mention operating, and even the plaque bearing the title of the 1st KMT

Youth Branch office was dislodged clandestinely from the wall of the building. Of opponents classified as independents, no one knew which building the KMT office was in.

But there were some "serious" students led by some "serious" teachers keeping on "tracking the KMT down all the way." And "they wouldn't stop looking for until they found it." After making an all-out effort, eventually, they found the building. And on the base of that building, they set up grills bluffing that if the KMT office didn't move out of the campus in time, they would mimic the going of *Chi Bi Warfare* or Red Wall Warfare in the *Three Kingdoms*, utilizing fire to attack that office.

I was extremely panicky, busying myself getting sort of directive to resolve this problem from Bu Tianpeng, the then secretary general of the Southern Taiwan's KMT Youth Headquarters. But he said to me: "As the KMT is still the ruling party, there is no reason for it to withdraw from the campus, isn't there? You must stonewall the tide and try to negotiate with the students!"

Having found out that seeking help from the secretary didn't get anywhere, I turned to President Maa for directive. Maa was non-committal, and didn't know how to deal with it either, and obviously in his mind, there was not a way out, at least for the time being.

I sat on my hunkers in the distance, watching them surrounding a gridiron barbecue. And peering through the crevices on the human wall, I saw the fire burning. And I thought to myself if this ongoing stuff couldn't be dealt with right away as an emergency case, there would be a great possibility for the students to smash the 2nd floor glass windows of the building by firstly throwing rocks and brickbats, and then tossing in torches. By then, the whole KMT office was on fire. If that happened, it would be a devastating damage to our school, too big to cope with. And I really didn't know how to clean up this sort of mess.

Therefore, I made up my mind to take immediate action. And with the help of Mr. Chi Canhui, party secretary of the KMT office, a volunteer worker, Cheng Shuyen, Paolien, my wife, and I, in the deep of that night, we had the important stuff on the 2nd floor of the building carted off to the upper floor of the North District Household Registration Building, and all the other items, books and magazines, to Chi's house and mine.

On the following day when they found out that the KMT office at NCKU had been emptied, they discontinued barbecuing down there any more, and a possible man-made disaster was narrowly avoided.

November 11 is the day of the anniversary of the founding of NCKU. According to the traditional practice, the school has to hold the NCKU athletic meeting. And the "Exercise Show" is the first entry listed on the NCKU Atheletic Meeting Guide, towering over a great number of athletic contests. Accordingly, teachers from the Department of Physical Education demanded that all the PE classes involved spare ten minutes to rehearse the show. Unexpectedly, this sort of maneuver caused the students to fiercely protest. They thought the rehearsals had unduly deprived them of "their regular class time," not only asking the teachers to apologize, but also lodging complaints to the office of the dean of discipline to prosecute them for their "derelictions of duties." The most disgusting stuff was that the complaints sounded bluffing. They proclaimed blatantly that if they couldn't get a satisfactory answer, they would "boycott" the "Exercise Show" all the way from the beginning to the finish.

What I considered was that the students were deliberately giving me a hard nut to crack. On the one hand, I continued talking with the president of the SGA, but on the other, got a severe measure of crackdown on them ready, and had conducted the sand table exercise. If on that day, there were students walking out to protest in earnest, we would let the security officers disperse them or drag them out of the stadium. Without doubt, having scented the hard-line stand of the office of discipline to crush them, the president of the SGA began to show signs of caving in. She indicated that if dean of discipline could give a clarification of this question: "The PE teachers use the class time to rehearse 'Exercise Show.' Is that right?" If the dean could, she would persuade the students not to boycott the "Exercise Show."

As dean of discipline, how could I be considered a guy who fussed about the students. If there was still "room" for me to move around helping resolve the protest, I would do whatever they wished to meet their demands. Thus, I showed up before the students who had lined themselves up for rehearsal in the stadium according to the time as scheduled.

Prior to my speaking, she spoke to the students down below from the grandstand, "That the school allows the Department of PE to deprive the time of the PE class to rehearse the 'Exercise Show' for the athletic meeting is just not right. But Dean Ma is here trying to explain what was going on there with us frankly. Please keep quiet!"

I took over the microphone saying that "the Exercise Show has been done for years at NCKU, one of the indispensables in the athletic meeting held by the university. And it can also be used to show that NCKU students' lives are all young sunshine and daring. As to whether taking away 10 minutes from the class time for rehearsal is right or not, I would like to rethink about it!" Once this word was out, seemingly, she found an excuse to get off the hook, and immediately asked me to hand the microphone over to her. Along the line of mine, she said: "Dean Ma has already promised that he will rethink about it, and that can be regarded as the right answer from the school!" Having finished speaking this, she made a good use of this opportunity to run down a flight of stairs from the grandstand hastily and left.

The students below fell out quickly. But when I was about to leave, I still saw some of the students staying in the stadium and qurreling with each other over "boycotting the Exercise Show" without letup.

On the day we celebrated the anniversary, and when the "Exercise Show" was on, there were still some students holding protesting signs made of cardboard in the stadium to protest. Nevertheless, when they

Leading the alumni and students into the 1990 NCKU Athletic Meeting opening ceremony.

saw the teacher-leader, who directed the whole show, was so composed and carefree, and the students, who participated in the show, were extremely excited, they had no choice but to throw away their signs joining in. And all of them stretched their arms and thrusted their legs to the beat of the music as rehearsed. That day, the whole thing done for the "Exercise Show" was uniformly beautiful and showed that the students at NCKU were full of life.

By then, the original motorcycle road rules at NCKU were not as flawless as deemed because it was stipulated that: "only faculty's, staff members', custodians' and janitors' motorcycles are permitted to run on the campus when they get on and off works, but during the class time, the engines must be shut off, and the 'machines' have to be pushed with hands to the parking lots. As to students' motorcycles, they are completely prohibited to enter the campus." Though the rules had been enforced for years, yet they were not fair having long been criticized by students. With suggestions from some faculty and staff members, I agreed that on each NCKU campus, side doors were built, and furthermore, on the grassy glades adjacent to the side doors, parking lots for the motorcycles were built. With rails erected on three sides, the motorcycles could be prevented from rampaging through the campus. The original rules for motorcycles were amended as: "All the motorcycles are prohibited running on the campus despite faculty's, staff members', custodians', janitors' and students.'"

I have worked 6 years as dean of students, and the thing that grieved me the most was that there were 26 students killed in accidents. Of these accidents, the most impressive one was that two students from the Department of Industrial Management in the College of Business Administration got drowned in the waters near South Guenshen Bay.

Around May, it had got into the brief spell of hot weather in the Tainan area. On a weekend, there were more than ten students who had agreed to go to the beach of the bay for playing volleyball game.

After having played for several rounds, all of them were drenched in sweat. Despite a sign bearing the warning: "No Swimming! Waters deep and dangerous," one of them from the township, Hehu, in Zhanghua County, ignored the sign and walked into the sea. While wading forward, he splashed water unto his body on the one hand, and kept on going on the other, one step after another. He went on and on, suddenly, out of sight. At this moment, everyone on the beach got nonplussed and stood on the beach shouting at the sea. At last, they saw him bobbing up and down in the waters and drifting to the expanse of the sea.

On the beach, there was a great commotion going on: some students ran to the nearby police station to report the accident, others kept on shouting at the sea. One of them from Heyu, one of the Penghu Islands, had confidence in his swimming skills jumping into the sea and trying to come to his rescue without considering the consequences of his recklessness at all. Goodness knows that his rash act and foolish behavior called *fenbi dangche* cost another precious life. *Fenbi dangche* refers to a fable story about a mantis which showed its bravery by stretching out its forelegs to blockade a carriage, and run over. A man shouldn't do what he cannot.

Two days later, their bodies were found: One was washed back unto the shore of the bay; the other, netted up from the sea by the fishermen from the seaport of Chijing.

When I participated in their funeral services respectively, I saw two sets of family greatly mourning over their boys' deaths by prostrating themselves before the caskets, pointing their fingers at the sky and stomping their feet. And I empathized with them, shedding useless tears, and became truly conscious of the then situation that the work for student safety was extremely important. I had to take action immediately by getting a project mapped out. Consequently, I firstly got the typical and lethal accidents, which had occurred on the NCKU campus, written and edited chronologically in the form of flyers, and then distributed them to all the students of the university in hopes that they could enhance their awareness of the importance of safety so that even if the deaf people could hear the warning, *zhenlong fakui*, or turning up the volume to the highest in the sound waves and letting the persons, who are even born deaf, get the message.

The thing that made me feel the happiest was the performances of various students' societies established at NCKU. And the majority of societies ran very well based on their guiding principles. Without doubt, there were a few of them incapable of standing the test of time "withering on the vine" due to the poorly managing. Among them, the most popular ones were the societies with the objectives to serve people. Members were not afraid of how rough the roads were in the remote mountainous area, going to help those disadvantaged children with their homework or sacrified their Sundays as guides to lead the blind people for a one-day tour. Furthermore, some of them went to *renai zhijia*, or nursing home entertaining those lonely souls of the elderly by singing and dancing as if they were troupers of a song-and-dance troupe.

In the universities across Taiwan, only at NCKU, there is such a unique student service that has been offering for decades. That is the NCKU student cart team. In fall, each year, when the school is about to start, the team members are pedaling the two-wheel cart to the Tainan Railway Station to help transport the freshman students' belongings. While pedaling, they are whistling and laughing all the way, echoing the traditional fraternity that has long been developed and valued at NCKU.

There are numerous student societies on the campus and they often hold workshops in different spots. If dean of discipline timely appears among them, it means a lot to them. Therefore, when free, I would certainly go to see them no matter where they were, at the seaside, or in the mountains. Accordingly, I have been to the offshore islands, Kinmen (Quemoy), Matus, and the Penghu Islands, let alone all the nooks of the island, Taiwan.

In 1993, the basketball team of the NCKU cracked all the other teams of the universities in the island and won the championship of that year and wanted to improve the basketball-playing skills via competing with the counterparts in the Chinese Mainland. From the inception of competing with the basketball teams of Fuchien University and Fuchien Normal University, the NCKU basketball team won all the way as if having easily cut the bamboo sticks. Namely, with the exception of that the strong team of Zhejing University and ours played to a draw, the team of the NCKU won by large margins having got overwhelmingly victories over others. When we got to Nanjing that day, the *Yangtze Evening News* reported that the NCKU Basketball Team, consisting of 19 members, was paying a visit to the city, the ancient capital of six dynasties in the history.

Young Chitung, Director of the Students' Advisory Committee in the Ministry of Education, saw that the student protests were spiking on all campuses throughout Taiwan, and accidents occurred one by one without letup, thus, he wanted to set up three student services centers in the northern, central, and southern Taiwan called: "The College and

University Coordination Center for Student Affairs" in the hope that the cases of the protests and accidents that had taken place on different campuses, and the ways they got resolved, were collected and edited in a book form and distributed to all of the schools for future reference. By so doing, "it prevents the problem from happening when it starts, and if something like this happens, people can use the book as the 'guiding lines' to deal with it." Since the center in the south was set at NCKU, naturally, I, as dean of discipline, became the head of the center spontaneously. And because of this part-time job, I had visited all the campuses of the colleges and universities located in southern Taiwan, the geographical boundaries are: Gah-I County to the south and Taitung County to the west.

Since 1993, the office of discipline has been renamed as the office of student affairs, abbreviated as *sho wu chu* targeting students' counselling in the main. However, the meaning of the word, "discipline," is lost. And worse, in Chinese, the abbreviated title is often mistaken for another office, *geo wu chu*, or the office of academic affairs because only the first two Chinese characters are different, *sho* and *geo*; the other two words, *wu chu*, the same. They need arduous explaining.

On July 31, 1995, I finished two terms of mine, six years in number. The incumbent president, also the academician in Academia Sinica, Wu Jing lavished some praises on me in the farewell party held in my honor using the words like these: ".... Dean Ma, over the past six years, gave the NCKU campus the most peaceful days. He is my winning card or trump card on my staff." Upon hearing this remark, and thinking of what I had done for the school, I didn't think that I had been that great. Instead, I felt sort of being embarrassed.

Overall, I worked five years as dean of discipline during Maa's presidency; one year, as dean of the student affairs during Wu's.

CHAPTER 33

REUNION WITH MY SISTERS IN HONG KONG

From the year of 1948 when I left the city of Jinan to the year of 1978 when I got my doctorate in America, for 30 years' duration, I didn't contact my family in Jinan.

When I was in the army, I was not allowed to write them due to the fact that I was an active-duty serviceman. Afterwards, discharged from the army and returned to civilian life, I became a civilian again, and because I was working in a public school, I was considered a "civil servant" and forbidden to contact them. Even though the image of my father frequently flashed on and off in my mind, I couldn't do anything but to stand on the seashore to watch the horizon and heave deep sighs.

When I was about to leave Southern Illinois University, I thought to myself that if I didn't write my family in Mainland China at this moment, when would it be the right time to do this sort of thing? Thus, I wrote a letter and mailed it to my home address in Jinan by using my friend's address as sender's. He was, at that time, working in the International Student Office in the university. And I told him that upon receiving any reply from Mainland China, he could put it into a larger envelope and forwarded it to Taiwan. This was my first time to try to contact my family, and I was ambivalent about it, puzzled, but to look forward to hearing from them.

About half a year later, I received two letters forwarded to Taiwan: one was from my eldest sister, Ma Zhonglan, who was residing in Nanjing now; another, from my little sister, Ma Yulan, who was living at the original address in Jinan and whom I had never met because when I left, she was not born yet. She is my half-sister.

Zhonglan briefly depicted several changes in my family after I left Jinan. The most important stuff was that my father passed away in the year of 1953.

After Jinan was liberated by the Reds, my younger brother, Ma Zhongxin, ended up being a sort of vagabond and wandered to the northeast shortly. At the prime of his life, age 36, he died of heart disease due to rheumatic fever. He was survived by his wife, Yu Shumin, three daughters, Ma Qing, Ma Hung and Ma Jun. And they are now living in the city of Mudanjiang which boarders Russia.

In 1951, my stepmother, Zhong Shi, gave birth to a baby girl named Yulan. They lived in the same family house in Jinan as I had done. Shortly after, my stepmother passed away, too. And this little half sis was brought up by the granny on her mother's side. Upon reaching adulthood, she wedded a man named Chuang Sheng and bore him a son called Chuang Peng.

Zhonglan worked in one of Jinan military clothing factories. When a move was made to Nanjing, she went with it. And there, she married a man named Ying Weicheng in 1956. Later they got two boys to raise: the first one is named Jianning; the second, Jiankang. They are all grown-ups having set their own families up respectively, and had their own children. Zhonglan's husband, my brother-in-law, was a senior educator having been the principal of a secondary school once. Its name is Ninghai.

My little sister described what a surprising news it was when she received my letter: "Since my childhood, I have been told that I have another older brother whose whereabouts is unknown to anybody.... Aside from immediately calling our eldest sister in Nanjing, I have your letter forwarded to her right away!"

These two letters were compared to great waves crashing in on my heart. I was of my opinion that someday, I would be able to see my father and younger brother in person, and now this "ruthless announcement" threw me into an abyss of despair, from illusion to disillusion. And there was a period of time in which I could neither fall asleep nor eat heartily. I sobbed privately looking like a ghostly figure wandering from one place to another and murmuring: "This is not true! This is not true!" My colleagues, Tian Tingfu and Miao Lizhong sympathized with me not only paying visits to me but making many phone calls.

In the year of 1987, the government officially announced to unban the Martial Law and permit *Waishengren*, or the mainlanders who had withdrawn to Taiwan with Chiang Kai-shek in 1949 to see their relatives in the Chinese Mainland. But I was teaching at a nationally-funded university at that time, being considered a "civil servant," and still not allowed to go to visit them. Not until to 1989 and as the Chinese New Year was in the cornor, could I endure this inhuman treatment any more, and decided to invite my both sisters to go to a third place, Hong Kong for a family reunion.

Zhonglan is four years my senior. And she is an open-minded woman, quick, well-coordinated in movement. During our childhood, we frequently got together and played a game called *tijianzi*, or keeping the feathercock in the air in our courtyard. She beat me every time.

Smarter than I, she is particularly great at the numbers. I often saw her blinking her eyes while calculating something.

When summer was on, she, wearing a light blue gown, came home from downtown Jinan by rickshaw creating a great sensation on Guanming St. And there was a lot of young guys whistling and yelling.

Though she had a wrinkled face in the 3.5 x 4.5cm photo she had mailed me, yet she remained unchanged looking attractive despite advanced age.

My half-sister resembles my stepmother, the image of her mother, with particularly two big round eyes, and two black solid braids. Based on her looks, she would look much prettier if she dressed herself up in the latest fashion.

As I had these two photos in my hands, I was not afraid of that I would have any difficulty identifying them at the Kowloon Railway Station.

Paolien and I had got to Hong Kong one day before they did for booking hotel. On principle, if we could save, we would do so. Because when the time was up for us to say "Goodbye" to them, I could afford to buy each one of them, one of "the three big pieces" approved by the then Chinese customs: a television set? A motorcycle? or a refrigerator?

As I can still recall, that morning, when the grey cloud in the sky was amassing over the Kowloon Railway Station area, it was extremely chilling, seeming as if having added something sad to our "sibling reunion."

Coming to meet my sisters who had been separated from me 40 years, I didn't think it was hard to imagine what kind of the upcoming scene it would be! I tried very hard to control my strong emotion and repeatedly remind myself of that only smiling face was allowed to show, and under no circumstances, was I permitted to cry. Because we had survived the biggest upheaval of the "great" times, we came to celebrate the reunion for the only survivors.

Finally, I saw Jiankang, my second nephew, who took my sisters to walk toward us, closer and closer, tentatively. At this juncture, I couldn't control myself any longer, but to run to them taking all of them into my arms. I forgot anything else and screamed myself hoarse and cried my heart out over this reunion.

The passengers, who had seen lots of scenes like this one in front of the Kowloon Railway Station, were not surprised at all. After crying for a while, I called a cab to take us to our hotel located in the Sheung Wan area in the western part of Hong Kong.

As soon as getting settled in that hotel, Zhonglan repeated talking about the vicissitudes of our family. However, when she was about to say something related to the cause of my father' death in the detail, she deliberately skipped the most important point of it only by saying a few of words to muddle through it. It seemed that my father's death became the saddest "taboo," having long been sealed up in her mind. Under no circumstances, would I like to tear it open, and nor would I like to keep asking why and how that "real thing" happened. If I kept asking, she would feel "stabbed" again. What I could do was that in the deep of the night when everything quietened down, I tried to piece a picture together about my father's death through what she had revealed.

My younger brother, Zhongxin, whose death was another sad story. In order to pay off the debt, he went to sell blood. And for the sake of the family's livelihood, he went to work with ailment. His rheumatic heart disease was deteriorating with puffy face and the swelling of limbs. He wound up to the extent that no medicine could be good for him and doctors were at their wits' end. When he was dying, Zhonglan, despite a thousand Chinese li away, went to keep him company for the final days of his life in the northeast.

While listening to the story of Zhonglan's misfortunes, I was nervous for her and in a cold sweat. She married a wrong guy in her first marriage having been beaten by her ex-husband. And there was one time when she was so down and unable to pull herself out of that depression hole, she had the idea of committing suicide by lying on the train tracks. Fortunately, she met a knowledgeable person who helped her out. And she was saved.

She was dexterous and hard-working having won the honor of model worker. After Weicheng and she tied the knot and built their own family, she bore him two sons. And henceforth, it seemed that she got something to depend on. Moreover, she got *hukou,* or residence permit in Nanjing. And Nanjing became her new hometown. When she was free, she thought of me and wondered where I was or whether I was still alive or perished from the earth.

My little half-sister is reserved. Overall, she withheld a lot of information from us when she talked about our father's death. However, the key point was that when our father passed away, she was only two years old. At the time she lost her mother, she became sort of orphan having no close relatives available if help was needed. And having stayed with her second brother Zhongxin for only some time in Jinan, she thought that he was the sole person whom she could trust. After Zhongxin moved to the northeast, she seldom had any opportunity to see him again.

The most touching story is that once, Zhongxin, *erge*, or the second older brother, came back to pay a visit to her. When the time was up for him to bid farewell to her at the Jinan railway station, he stuck 20 yuan into her pocket that was the only sum he had. And as she suddenly thought of the long journey ahead of this *erge* that he would go hungry all the way to his destination in the northeast without this money, she rushed herself to return it but alas, it was too late because the train started chugging and letting her have no other alternative. She stood there stomping her feet on the platform, but in vain and saw him go far, farther, farthest, and finally out of sight.

Zhonglan said: "Zhongxin loves this little sister dearly, and all of our family love her because when she was born into our family, we were all grown-ups. Our Father loves her the most."

The Chinese New Year, 1989, was gone with the mixture of love and sadness. On the third day, the streets of Hong Kong were fully back with cars, buses and people. Paolien and I took them to tour the city. Zhonglan exclaimed: "This place is really more prosperous than any other one she has ever visited!"

By then, Hong Kong was compared to the pearl of the East and if there had been no such an opportunity of touring it this time for our family reunion, making a tour of this fabulous place would be delayed at least a few years later.

CHAPTER 34

A POETRY JOURNAL

If one wants to talk about the poetry journal titled the *Seagull Poetry Semiannual*, one must turn the clock back to the time when the Seagull Poetry Club started. Poet, Qin Yue writes an essay entitled: "The Seagull with Broken Wings" and has it published in the 39th issue of the *Seagull Poetry Semiannual*. In that essay, Qin described the history of this poetry magazine as follows: "In 1955 when Chen Jinbiao, a student-poet, was studying at Hualian Senior High, and encouraged by senior poet, Hu Chuqing, he set up a poetry club called the Seagull Poetry Club. Included in it were: Yi Sheng, Chiu Ping, and others. Their works were published in the *East Taiwan Daily News*, whose editor-in-chief, Jitang Zeng, supported them, and furthermore, half a page of the supplementary edition called the *Wenye Weekly*, or the Literature and Arts Weekly was saved to run their works once a week. And this half page used to publish only their poetry was given a title, the *Seagull Poetry Club Page*. And it could be compared to its counterpart, the *Modern Poetry Page* in *The Independence Evening News* in Taipei. After having issued its No. 90, *The Seagull Poetry Club Page* came to an end suddenly. With its title changed into *The Seagull Poetry Page* with the word, "club," left out, they kept it going. In the end, when the newspaper was transferred to a new owner, it terminated.

In 1957, Qin Yue and Li Chunsheng fell victims to the informants (literally translated as political warriors in the army) who mistakenly accused them of their wrongdoings and Marxism thought. They were sent to Yanwan Reform Center in Taitung County for correction. However, the officers who were held responsible for reforming them could tell that they were not "bad apples" at a glance. And on the contrary, they considered them the young talents who were literary-oriented, being capable of editing and writing and independently thinking. Aside from being asked to lead a sort of self- disciplined life as done by others in the center, they were not under surveillance any more in terms of ideology.

They were likened to two pieces of stones in the dirty latrine, though stinky but steely. And in the worst environment, they struggled for what they wanted to do without letup. With their pens as creative tools, they wrote poems and used them as songs singing, "Life is good!"

With their well-wrought plan, they set up *The* East Sea Poetry Club in Taitung County. And on the supplementary edition affiliated to *The Taitung New News*, only on Sundays, they got *The East Sea Poetry Page* out, and later, it was renamed *The Poetry-planting Page*.

Even though these two pages were short-lived, they got a poetry movement started in Taitung.

In September 1961, Qin Yue and Li Chunsheng were discharged from the army and both got in STTP Program at HTTC. Introduced by the same teacher-poet, Chuqing, they made friends with local verse lovers. With their concerted effort, they got *The Seagull Poetry Page* back. Of the old members, I could name only one, Chen Jinbiao. As to the new ones, with the exception of Qin Yue and Li Chunsheng, Wang Shou and Lu Wei (Zhou Tingkui) joined the club as well. For a short span of time, this poetry club in the school became a concentration of a galaxy of talents, and the poets enjoyed visiting this club and recited their poetic works. Unfortunately, after *The Seagull Poetry Page* got to its 15th issue, it came to an end as expected because most poets graduated and were sent off to the elementary schools located in the different parts of Taiwan. Thus, the publishing business of *The Seagull Poetry Page* terminated again.

One day in 1991, Li Chunsheng, Lin Ling, Lu Wei, Chu Long, Shou Lan and Sun Tsuingliang gathered together at Qin Yue's home to talk about how to republish *The Seagull Poetry Page*, and they came to a conclusion that this time, the page should be published in magazine form, the title should be changed into *The Seagull Poetry Semiannual,* and the Relaunch No. 1 should be marked with the date, August 1, as the jumping off point. It needed all of the members to share the work. Without having my endorsement, Li Chunsheng appointed me the proprietor of *The Seagull Poetry Semiannual.*

At that time, I had not tried my hand at writing poetry for years. Even if I wanted to restart, I didn't think that I could get to their level as expected. Furthermore, I did get myself estimated and concluded that I was not gifted at writing poetry at all, thus, not daring to blaspheme the Muse again. However, Li Chunsheng said repeatedly, "Keep trying, you will be on your way!" With my old friend's firmly supporting, I became speechless. Therefore, I wrote a short as the preface for *The Seagull Poetry Semiannual* plus several short poems. Of them published on the first issue, one poem entitled, "Typhoon" was highly praised by a poet named Jiang Tian who resided in the Wuhan area in the Chinese Mainland. His kind and generous words rekindled my passion for writing poetry. Henceforth, there was a stream of my poems appearing on every issue of the Seagull. Meanwhile, I had my pen name changed from Ma Ting to Ma Con because in Chinese pronunciation, Ma Ting sounds like Martin tinged with Western style.

When *The Seagull Poetry Semiannual* had got out its 7th issue in August 1994, the 15th World Poetry Symposium was held in Taipei. And certainly, we didn't want to be absent from it. For that reason, Chu Guenhe, English teacher by then at Nantou Senior High and I translated some of the poems that had been published in our magazine, and got them collected and edited into sort of booklet form with the Chinese-English bilingual format. And we struck out many copies and displayed them in the symposium as one of the "poetry journals" for the participants to browse.

Li Chunsheng's wife, Lin Ling, is an outstanding prose writer. She is also the behind-the-scenes mastermind for our magazine. Whenever she met with me, she never forgot to lavish some praises on me: "In your group, you are the greatest, because you have got to the level of the professorship of a university!" What she doesn't know is that amidst these literary friends, I am the least gifted man in terms of creativie writing. Furthermore, I do have deficiency in Chinese, and so do I in English. In fact, I am sort of guy of *ban ping cu,* or half a bottle of vinegar, meaning a bungler.

Unfortunately, in her prime, she suffered from malignant brain tumor. When she was in Taipei Veterans' Hospital waiting for operation, I went to see her. She looked collected as if she had let go everything including the matter of life and death. With her looks of that kind shown, I felt a little bit relaxed.

After Lin Ling's death, Chunsheng moved from Pingtun to the city of Tainan and lived with his oldest son, Li Lin. Accordingly, there were more opportunities for me to visit him and hangouts with him.

Mostly poets are born romantic. Shortly after Lin Ling passed away, he remarried a poet named Dong Xiaowen, one of grads from the Department of Chinese Literature at Henan University. Nevertheless, this talented girl couldn't get herself accustomed to living in Taiwan. Shortly afterwards, she wanted to return to the Chinese Mainland with no definite date to come back. Therefore, this situation made Chunsheng fall head over heels so that he called her continually. In order to divert his attention from this beaten track, I frequently got him out to dine with me in eateries, and then accompanied him to go to Tainan Park for taking a walk.

On April 2, 1997, Chen Jinbiao, the founder of the *Seagull Poetry,* called in the members and verse lovers to Hualian County to attend the syposium held for celebrating the 42nd Anniversary of the Publication of the *Seagull Poetry.* And I went with him by taking the one-flight-a-week plane from Tainan to Hualian. When taking the breaks in the symposium, I saw him constantly fingering a string of Buddhist prayer beads and simultaneously doing the silent OM chanting. I immediately realized that he was in trouble seeking help from Buddha. And these signs foreboded something bad that would befall him soon.

Around May 1997, I suddenly got a call from him at Qimei Hospital in Tainan saying that he had been admitted to the hospital, and I headed straight for Qimei. What I had seen on his two swollen legs was the millet-sized red spots all over. The doctor said that:

"These are the symptoms of kidney failure needing dialysis treatment immediately. However, he was opposed to the renal dialysis unit firmly. It gets stuck and I don't know what to do."

I advised him to accept the Doctor's diagnosis but he didn't give a damn care of the word of mine at all.

On July 28, he passed away in his home in the city of Pingdong.

During his lifetime, Li Chunsheng wrote poetry and poetics. He was awarded a medal for his book, *Nine Essays on Modern Poetry* by the ROC Wenyi Xiehu, or the ROC Literature and Arts Association, poetics by genre. Later, he fleshed it out with several critical writings, and it was republished and retitled, *Poetry: Its Tradition and Modernization*. Because of this work, he is employed as a part-time instructor by the Wenyi Zu, or the Literature and Arts Program affiliated with the Department of Chinese Literature at the Chinese Culture University.

That the real stuff, worthy of being exalted by his friends, was done by him since 1978, was that he came up with two sets of poems (24 pieces) based on the Chinese Zodiac signs, totally 12 animals, each animal representing a Chinese New Year, and had them made into beautiful greeting cards. Therefore, when the Chinese New Year was in the air, he would mail them to his friends wishing them a happy new year. He loved poetry to the full wishing that during his lifetime, he could link the Chinese Mainland to Taiwn, though separated by Taiwan Strait, yet united by the sky called "The Vault Sky of Poetry."

The Seagull Poetry Semiannual was originally edited by him and

Zhou Tingkui. After he had passed away, the editor's job fell on me. Firstly, I went to the city government of Tainan to have it officially registered at the Department of Cultural Affairs, thus, enabling the magazine to get on the catalog as one of the ROC's publications. Secondly, I made some efforts to promote our magazine having got tens and tens of subscribers, and a sponsor who had donated 10,000 yuan.

Because Qin Yue studies at the National Taiwan Normal University and during his undergraduate program years, he participated in the Poetry Society established by the verse lovers on the campus, he recruited five professor-poets to join us when the *Seagull Poetry Semiannual* got to the time point of publishing its 20th issue. Firstly, Gu Tianhung and Chen Pengxiang got in, and so did another three, Yu Chongsheng, Zeng Zhenzhen, and Chen Mingtai later with the recommendation of Professor Gu Tianhung. Suddenly, the seagull was getting strong with its wings outstretched. And in turn, it enabled itself to be listed as one of the publications in the poetry magazines category in Taiwan.

At the time Prof. Gu Tianhung worked as editor-in-chief, aside from the proof-reading that needed improving, the others such as the qualities of poems and poetics became obviously better. As to the poems, he advocated writing the long ones based on what had happened in Taiwan. As to poetics, he advocated getting the foot out of the mire of surrealism. Afterwards, he was transferred from the nationally-funded university, Shida, to the privately-funded university, Ciji, in Hualian and found himself unable to do the editing any longer. And for that reason, the prosperity of the *Seagull Poetry Semiannual* was likened to a meteor crossing the sky and instantly dimmed in the universe.

All in all, Qin Yue did all the work such as: the more important job of publishing the magazine; the less important, editing. He grumbled no one for these "trifles." And especially, during the last few years of his life, though being on dialysis, he strove to get the new issue of our magazine out on time till the last issue. He deserved all the credits.

There are two reasons for shutting down the *Seagull Poetry Semiannual business*: No. 1 is that the owner, also the manager of the print shop with whom Qin Yue signed the contract, runs his shop so badly that the membership fee we have turned in is lost (according to the contract that has been signed via Qin Yue, if the print shop cannot have its obligations fully executed, the owner should return the membership fee to each one of us unconditionally). No. 2 is that the original members are getting older and older, while the younger ones need to make a living. Most importantly, in this modern society, as everybody looks up to the monetary stuff, is there anyone who is willing to contribute money, time and energy to do the work of this kind without pay? I have attributed all these failure factors to two words, "karmic relationship." When the "karmic relationship" ends, nobody can hold us together. Therefore, nobody ought to be blamed.

However, to make an exhaustive review of the entire thing, I have figured out the *Seagull Poetry Semiannual* benefits me as follows:

1. When the students' protest was spiking on the campus, I found I had no way out. And there was such a magazine there that upheld me to rack my brains to form a piece of poem in my head, jot it down on the paper, and send it out to get published, and to me, the magazine became an excellent outlet for unwinding.

2. In October 1995, I collected 60 pieces of poems published in *The Seagull Poetry Semiannual* and handed them to a publishing house named Literature Avenue in Taichung City and had my first anthology published out of my own pocket. I entitled it, *Birding in the Winter Time with Binoculars*. Unexpectedly, I received a lot of feedback from readers and critics. And of the critiques, there are two pieces considered more significant than others: one is "A Mixture of the Current Thinking and the Romantic Charm in the Ancient Chinese Literature" by Prof. Wu Kaijin of Shandong University; the other, "The Analyses of Ma Cong's Three Poems" by Associate Prof. Liu Qintai at NCKU.

3. One of my poems, "No Title," published in *The Seagull Poetry Semiannual,* was valued and selected by Bai Ling, the chief editor for the *1995 Ahthology of selected Poems, ROC*. Attached is a short critique by senior poet, Xinyu. That was the first time I was recognized as a poet since I started writing poetry in 1952. The whole thing is as follows:

Ever since a group of soldiers planted in my head a row of windbreak trees
I have lost my freedom to be driven out to the vastness of the sea
And the global concept has also been blurred

Like a stray soldier,
Lifting my gun
I aim at nothing
But to scare away a flock of birds perching on a tree

The sea is beyond the island
And the sky is beyond the sea
In the rays of the setting sun,
Birds are making noises to the utmost
The core value of the two-word combination of hometown is abstract
Further, the hometown of today is not that of the past
You cannot comb one of the phoenix's feathers out of a crow.

Accordingly, I am:
One base-isolated building in the storm
One piece of stone in the mire
(I hate human feet)
One length of night in the pitch-darkness
One tree denuded of leaves

Against the wind
I am listening to
The spring tide in the distance rolling to me

As I recall my poetry-writing career, if there had not been a guy like Li Chunsheng who constantly encouraged me to keep writing, my interest in poetry would have been lost. And if there had not been him, I would not have joined the Seagull Poetry Club.

When Li passed away, I wrote two reports about his death: one was published in the supplementary edition connected with *The Taiwan News* in Kaohsiung; the other, *The United Daily News* in Taipei. Moreover, I was also asked to write an article by the editor-in-chief, Feng Taping, of *The Wenhsun Magazine Monthly*, or the Newsletter for Writers to commemorate him. And the title of the article is "The Sky of Poetry."

In December 2009, I resided in a small city of Cupertino, California, U.S.A. and one day, suddenly, I bethought myself of him. And the old story of how to strike up our friendship was brought back to my mind. As my thoughts were racing, I couldn't help but write a poem. After messing around with it, I came up with a piece entitled, "In Remembrance of My Friend, Li Chunsheng" as follows:

Northern geese flew south
But the way of their honking was different
One was craning its neck and honking with strong Shanxi accent
The other was craning too and honking with bad Mandarin
When we were teenagers the similarity between us was
We lived a life for a period of time in the army on the Penghu Islands
And wrote poems

In the strong monsoon wind

We practiced our marketman's skills
Swallowing the husked rice mixed with sand
We tried to make our stomachs as strong as wrought iron
With red shorts and straw sandals on under the scorching sun
We wanted to boost our revolutionary spirit
With the fishing lamplights here and there on the sea
We learned to write modern poetry

Through mutual encouragement
Based on the example set by the wild cactus in the field
We were growing up in the desert
To the hua la la, the sounding of waves, on the beach
We sang "Life is beautiful!"

The *Epoch Poetry Quarterly* had it run on its 162nd issue, in
March 2010

CHAPTER 35

THE TOMB-SWEEPING TRIP

In 1991, the government continued loosening stringent restrictions on mainlanders to visit their relatives in the Chinese Mainland. And this time, civil servants including teachers who were teaching in the public schools were included.

I still remember that when my mother passed away, her body accompanied by Zhonglan, Zhongxin and me was transported to my native village for interment in the Mas' pear orchard. The burial place was nothing but an accumulation of earth and stone erected over the grave. After my father's death, though buried in the same grave with my mother, there was no headstone erected.

Before my leaving for the Mainland, I got the idea of constructing a headstone for my parents. Therefore, I asked Prof. Xu Jingzhong at the Department of Chinese Literature at NCKU to write an epitaph by using Chinese brush-art calligraphy and mail it to Zhonglan in Nanjing. And I asked for her to get the best headstone material in Jinan and find the best stonemason to do the carving.

In May, I received her reply as follows:

May 25, 1991
My Dear Brother, Chungliang:
    "As soon as I got your letter, I wrote our little sister, Yulan, in Jinan, telling her the matter of returning to our native village to erect a headstone for our parents' grave. On May 12, your brother-in-law and I went to our little sister's home in Jinan, and on the following day, based on the epitaph you mailed to us,

we went to a local masonry to get the stone material fixed. The headstone is 1.2m high and 0.5m wide with a base. Fifteen days later when it got done, it was shipped to Large Horse Village on the same day with your brother-in-law, me, our little sister and her husband in attendance.

Back to our native village, with the help of our relatives and fellow villagers, we located the grave very quickly and added fresh earth to the mound grave and erected the headstone successfully. A ritual was held in front of the grave. And in the meantime, though you live overseas, we passed on what on your mind to our deceased parents underground.

We stayed in our eldest aunt's home on our father's side for two days, and then headed for Jinan on May 19. We were scheduled to return to Nanjing on May 25. When you'll be in the Chinese Mainland, we will go to our native village to pay tribute to our ancestors together."
With the best wishes.

Zhonglan[71]

At the beginning of 1992, we decided to make a trip to our native village. And first we planned to celebrate the Chinese New Year in Nanjing with Zhonglan, and then, we would set out together for Large Horse Village by way of Jinan. Overall, it would take us three weeks as planned to get the whole thing done.

I was told by those who had returned from Mainland China for the same purpose that though the ordinary people there were not worried about food and clothes any more, yet the outdated fashion trends were still on. Paolien specifically picked out some pieces, worn but still wearable, getting them into two large canvas bags full, seeing in what way could these clothes be put to good use?

As our daughter, Ma Hungling, a NCHU undergraduate student, got a winter break having nothing to do, she indicated that she wanted to go with us to experience the customs and habits of my native village in person and see that part of the world in Shandong Province.

Like other people who had already made the trips to their hometowns for paying tributes to their ancestors at graves, and once, boarding the plane, I couldn't help sobbing, face drowned in tears. At the time we had a connecting flight at Hong Kong to Nanjing, I did the same thing. Those events of the past that had been kept in my head for 44 years came alive now as if they had had wings outstretched swooping down on me. I couldn't get them straight, and nor could I put them in time order telling which events happened first, second, third and last. Not until the plane got to the Nanjing area, did I come to myself stopping digging into those past events and being brought back to reality.

The aircraft landed at a Nanjing military airport with tight security.

When we went through customs, the security officers, seeing us pull two small carry-ons with another two large canvas bags, took us for a sort of self-employed businessmen who engagaged in selling second-hand clothes. Therefore, they arrogantly told us: "These two large pieces need disinfecting, firstly, go to the window on the right-hand side, and turn in fee, and then pull them into the room on the left-hand side to be disinfected. One hundred Renminbi per piece!"

We did as we were ordered. Having turned in the fee, we pulled them to the designated room to be sanitized. What we saw was a guy who carried a fire extinguisher-like thing and did a symbolic gesture of spraying. Afterwards, he said: "Okay! Okay!" This was not disinfection at all but being in a flagrant way to "rip off" his fellow countryman from Taiwan.

After having checked out, my two nephews, Jincong and Jinning were waiting for us at the exsit. They said to me abruptly that "this was the airport from which the KMT withdrew four decades ago. And a new international airport is under construction by the People's Government of Nanjing City somewhere else!"

Having got on the van sent by their unit, we were on the way to the city of Nanjing which had been China's ancient capital of six dynasties.

Along the road, I saw farmhouses here and there lying between farmlands and wildernesses. As it was in the winter time, the trees on either side of the road became skeletal, with branch fingers, clawing at the blue sky and creaking and moaning in the bitterly cold wind. This is a bleak winter scene in the wintry season. When our van was nearing the city, I saw the magnificently brick-built wall renovated during the reign of the Ming court.

There was a row of bungalowes on Ninghai Rd. Of them, one was Zhonglan's. One could call it anything but a home because it was so poorly furnished with its kitchen in the open, the floor space was terribly limited. Unexaggeratedly speaking, it could be called *guaju*, or the "shell of a snail." In this home, besides I saw my brother-in-law, Zhonglan's husband, the first time, and so did I see my sister-in-law, Zhongxin's wife, Yu Shumin and her third daughter, Ma Jun. Both of them travelled a long way to see us from the northeast.

They installed us in a room with toilet facilities in a sort of hotel. In the daytime, we went to Zhonglan's home having nice chats and getting meals; at night, we returned to it for the overnight stay. Moreover, my older nephew, Jinning was with us back and forth for fear that if by ourselves, firstly, we might get lost in the city; secondly, when we were crossing the street, we might get hit by bicycles as many as *guojiang zhiji*, or the Yangtze River is teeming with carp fish that are trying to cross the river. Though we kept reminding ourselves that we had to be extremely cautious, yet Paolien was still knocked down by a cyclist. Fortunately, she got only bruises, no bone fractures.

On the Chinese New Year eve, Zhonglan prepared a tablefull of dishes including the Shandong dumplings. After I had got three *ganbei*, or drinking the good stuff bottoms-up three times, and a larger number of dishes tried, I became tipsy. Looking at my sister's white hair atop her head and keeping relishing the dishes she cooked, I did the utmost to contain my tears in my eye sockets saying: "This is the first time for me to have a Chinese New Year dinner on the homeland after 44 years' separation. Let bygones be bygones. And we should toast one another for the welfare of ours now." My sister firstly tilted her head to one side and then turned her head back, covering her face with one of her hands, and finally facing me smiling, eyes glistening with tears. She said: "Yes, we ought to do what you have said!"

When we were back to the hotel, it was the hour of midnight. I lay on my bed with my clothes on and was between the borderlands of sleep and wakefulness. I heard firecrackers crackle from time to time. Though there was no difference of the explosion sound heard between Nanjing and Taiwan, why did I feel that lonely here?

On the first day of the Chinese New Year, my little sis, Yulan, and her husband went back to Jinan with the purpose of preparing the tomb-sweeping stuff.

In Nanjing, for the rest of the five days, we found nothing else to do but to do the sight-seeing. This time, my younger nephew, Jingcong, worked as a local guide, taking us to tour the scenic spots: *Ming Xiaoling,* tomb of the Hongwu Emperor, founder of the Ming dynasty, *Zhongshanling*, Sun Yat-sen Mausoleum, *Fuzimiao,* Temple of Confucius, the Qinhuai River, Xuanwu Lake, the Yangtze River Bridge, and Yuejiang Tower. My brother-in-law said to me: "Walk around. If there is an inspiration striking you, put it into words."

As I was teaching at an institution of higher learning in Taiwan, my brother-in-law also took me to tour Nanjing University which is just located a stone's throw away. Furthermore, one of his old friends who had once worked in the university was asked to be the tamporary guide. Like many other esteemed universities in the mainland, Nanjing University was founded by missionaries as well. The earliest name was Huiwen College affiliated with a Missionary University. In the 10th year of the Republic of China, it was upgraded to an institution of higher learning named the National Southeast University. And later, in the

16th year, it was renamed the National Central University, and finally, the National Nanjing University. Dr. Wu Jianghxiong, a physicist, recognized as the Chinese Madam of Curri, is one of its outstanding alumni. The school legacy consisting of an 8-character couplet is *"cheng pu xion wei; li xue dun xing."*[72] The first part is referring to the noble virtues of integrity, simplicity, fortitude, and greatness; the second part is composed of two verbs, the first verb, Li Xue, generally meaning that the students in this school ought to pursue knowledge diligently; the second, Dun Xing, what students have learned ought to be translated into practice. Obviously, the university lays much emphasis on the balance between the inner and outer self, namely, implementing the "holistic education" policy.

The holidays of Chinese New Year finally came to an end, and so did the sight-seeing tours in Nanjing. On the night of the 5th day after the new year, we, a group of 8 people: Zhonglan, Weicheng, Shumin, Ma Jun, Jingcong, Paolien, Hungling, and I set off starting from the Nanjing Western Railway Station (another name is Xiaguan Station) to Jinan. Because we had the travel papers called "The Mainland Travel Permit for Taiwan Residents," Jingcong could get us three tickets for *ruanwo*, or a railway sleeping compartment; Weicheng, Zhonglan and the rest, took *yingzuo*, or seats as general passengers take. There was one time that I thought we could exchange our *ruanwo* with their *yingzuo* letting them have a light sleep, but the security guards mounted on the train said, "No!"

Having crossed the Yangtze River, the train flew on the flat and open land of central China like a dart. And those events of the past like waves began crashing upon my mind again.

My father is extremely cautious in his daily dealings with people. In my childhood, I often saw him that once getting off his work, he closed the front door earlier than expected. He could shut himself up in his room all the time. And there was nothing on the street that interested him, no matter what the hurly burly was. Moreover, he never struck up a conversation with anyone else whom he didn't know well, and nor was he seen to socialize himself with our neighbors. However, if a close friend of his came to visit him, it was not a rare thing that they sat talking deep into the night.

My Father is a quiet breed. When he has something to say to us, he just uses a few words, for instance: "don't make the same mistake again if you come across the same thing next time!" and "one cannot become smarter until one has got burned!" The only time he gave me a tongue-lashing was when I used my Chinese brush and ink to learn to write Chinese characters, the brushstrokes I executed got out of the box. He shouted reproachfully: "you must write within the checkbox-like space on the calligraphy grid paper," meaning I had to obey the rule.

In the early 1940s, because the battles plagued the country in succession, and in a city like Jinan, God knows how hard it was to support us of a big family? He was not only able to raise a 5-mouth family, but able to abide by the saying: "Little drops of water make a might ocean." And within a span of less than three years, he bought a *Siheyuan*, or housing complex, in the Tianqiao district. If not sharp enough, how could he make it?

My mother is a daughter of filial devotion, her virtuous deeds spreading through her maiden home village. When my grandpa on my mother's side became very ill, he had difficulty passing stools. And my mother used her fingers to "dredge" the hardened stuff stuck within his anus one piece after another to the final "clearance."

Though a woman, my mother is able to keep her head on her shoulders in the midst of crisis. There was one time that she and I were on our way to Zhang Jiamiaoguo and lifting our heads up, we saw three Japanese fighters flying by at the lowest altitude with their wings slanting. She hastily pulled me down to the ground. Seeing that I was terrified and shivering all times, right there, she said: "Don't panic! Don't panic! These air crafts don't lay eggs!"

My mother does what she is supposed to do without irresolution while facing adversity. At a time, we, the whole family, were fleeing a sort of engagement, and my younger brother, Zhongxin, for an unknown reason, was howling and misbehaving himself on end. The more, she indulged him, the worse, he became self-willed. Outrageously, she dumped him onto the roadside letting him cry on and on until he quit of his own accord. Furthermore, she commented on a hardscrabble journey abruptly: "we cannot let you, just one kid, get the whole family killed!" At the time, we were half a Chinese li away from him, one of my uncles named Jiang Guitian, went back to fetch him.

Throughout this whole journey, I did nothing but to try very hard thinking back to those events that took place in the dim and distant past. When it was just dawning, we got to Jinan safely.

Once we stepped on the platform, several young folks rushed forward and pulled our belongings to run. At the beginning, I thought that we had bumped into "Shandong bandits," and in a wink of the eye, I realized that they were the so-called redcaps, porters, offering services to make some money by carrying passengers' baggage. Seeing what they were doing, I had to make a few quick steps to catch up with them and run after them elbowing my way through the crowds and out of the Jinan Railway Station. Holding up my head, I saw Yulan and her husband were waiting for us there.

With the ever-increasing number of the people who wanted to return to pay tributes to their ancestors at graves, the fees fixed by this "trade" for carrying passengers' luggage were hiking up. Initially, they charged 10 yuan a piece, then, 20 and 30, and finally, 50. The service charge of this kind soared successively as much as 4 times. If there was a large piece to be dealt with, they charged extra fee. As we had three pieces in total, they randomly charged us 200 yuan for them. After haggling over the price, we drove a hard bargain, and the deal was 160 yuan.

After having got settled in the cab, I was in the state of drunken stupor, thinking to myself that the *siheyuan* or the complex I had not seen for 44 years must be in a dilapidated condition with the wall partly damaged and the paint on the front door sooty and chipping. Nothing original remained but a ruined *siheyuan*. However, as we got to our doorstep, we saw the blue tile-roofed and red brick-walled houses, standing bolt upright. All these good maintenances ought to be attributed to the present occupiers, Yulan and her husband, who obviously took good care of it.

Guang Ming St. remained the same as it had been but neighbors became all strangers. Here I could find neither my childhood playmates Liu Peiji and Wei Xingan nor Zuo Shaohu whom I called big brother. Zuo and I went to the same school, the Municipal Jinan Secondary School but in different grades. On the whole street, there was no one whom I knew except for another big brother, Mr. Bi and big sister Mrs. Bi whose home was located at the east end of the street. Bi had once served in one of the units in the Nationalists Army ranking first lieutenant. When the Nationalists Army withdrew from the Chinese Mainland in 1949, he had already reached Xiamen also known as Amoy and couldn't bear to leave his newly-wed wife and returned to Jinan.

I paid a visit to the son whose father was my father's teacher named Zhang Huailin in the traditional school. The son's name is Zhang Hede. Though I called him Little Uncle Zhang in name, in reality, he and I are of the same age. After the whole country having been liberated, he once assumed Office of Party Secretary of the Communists in the People's Government of Jinan City. High and important as his post was, he never forgot to take care of our family members left there. When I called upon him, he said nothing to me, but to pick up his Chinese brush with ink writing me two big Chinese characters: *qui yue*, or autumn moon like the size of two rice containers. Of them, the character, *qui*, was written in the Chinese classical language. If taken apart, *qui* can be divided into two individual characters. The character on the left is *he*, or stalk while another on the right is *qui*, or tortoise. Putting them into one character of *qui*, I find that there are 21 strokes in it. To me, it is very interesting indeed.

Zhonglan often speaks of him to me and lavishes praises on him that every Chinese New Year's Eve, he makes a phone call to Nanjing wishing her a happy new year. Nowadays, people's minds are not what used to be; furthermore, isolation prevails; and worse, crass behavior goes on without a check. Making a phone call is a petty stuff, but it can prove that what kind of person he really is!

I retoured the scenic spots as I had often done in my childhood: Daming Lake or Lake of the Great Splendor, Baotu Spring, Black Tiger Spring, Lixie Pavilion, Ancestral Hall of Lord Tie or Tiegong Ci, Beiji Temple, Memorial Hall dedicated to poet, Li Qingzhao. I also paid a visit to the elementary school I had attended inquiring if there was anyone who knew where my former teachers and classmates were. They said to me that due to the elapsed time, it was very hard to truce them, and the names I had mentioned were never heard of.

The unit of my half-sister's husband, Chuang Sheng, provided us with a van. On the fifth day in Jinan, we set off for Large Horse.

When we were getting by the Yellow River bridge, and as it was in the period of the lowest water level in the winter, we didn't see the muddy water rolling. What we saw was a narrow yellow stream in the center of the broad river bed. However, as it had frozen, and under the sun, the refraction of its rays hit our eyes.

Along the road, I saw some places which looked either familiar or foreign to me.

Once we got into Ling County, the van firstly ran very fast on the wide asphalt-paved road, and then as it turned unto the dirt one, it began moving jerkily. Aside from the farmlands on either side of the road, many a two-story high oil-drilling machine stood. Surprisingly, there are oil deposits, black gold, in my native county! This oil zone is named "the Victory Oil Land."

Everything had to be done according to Zhonglan's detailed itinerary: Firstly, we would have an overnight stay at my eldest aunt's home in the village of Li, and from there, they would be able to release the news to our close relatives: "The prodigal has returned home!" And then, on the following morning, all of us would go to pay a visit to my immediate uncle, Du Zhangte on my maternial side in Zhang Jiamiaoguo. Finally, at the noon hour around 11 a.m., we would gather together at Large Horse to offer sacrifices to our ancestors at their graves.

This eldest aunt of mine had suffered from stroke for seven years and remained bedridden more than one year. As I lowered my body to talk to her and gave her some money wrapped in a red envelope as a gift, she tried very hard by twitching her lips many times to say a word like this: "Finally I have seen my dearest one!" Afterwards, she kept her mouth shut without saying anything, but to stare at me with her glazed eyes.

Her husband, my uncle, was still lanky as he had been in those old years, nothing particularly noticeably changed but aged. But he has a good memory. When I mentioned one thing that had happened to me during my eary teens: one day, I had a donkey-back ride past a patch of his water melon farm, and he treated me seedless, yellow-colored pulp and green-skinned melon. He shook his head violently heaving deep sighs and said: "That thing took place many and many years ago, and how do you still remember it? Look, I am an old man now and cannot work on the farm any more."

After the upheaval of the whole country in 1949, my immediate uncle, Ma Jiaxin, moved out of Zhejing Province, south of the Yangtze River, to one of the provinces in the northeast. And he was accompanied by his two sons to join the tomb-sweeping ceremony despite the hardship that they traveled thousand Chinese li and caught the connecting trains. To me, this was wonderful! When we met at this aunt's home, we held hands firmly. And then, we talked about the stuff especially related to the time after our separation at Longyu. We sighed deep sighs and felt as if the we had been living in a different world.

Next day, we got our breakfast at Zhangjia Miaoguo. I saw not only Uncle Du, but also the third aunt, my mother's youngest sister who was the only survivor of my mother's sisters. Uncle, Du, coughed all times now, his health going downhills, *fengzhu cannian*, or he had one foot in the grave. This aunt, No. 3, though very old, was in good health. However, I could see the lines were all over her face, noticeable signs of the aged. As she sensed that I had that kind of weird look, she deliberately said to me: "I haven't seen you since the interment service held for your mother. You have completely changed. If I bump into you on the street, I am certainly unable to recognize you!"

Around 10 a.m., all of us gathered together at Large Horse.

Forty-some odd years ago, the Mas' houses that stood one by one on the block from the front to the rear had been levelled. Instead, a large emptied square was before my nose. I stood there getting lost in somewhere. There was a strong gust of wind arising and blowing up a cloud of dust, and I got blurry vision because of tears, certainly not because of dust. And suddenly, my displaced soul was slipping back, and suddenly, I realized the purpose of this trip.

My cousin, Ma Zhongrong, received us, and we took a rest for awhile at his home and then went to the grave site.

As soon as I saw my paraents' grave and the newly-erected headstone, I couldn't put myself under control any longer and began sobbing. I told myself: "cry, cry, and cry my heart out!" Simultaneously, I murmured a prayer to my parents underground: "Your son without filial piety comes to do the kowtowing to both of you!"

Zhongrong led me to the graves of my grandparents' and my second grand-uncle's and my third grand-uncle's to pay tributes through libation ceremony.

After having finished the whole thing, we returned to Zhongrong's home again where he introduced the relatives and people from the same village who had attended this service. Of them, there was a young girl coming from the village of Xiajia Daokou. She is the only daughter left by my youngest aunt on my paternal side.

With Zhongrong's suggestion, and in order to express my gratitude to all of them, I left a certain amount of Renminbi with him to reward all involved by a "feast" hosted by Zhongrong on my behalf.

On the afternoon of the same day, we returned to Jinan.

CHAPTER 36

THE BEIJING TRIP

After having returned to Jinan, on the early morning, the following day, we bid farewell to all my relatives and got on the sightseeing tour to Beijing. With the rhythmically chugging sound of the train, Hungling, Paolien and I sat appreciating the wintry landscapes through the windows. And we felt quite relaxed and comfortable.

In spite of the fact that I had not been in the mainland for 44 years, I was still able to understand the dialects spoken in these three provinces: Hebei, Shandong and Henan, not 100 percent but almost. Furthermore, Ling County borders Hebei, and the dialect the Ling people speak is the same one spoken by Hebei people. The difference lies in that our dialect lacks retroflex consonants. Other than that, there is no language barrier existing. It was no problem for us to tour Beijing on our own.

As the train chugged in the Beijing Railway Station, we let the cabby take us to one of the hotels. Once the pieces of baggage of ours were in our room, we rushed ourselves to do the sightseeing. At that time, for the tourists from Taiwan on their own, the simplest way to get to scenic spots was to get a cabby and pay him based on daily basis, not on taximeter. On principle, the more days, the service of this kind was offered, the cheaper, the fare would be. Of course, paying by the hour was the most expensive.

The first scenic spot we wanted to see was naturally the Great Wall. With the suggestion of customer services in the hotel, "the Badaling section is beautiful, majestic and well-maintained, representing the spirit of the Great Wall. Therefore, I thought to myself that if we were able to climb up the best part of it within two hours, having seen its depth and thickness, and if we could stand on the commanding position having seen this great wonder zigzaging up and down, we would be quite content.

At the Tiananmen Square, we got a cab and paid 200 yuan and made ourselves clearly understood beforehand that once having completed touring Badaling that day, we would continue our sightseeing tour to *Yiheyuan*, the Summer Palace. And by the end of the day, the cabby was obligated to take us back to our hotel.

After having hopped in the car, I immediately realized that this cabby was not only a "master" (by then, people called drivers or chauffeurs *shifu*) but also a "kingpin" of the trade because he struck up a conversation with us by saying something which sounded to please us, "People living in Hong Kong, Macau and Taiwan are all fellow countrymen, why are their admittance fees so high? They charge nationals one yuan and people like you five!"

He pulled up at the base of Badaling. Hardly had we got off the car when the cold front hit us. Though we felt that the winter clothes we had had on could keep us warm, the headgears on us were no good. For this reason, we ran into one of the stores nearby and picked the new ones made of fur to replace the old ones.

That day, the gray cloud was closing in, the northerly wind was blowing violently and the temperature suddenly dropped to 5 or 6 celsius below zero. We sat on the parapets posing just for a few of pictures and had to climb strenuously upward. We couldn't make any pause because once staying still, we were shivering with cold. And we couldn't stop our teeth chattering.

In the watchtower, on the one hand, we rubbed our hands together and on the other, we stomped our feet. And in the meantime, it made me think back to what the situation looked like when the sentries in the ancient times to do the guarding in this sort of place. In such a bitterly cold weather, they would have surely frozen to death, not to mention getting out of the pass to fight with the enemies. How did they keep themselves warm? What did they do here whith the "Chinese iron armour on?" Were they walking back and forth in this watchtower or sitting against the cold wall with their weapons in their airms and daydreaming?

My nose turned red. If staying on in that place, we would fall victim to hypothermia. Despite the two-hour sightseeing trip earlier planned, we had to subtract 1 from 2. In another word, we had to end it this way.

In one of the stores for selling Chinese landscape paintings, I picked three pieces: one is the landscape of the Great Wall; two others, plum flowers. All three of them are the black and white ink art. Without any delay, we got on our cab returning to Beijing.

It was 3 p.m. when we got to the Summer Palace. And as we all felt hungry, and right there, we sauntered into an eatery that sold dumplings exclusively. What made us feel curious was that it sold the products by weight on a scale of the catty system, not according to the number customers ordered. By then, I had no concept of the catty and tael system in the mainland, and nor did I know of how many dumplings equivalent to the weight of one tael? Therefore, I just ordered four taels for three of us as I wished. And goodness knows that these four taels of dumplings wouldn't be enough to get three stomachs filled. When we felt like making the second order, it became overcrowded. To get more time to tour the Summer Palace, we couldn't wait. Waiting would reduce the time needed for cruising the palace.

Before we got in the Summer Palace, we saw a Mongol, full of side whiskers, stand there with a rather big camel on leash. Obviously, it aimed at providing tourists for getting on and having pictures taken with it. As the guy beckoned to Hungling, she just ignored us and got on the camel right away with the help of a stool by its side. And with her sitting on it, a very nice snap shot has been kept since then.

The Summer Palace is a big garden originally designed to provide the royal family for retreat. With its numerous scenic spots, we found out that it was impossible for us to see them all within this short span of time. We just walked along the bank of Kunming Lake and toured the palaces that are of more significance to us. Therefore, only two buildings, *Renshoudian*, or Palace of Benevolence and Longevity, and *Yulandian*, or Palace of Jade Ripples were more closely scanned. During the late Qing dynasty, that the empress dowager emphasized the importance of retreat was nothing wrong, but that she embezzled the fund originally budgeted for the build-up of the navy to renovate her family garden was absolutely a bad example set. What she had done was a proof that she didn't understand the on-going of the nation. Thus, that she brought the courtiers' and opponents' protests upon herself was natural.

On the following day, we toured the Forbidden City, visiting the outer court: *Taihedian*, the Hall of Supreme Harmony, *Zhonghedian*, the Hall of Central Harmony, *Baohedian*, the Hall of Preserving Harmony; the inner court: *Qianqinggong*, the Heavenly Court, *Jiaotaidien*, the Hall of Union, and *Kunninggong*, the Palace of Earthly Tranquility. Occasionally, we followed the heels of one of the tourist groups and listened attentively to the local guide's elucidations about the history of these varying palaces.

In 1992, shortly after the Chinese Mainland adopted the open-door policy, again, China was in its initial stage of modernization groping forward in the darkness. On the one hand, "it busied itself getting rich," but on the other, "its progress couldn't keep up with the pace of the developed countries" The most concrete example was the attitude of services to customers. The employer or the employee of a business in the private sector grinned from ear to ear and touted his business to potential customers enthusiastically. Conversely, the employee of the state-run business gave the cold shoulder to the potential customers with nothing short of a "poker face," for example, a female employee sat behind the counter with head down doing the crocheting. When some one went up to ask her, "How much is this? How much is that?" she just replied by saying few words. This is state-run business! To her, there is no difference between those who work hard and those who doesn't in terms of getting paid. "Not a damn dime short of mine!" if she kept working that way.

Quanjude Restaurant is noted for Beijing roast duck throughout the world, and we would like to have a try.

It was not easy for us to squeeze into the bus for Quanjude. Hardly had we gained the footing in the bus when we felt that there was a sort of grim atmosphere hanging there. What we saw on the bus was that all our fellow countrymen were all clad in one-colored Chairman Mao's suit. These fellow travelers were cold-eyed and arrogant. And they saw through us whose clothes were different in colors as though we had not been standing there. Although they were hostile to us, we had to be courteous to them for, later, we had to get the information from them regarding which bus stop was the right one for us to get off near Quanjude. Finally, I plucked up courage with a toothy smile to ask a guy who just stood on my right:

"We want to go to Quanjude, roast duck restaurant, would you kindly tell me at which bus stop we should get off? And which bus stop is the closest one to it?"

He looked at me as if he didn't get what I had said and stood still there. He was under the sway of the running bus.

I used the same word to ask the person on my left. The answer I got from this one was the same. At this juncture, all the passengers' eyes in the bus were on us now. And there was no one speaking nor even a cough heard. The air in the bus seemingly became heavy. Turning to Paolien and Hungling, I said to them: "we will get off next stop!"

We paid the fare and said "Execuse me! Execuse Me!" to get off the packed bus. Closely followed were several other fellow travellers. Among them, there was one who spoke to us now:

"You got off one stop earlier. Quanjude is located near the next stop!"

It seemed that he got a sort of "compensation" from what we had suffered. And I became speechless for this late answer!

The "feast" in the restaurant redeemed this "slight mishap" completely that we had run into it on the way for this Beijing speciality. We, three, had got half a roast duck down, and had another half buckled up when we left the restaurant.

On the morning of the third day, we flew Dragon Airlines to Hong Kong. On board, I was hit by an interesting stuff. Though years have elapsed, even to this day whenever I think of it, I cannot help chuckling. It is so funny.

Just one row before ours, a foreigner sat there, and I judged from his accent that he was an American. He looked *sisiwenwen*, or refined but in fact, he was an alcoholic. He kept on asking for drinks from a stewardess. After having finished one drink, he turned to her asking for another: "One more please!" She refilled his glass as told. This way, he continued enjoying his drinks all the way to Hong Kong. After the captain announced that the aircraft would land in a moment, he contuined asking: "One more please!" This time, the stewardess rolled her eyes and said to him impolitely: "Not any more!" getting his seat and the fold-out table returned to their upright positions.

We stayed in Hong Kong for three days. For Paolien and me, this was our second time to tour Hong Kong, but for Hungling, her first.

My daughter, Hungling, enjoyed camel-back riding.

CHAPTER 37

Acting Chairman of Graduate Institute of Education

In the summer of 1995, my two-term dean of the student affairs, 6 years, ended. Finally, I disburdened myself of the students' affairs. And I returned to the DFLL to restart focusing on the teaching and researching all times.

By the end of August 1996, as I led a 13 months' carefree life, Prof. Lee Jianer, the incumbent dean of Academic Affairs came to see me inquiring if I'd like to be the acting chair of Graduate Institute of Education which had just been approved by the Ministery of Education. He indicated that the newly appointed chair, Prof. Lin from the National Kaohsiung Normal University suddenly changed his mind and returned the contract he had signed. Now the new school year was about to start, and launching a recruitment campaign was too late. For that reason, he recommended me as the acting chair.

Honestly speaking, I had been thrown into university administration jobs as chair and dean for 11 years and contributed what I could and should. And I was 63 years old now feeling that I was not as strong as before. Moreover, it was two years away from my retirement according to the age limit. For the well-being of myself, the less I involved myself in administration, the better I would be. In another word, getting retired without making a fuss was my best strategy.

However, thinking the other way around, I realized that the school had run into a "bottleneck" on this. Considering that I was a EdD holder and the right candidate for the acting chair, accordingly, dean of academic affairs was approaching me. If I persistently declined to take it, might I not be considered a weird guy who at the time of school's difficult time didn't want to help solve the problem? Furthermore, was I really able to avoid being deemed as a guy who assumed an air of importance not considering the interest of the school?

However, in another thoughtful turn, the university administration jobs I had taken on before were in the DFLL, the CLA, and the university. Right now, I was asked to head an academic unit in a different college. And how did my colleagues of the DFLL and the college think about me? "Has Mr. Ma been addicted to power? Doesn't Mr. Ma take up that post as the acting chair of Graduate Institute of Education for self-profit? Can't this act of his be considered going too far?"

These questions perplexed me in my head immediately. And I couldn't make a decision right away. However, I let the state of being uncertain take its course. Anything can be a drag needing more time to round itself off. For that reason, I asked Dean Lee to give me more time so that firstly I could let it take a break and then find a perfect answer which would be satisfactory to everybody.

Having gone through the process of consultations with senior professors including former president Maa JerRu in the know on the campus, I got all the feedback that was positive. Consequently, I agreed to being the acting chair and made it understood that I would like to do the administration job only, not offer any course in the institute.

After having taken office, I had the first problem troubling me—finding a spot for the institute to get it started on the extensive campus. By then, though NCKU had 180-plus hectors of land, yet every unit would rather let its extra property remain idle than loan it to us. Because it feared that once, it lent it to us, it could never get it back.

Having gone through several frustrations, eventually, we were able to get two classrooms in the Mechanical-Electrical-Chemical Building on the Cheng Kung campus. The first classroom was partitioned into two sections: one was used as the chairman's office; another, staff members';

and the second classroom, two sections, too; one was used for students' classroom; another, conference room.

When we hung the black-lacquered wooden plate with five gold-gilt Chinese characters, *jiao yu yan jiu suo*, or the Graduate Institute of Education, on the front wall of the building, our entire faculty and staff members burst our sides with laughter. And "the so-called all of us" was only referring to five people: Associate Prof., Yang Huijin, Associate Prof., Rau Mingshuao, administrative assistant, Li Huizhen, custodian, Tung Yongshun and the chairman, me.

The second problem I had to deal with was the Teacher-training Program. Before I took office as the acting chair, I had heard of this thing that the institute would be held responsible for running the Teacher-training Program. Once in office, Mr. Yan Boliang (one of my former students) who, by then, worked in the section of curriculum development under the office of academic affairs handed over to me a large stack of documents and data including the first draft of "The Project of the Teacher-training Program for Secondary Schools, NCKU" (he was one of the original planners as well as writers) and a copy of *the Law of Teacher-training Program* issued by the Ministry of Education. And furthermore, he said: "documents and data are piled up so high on his desk." Thereafter, there would be more like snowflakes falling so that he couldn't cope with them and be unable to fall asleep. With a broad grin, he said: "Everything is all right now!" That is an implication meaning that he finally has found a "scapegoat!"

At that time, I didn't know anything about the Teacher-training Program in detail. The only thing I knew during the mid-1990s in Taiwan was that there was a great deal of changes in the traditional teacher-training system. That was that it had to break up the monopoly system that only the normal university or the teacher-training college could produce teachers for elementary and secondary schools. In another word, the teacher-training business had to be open to the top universities or colleges across the country.

The job for solely running the institute kept me busy enough. Now added to it was to run the Teacher-training Program. How could I manage two jobs without going crazy? More disgusting was that hardly had I got the Teacher-training Program under way when I had to prepare a report for the evaluation which would be held by the Ministry of Education. Therefore, in the school year of 1996, on the one hand, I had to work out a plan regarding how to select the most eligible students for the program on the campus and how to do the curriculum offering, on the other, I had to figure out how to deal with the forthcoming evaluation conducted by the Ministry of Education.

That year, 12 graduate students passed the entrance examination and enrolled in our institute. In the days that followed, 100 undergraduate students who had succeeded in passing the given tests enrolled in the Teacher-training Program. And they were divided into two classes, each class having 50 students.

Within the limited human resources and limited space of this kind, I tried to keep the institute and the Teacher-training Program going along two parallel lines. Sometimes, I had to use the strategy of "Do what I can and see how it goes." Based on the faculty and their specialities, I got the time schedule done. In another word, their specialities determined the curriculum offerings. The most urgent stuff was that there must be courses available for students to take when the school started.

At that time, there were only two full-time associate professors in the institute: Rao Mengxia and Yang Huiqin, the former offered psychology and counseling; the latter, curriculum and instructions for the first-year students in the institute. As to the other core courses, we hired part-time teachers. And thanks to that the campaign for recruitment was quickly launched, and Associate Prof. Lu Weiming, with the academic background of education statistics, succeeded in passing the interview of the Screening Committee set by the institute and joined us timely.

Having experienced the scheduling for our institute, I had no difficulty doing the same stuff for the Teacher-training Program. And this time, I got it done easily.

All scheduling being all done, I immediately started writing "The Report of Evaluation for the Secondary School Teacher-training Program, NCKU." Though the day for evaluative team to come to NCKU fell on the second semester of the school year, we had to "make hay while the sun shines." Because when the time was due, and if we did find some errors in the report, it would give us a little bit "leeway" to get them straight. Therefore, in those days, I sat in my office day by day trying very hard to write a good report.

I was held accountable for writing the part of objectives and the characteristic features of our Teacher-training Program. As to the aspect of curriculum planning: core courses, elective courses and *jiaoyu shixi*, or the trainees' teaching demonstrations, I asked other three full-time teachers to write them. Due to our collaboration, in less than two months, a thick copy of the report to deal with the evaluation came out of our concerted effort. As I was very proud of my ability, not bad at all, secretly, all of a sudden, I found out that there was something lacking in the report. In nowhere was there the list of senior and junior schools that provided the trainees for teaching demonstrations, and nor was there a list of reference books in the field of education found.

Getting the secondary schools for the trainees' teaching demonstrations cannot be done at one blow but making a list of the potential secondary schools for trainees' teaching demonstrations can be easily done. If further elaborated, paying visits to them in person one by one is extremely difficult. Only the work for making appointments with the principals will be unbearable. Sometimes, even though an appointment has been scheduled, but owing to the reason, at the given time, principal, by accident, is on an important mission out of town, a reappointment has to be made. As this is a matter of seeking help from him, not am I sought to help. Therefore, I have to be more polite and humble myself.

Being the schools of the NCKU trainees' teaching demonstrations, they dodn't have to pay our students anything. Conversely, they can get a variety of services from our students: providing help in teaching, checking school assignments, and helping students to learn and supervising labs. Was there any great deal like this one under the heavens? Consequently, there was no need for me to do a lot of talking, and I got all the agreements signed by the schools that I had contacted.

But there were some technical problems for me to get the signatures affixed on the agreements from the 5-star senior high, for example, Tainan First Senior High and Tainan Girls' Senior High. They were selective in terms of the trainees who would be sent to their schools with such a purpose. And they indicated to me that they'd like to accept the students from the Departments of Mathematics, Physics, Chemistry, Biology, Electrical Engineering and Mechnical Engineering.

In order to get the enough number of these schools, we didn't stop working until we got all the junior and senior high, and vocational schools in the Tainan area and the close area to Tainan on the list.

As well known, NCKU is noted for the College of Engineering. The library has countless books on engineering studies on the shelves; there is a Chinese proverb good enough for describing its magnitude, *hanniu chongdong*, literally translated as that: "Numerous books make a pack-ox sweat when books are carted off to a new place, and when stored, the books can fill the building full all the way to its rafters." Our institute was a brand-new setup and though we wanted to make all-out effort to buy books of education, it simply wouldn't work out that way because we couldn't get the purchases done overnight. The only way to get it around was to get books, such as books of engineering education, business education, medicine education and general education in. "We cooked up the number of the books," the more books we had put on the list, the better, the report would be, really looking like something desired!"

After several rounds of supplementing, "The Evaluation Report for the Secondary School Teacher-training Program, NCKU" appeared extremely remarkable. As I looked at this thick copy of report, and "under the influence of self-promotion" I couldn't help marking 95 points on the 100-scale system in the box of self-evaluation.

Here, aside from giving my heart-felt thanks to three Associate Professors, Lu Weiming, Rao Mengxia and Yang Huijin for their help, I was very grateful to Ms. Lee Huizheng's doing. She did the share of her work at her own pace, getting everything in order. Furthermore, she has the stamina which stunned all of us. In order to catch up with the progress, sometimes, she got the page typed as soon as it was handed over to her. If there were any wrong words and sentences left out, she exercised her patience to get them corrected, never showing a frowning look.

At the time there was one unexpected event taking place but it was not related to the institute.

One afternoon, Prof. Zhou Zechuan of the Department of Chemical Engineering met me on the Cheng Kung campus. He indicated that there was an American visiting professor, who had finished his contract, would go back to the U.S. in the near future. And he wanted to send him a bronze to express gratitude to him asking me a question, "Chairman. Ma, what is the English translation of *Chunfeng huayu?*" (*Chunfeng huayu* is a Chinese proverb that can be literally translated as: the life-giving spring wind may finally bring the rain to the world. But here it really refers to the possibility that the students who have been encouraged by a good teacher, may grow in their academic performances, from B students to A students). Though I am from the Departmen of Foreign Languages and Literature, having taught English for years, he got me there. After having returned to my office and thought very hard about what the best translation might be, I finally got it rendered as such, "Under you, everybody is educable." In it, there is neither the word, "wind" nor the word, "rain." And it doesn't match the three translation principles set by Yang Fu, the greatest translator in

China: *xin*, or faithfulness, *da*, or fluency and *ya*, or elegance. However, my rendition echoes sort of essence of that proverb. My second thought is that if I get this English version translated back into Chinese again, I will think that *youjiao wulei,* or providing education for all without discrimination is also appropriate. Isn't it?

After the second semester of that school year just started in spring, the former Vice Minister of Education, Shi Jinchi, led the evaluative team to come to our school, and I was one member of the evaluative team, too. In order not to violate the rule, "The ball game player cannot be the referee simultaneously." Therefore, I asked Associate Prof. Rao Mengxia to do the briefing.

Aside from our three faculty members in the opening session, Prof. Mao Qiwu of the Department of Electrical Engineering, one of the supervisors in the trainees' teaching demonstrations course, was also invited to participate in that opening session demonstrating how the "Mathematics Cubes" invented by him to teach Math.

I took 10-some odd members of that team to inspect the Center of Teacher-training Program including our teaching facilities and equipment and our general library. All of them indicated to me that within such a short span of time, the fruits we had made were incredible. It was regretted that the Center of Teacher-training Program and the Graduate Institute of Education shared the same office for two different educational purposes. And they considered it inappropriate and it should be marked as a weakness. And they said they would make a recommendation to the school authorities that the Center of Teacher-training Program ought to have its own office.

The outcome of this evaluation conforms to our own anticipation—the Teacher-training Program of NCKU is on the list of excellence. Besides the outcome of the evaluation was published on the major newspapers, the then President, Weng Zhengyi, lavished praises on what we had done.

After I finished "the scheduled milestone of something," it was about the time for me to retire. A farewell party was held in my honor, and after having enjoyed a sumptuous "feast," I quit the National Cheng Kung University because of the age limit.

CHAPTER 38

Enjoying My Retirement

On December 31, 1998, I retired. On the following morning, firstly, I drove to the NCKU campus, then, to Houjia Junior High, and finally, to Tainan Stadium on Jingcong Rd. to see if there was any fitness program that fit me.

In Tainan Stadium, I saw a Taiji Quan master demonstrating 40 steps, Yang's style, one posture after another. He is an imposing man, full of life, and highly trained in the field. Upon inquiring, I came to know that his name was Liang Xianyun from Wushu Academy in Beijing.

Henceforth, I was captivated with Taiji Quan. And I started learning from 37 steps, Zheng Manqing's style, through 24 steps, 42 steps, 48 steps, Five-step Quan, to Ring Quan. As to Taiji Jian, sword, a sort of hand weapon with a long metal blade and a hilt with a hand guard used for striking, I learned from 32 steps through 42 steps, 49 steps, *Xingyi*, or shape-and-will, *Wudang*, or Taoists's style in Mt. Wudang, *Yunlong*, or cloudy dragon to *Panlong*, or coiled snake. As for Taiji Dao, boardsword, I learned from 33 steps through Elementary Form, Master Chen's 48 steps, Plum Blossom Form to Little Li's Form. As for Taiji Shan, fan, I learned from Lotus Form through Yang's style and Chen's style, Gonfu Shan: Part one and Part two, Double Shan to Mulan Shan. As to Taiji Gun, a wooden stick, I learned two forms called *Longhu*, or dragon and tiger, and *Qimei*, or if standing upright, the stick and the brows are of equal height. The long spear, 10 feet long called Yang Family's Spear also took root in my mind. Overall, whatever our teachers had taught, I learned them all.

Every day, I got up around 5:30 a.m. After having finished toileting, I went to the stadium to practice the Taiji stuff.

Our masters were demanding and making us do each posture correctly. But I was of my opinion that at my age, that I could get up at such an early hour and drove to the stadium to practice Taiji Quan was not easy at all. I couldn't be trained the way as those Taoists in Mt. E. Mei who want to get to the degree of being celestial beings. Therefore, I frequently and secretly warned myself that even though I couldn't do it exactly as demanded, yet I could execute each posture as accuratly as I could. Furthermre, I wouldn't like to go beyond. If I would, I might get hurt. With this in mind, I didn't think every posture done by me could reach the level set in the Taiji field. For that reason, I often felt ashamed of myself about what I had done, and simultaneously, because of this feeling, a piece of poem entitled, "Sword-practicing" came by itself. It is used to encourage myself:

I practice Taiji sword in the early morning light
Even one leaf of a tree doesn't fall
My view is wrapped up in mist
And there is not enough qi, or strength, in my arms
And my eyes can't follow where the sword is striking
My mind can't coordinate the steps of my feet
The soldiers have crossed the river already in the Chinese chess game
Every posture of his becomes ridiculous and deviated from track
The "fire" in the dantian, or the lower part of abdomen, has burned itself to ashes
But if I keep on practicing the Taiji sword without letup
Sparks will be shooting out from the tip of the sword
I shall be able to run to another spring

There are lots of people in the Tainan Stadium Taiji Group who can be compared to "crouched tigers in the deep mountains and coiled dragons in the deep waters," or all sorts of talented people are obtainable there. Of them, there were two "masters," Liu Ming and Liu Zuochang. The former played guitar very well; the latter was a master of *qigong*, or air strength. Though both of them were octogenarian men, yet they were healthy and full of energy. Ming taught me the 37 steps; Zuochang, the secrets of *qigong* named Sun and Moon.

In order not to waste the academic stuff that I had got for years in the school, I kept on teaching at the DFFL four hours per week on a part-time basis. Aside from that I tried my hand at writing "modern poetry" to entertain myself.

God knows that having just had this kind of carefree life for two years and a month, I was asked to take up another "Mission Impossible."

CHAPTER 39

SETTING UP THE DEPARTMENT
OF APPLIED ENGLISH
FOR LEADER COLLEGE

Around January 2000, while walking on the Gunfu campus at NCKU, I met the former chairperson of the DFLL, Chen Rende. After he and I exchanged pleasantries, it seemed that he had something to tell me, but to withhold it. At last, he couldn't help getting out bluntly: "Dean Ma, there is a privately-funded institution called the Leader College of Management which will be established. There is an opening for chairman of the Department of English. I am wondering whether you're interested or not?"

By then, I was often told that a NCKU professor so-and-so, who after having retired, was employed as president of a private university, while another professor in the same token, chairman of a department by another private university. Frankly speaking, to me, the talk of starting the "second career", I was more than happy to see they had been reemployed. Given that how many books has a 65-year-old retired professor consumed? How many research projects has he done? And how much life experience has he accumulated? These questions will be given the answers by themselves. If he is still healthy and inspiring, and if there are still students who'd like to take course with him, why does the school compel him to retire because of the age limit? No other thing in the world can be compared to the squandering of human capital like this! If it is said that he keeps the younger generation from climbing the rung of academic ladder, based on my own perspective, it is completely out of the line. If I belong to the younger generation and am really "a talented guy," who can be in the way for me to get promoted?

However, this "windfall" causes a ripple of excitement in me.

From the positive point of view, I have done the nationally-funded university administrators' jobs for more than ten years. Based on this background, I can set up a brand-new department with facility. Moreover, getting something started is always hard at the initial stage, and once I get it kicked off, everything ought to go smoothly. Simultaneously, I am of my opinion that if there is somebody asking me to take up a post like that, it means he looks up to me as a right candidate. If I am not qualified, though I beg him in earnest to take me, it will be of no use.

From the negative point of view, at the time I was 67 years old and looked still robust but advanced in age. If there is any pressure imposing upon me and due to that pressure, I will be made to have the loss of appetite and the difficulty falling asleep, what will I do? Furthermore, I have got used to the publically-funded university environment already. Once in the private one, I'll probably meet some of the people who may be "snobbish" and get into the occasions in which I'll have been condescended to. What am I going to do? As soon as I thought about this, I became hesitant. Therefore, I grabbed the phone and told Chen that I'd like to thank him for his kindness to recommend me and made a decision not to take the job. Unexpectedly, from the other end of the telephone came the words: what I had worried was something drawn on imagination because the Board of Trustees of the Leader College of Management had employed the former chair, Prof. Shik Hungchi, of the Department of Urban Planning and Development at NCKU as the first president.

Prof. Shik is able, savvy, and experienced. And once a decision is made, he will stick to it in spite of whatever difficulty lies ahead. When President Weng Zhengyi was heading the NCKU, he was dean of general affairs. Despite the fierce protests from the faculty, staff members, custodians and janitors of the university, he hiked up the parking fee to 2,000 yuan. And when he was chairman of the Department of Urban Planning and Development, I was in charge of the DFLL. We sat through countless meetings. Though he may not be regarded as my crony, at least, he is a sort of my friend. Thinking of this type of relationship between him and me, I promise to go to the college giving a try.

But when I saw him in his office, he told me that a change had been made. He wanted me to assume the office of dean of the student affairs.

The education facilities, the hardware part, of the college were under construction in the Annnan area of Tainan City. The site for the school is ringed by sugarcane farms, and let out under a lease from Taiwan Sugar Company. Aside from the loud noises of pile-driving, "Din! Din!" and clouds of dust which blanketed the sky, there was nothing seen there. And even the preparation committee didn't get a place for holding a meeting. Having no choice, we had to move back to the NCKU compus and borrow a conference room from the Department of Urban Planning and Development for such a purpose.

In the meeting, besides the appointed dean of general affairs, Dr. Zhen Deying was new to me, the rest were all my old colleagues at NCKU. Of them, Prof., Lee Maoxiong, former secretary general of the president, Xia Hanmin, was appointed dean of academic affairs; Associate Prof., Liu Qingtai, former dean of academic affairs in the evening school program, chairman of the department of English; and former chairman of history, Prof., Huang Yaoneng, chairman of the department of Japanese. All these old colleagues gathered together and tried to voice their opinions about the potential problems of how to recruit students. Two key points were considered the most important: one was how to make a name for the college; another was how to get the quota full, the number of students, fixed by the Ministry of Education.

Though I was reappointed dean of student affairs now, yet under me, I had neither "soldiers" nor "cadres," namely, "a general without any following." The most urgent thing was that I had to try very hard for the prospective students who, coming from afar, could move into our newly-built dormitory without any difficulty.

Where does the President of the Board of Trustees, Wang Rongchang, hear about such a term, "Community Service?" I don't know. But he sent me on a "pilgrimage" to the Zhaoyang College of Technology, in which the community service program had been conducted for years, to get "sutras," or to learn the program. He said: "The Leader College of Management is a brand-new school, and once the school gets started, we must conduct the sort of "Community Service" education, and have students build the habit of enduring everything.

In reality, "Community Service" is nothing else, but to do the cleaning work for the school and on the list of curriculum offerings, it is a compulsory course with zero credit. And all students have to take it for one year. If failed, students cannot graduate. Frankly speaking, it is Wang's mechanism of running the school, and the cost for employing janitors must be taken into consideration.

By then, all of the job openings in the varying sections under my office had almost been filled. And all these sections were about to operate. However, at this juncture, the appointed chairman of the Department of English, Liu Qingtai, was suddenly transferred to the Office of Academic Affairs, and held responsible for recruitment. President Shik asked me to do one more job charging me with heading the Department of English. He said this was nothing, but to be just a little bit of extra work for me to do for the Department of English.

As the Leader College of Management was at the stage of pioneering called *bilulanlu,* or to blaze a trail in the hills. With limited manpower, "everybody is worthy of ten men, ten men, one hundred." This way, the college could be run economically, and I certainly understood the implication of this saying. Because of this "tacit understanding," I had nothing to grumble at, but to accept the job at such a "crucial hour." But I felt it was rather late because the school would start immediately.

Once I was in office, the first thing that puzzled me was the translation of the title of the department. If I translated it from Chinese into English as the Department of Applied English, it would fit the first one of the three translation guidelines "faithfulness," not the other two of "fluency" and "eloquence." Worse, though I had looked up through the American university catalog, I was not able to find any title like that, only the Department of English or English as a Second Language Program could be found. However, if I translated the department of applied English into the department of English, then what the difference between these two departments could be told? After giving much thought to this, I favored my first translation, the Department of Applied English. Later, I did find there was such a title in the Australian university catalog, for example, the Department of Applied Physics. Based on this finding, I emboldened myself to get the English translation of the title of our department finally fixed, the Department of Applied English. In fact, English is English, why do people distinguish the difference between literary English and practical English? That is the expedient solution only.

The second problem was the shortage of qualified teachers for the department. Getting the qualified ones to teach core courses is easy. If unable to get the qualified ones on a full-time basis, I can get some on a part-time basis. However, getting a native speaker in timely is out of the question. Moreover, by then, an Applied English Department, which didn't have a native speaker, didn't look like the Department of Applied English at all. Accordingly, I, *shang qiong bi luo xia huang quan*, or searched high and low, everywhere, in hopes that I could find one who possessed master's degree in this shortest period of time. If I couldn't find one on a full-time basis, a part-time one would be okay. Whatever the case it might be, I had to get one for the first semester, and afterwards, I'd work out a long-range plan.

As one week was away from the start of the school, the progress for getting a native speaker got nowhere. It seemed as if I were in the state of *zon kun chou cheng,* or being walled in by my own worries. Suddenly, there was an inspiration striking me that why didn't I go to the Chinese Language Program of the Language Center at NCKU exploring the possibility of those international students who came to Taiwan to learn Mandarin? The outcome is that the majority of British, American and Canadian students in our Chinese-learning program in southern Taiwan possess only bachelors' degrees. Few of them are masters' degree holders.

While searching through everywhere and "exaggeratedly speaking, wearing out a pair of endurable shoes," I couldn't find one. Fortunately, I met Chen Shuling who was serving in the Language Center by Cheng Kung Lake. She said: "a former foreign student, Damien Trezise, graduated from the center is Australian. He is not only a master's degree holder but also a Chinese major from Monash University in Australia. He is decent and easy-going. I can assure you that he is an ideal candidate. But right now, he is teaching English to children in Kaohsiung City, and I can call him on your behalf inquiring whether he is interested in teaching in Leader or not." I told her that if the answer was positive, she could fix a time and a place for me to interview him.

Mr. Trezise of Australia exudes the wonderful personality traits of an English gentleman. At first glance, I can tell that he is a guy with middle-aged man's maturity and young man's vitality. His eyes are the reflection of honesty and his lips curling up make him look as if he was about to smile. All these personality traits make me feel comfortable and free while being with him. He indicated to me that he would be very happy to have such an opportunity to teach at the Leader College of Management. However, he was bound by a contract with someone in a preschool program in Kaohsiung. Not until he had fulfilled that contract in October, was he able to come to Leader. I told him: "there won't be any problem for you to do that. The classes scheduled for you will be on hold. Once you report to our school, you can find time to do the makeups."

The original plan submitted to the Ministry of Education for the Department of Applied English, Leader, is to get two classes of 100 students. Due to unspecified reasons, only one class has been okayed by the Ministry. After receiving the notification from the Ministry, I have to do my utmost by lodging an appeal. And besides explaining our desperate "needs," what I must do is to do the wording again and again. Anyway, on the following year, we finally got what we had wanted.

At that time, I was doing two jobs: One office is located on the 4th floor of our administration building (dean of Student Affairs), another, the 6th floor (chairman of Department of Applied English). I was running up and down between these two offices. Although hard, yet when I saw a brand-new school set up from its scratch and grow rapidly like this, couldn't I be happy? And furthermore, in numerous meetings, I repeatedly made suggestions to the school authorities that the school should increase the English-speaking and -listening skills for the entire Leader College students. Consequently, the school might become an institution of higher learning with some of the features. Listed below are my suggestions:

1. On each floor of the student's dorm, a counselor is available to students in terms of English-learning. And the post should be assumed by someone who comes to the NCKU Language Center to learn Mandarin. The school should provide him with board and lodging. Living together, this counselor and students will learn the languages, English and Maindarin, from each other.

2. Aside from audiovisual classes regularly scheduled, in the Department of Applied English a speech club should be organized, and hosted by native speaker. By so doing, students are provided with the one-on-one opportunity in which they can sharpen their speaking and listening calibers. Furthermore, students can get rid of their fear and bashfulness while speaking the language with foreigners.

3. The Department of Applied English should encourage the graduating class to stage an English play every year so that the fruits of their learning over the past 4 years can be shown. And by doing so, Leader can display this endeavor as one aspect of students' extracurricular activities.

4. An English newspaper entitled, *The Leader Students*, will be periodically issued. Students organize their own editing committee and get all the work of interviewing, editing, proof-reading, printing, and circulating done. At the time student reporters have turned in their written works, one of the native speakers will check with them and correct the grammatical errors student reporters have committed.

It was pitiful, only No. 2 and No. 3 were implemented. The rest died during the period of planning.

When everything in the school was in full swing and the Leader College of Management was nick-named "Little Chengda, little NCKU," unfortunately, I became exhausted physically and mentally. In the daytime, I fell into a trancelike state, and at night, I couldn't fall asleep. Therefore, I rushed myself to see doctor at the hospital affiliated with NCKU. The doctor said: "the symptoms are derived from pressure!" hinting that I had to resign all the college administrators' jobs I was holding. Agreeing to this admonition from this medical professional, I immediately did what I was told. Simultaneously, I had made up my mind that I'd like to quit the school with no hesitation if the resignation would be turned down.

President Wang of the Board of Trustees and President Shek of the school, understood what my problem really was, and permitted me to quit all of the administrators' jobs.

It took me a lot of time to recover from this "nervous breakdown." Hereafter, I concentrated on teaching and researching only.

CHAPTER 40

"PURSUING THE STAR"

Written for the 50th Anniversary of the Founding of the DFLL at NCKU

Around April 2007, I met the then chairwoman, Liu Kailing, in the hallway of the DFLL building. She told me that in the near future, she would hold a ceremony to celebrate the 50th Anniversary of the founding of the DFLL hoping that I could write a piece of "modern poem" to do the poetry-reading as one of a series of activities in the opening ceremony. Because I knew that writing a piece of poem to heap praises on somebody or on something was not easy, I wouldn't like to commit myself to giving her a definite answer right away, but only to promise her that I would certainly like to give a try. I also told her that the deadline for turning in that piece was unpredictable, maybe tomorrow or never.

Writing poetry needs inspiration. If there is nothing that comes as fast as lightning, a poet won't be able to produce high quality works. Only bad poems are made from a burner of middle night oil.

From the moment I was entrusted with such a task, I walked around Cheng Kung Lake thinking very hard about how to write such a piece of poem. As well known, it is not the length of the poem that matters but the real stuff. In other words, there must be a spirit in it. It cannot be too complicated because it will be read out loudly in public. It cannot be too simple either. If it is made too simple, the poem will lose its "poetic charm." The poem cannot be used as a calculator to calculate the strengths of the DFLL, and if so done, the poem will get into an ingratiating manner only to blindly lavish praises on the department.

That the good words are too many will be nothing but excessively flattering. Nor can the poem be utilized to enumerate the weaknesses of the DFLL and if so done, the poem will lack something encouraging for the DFLL.

"Oh! Oh! What should I do?"

Under the scorching sun, I kept walking around the lake once, twice, thrice and so on. Suddenly when I heard the bell chime on the hour and saw a student jumping on a flight of stairs to Xiuqi Building and rushing himself to his classroom, seemingly, I had the idea of personifying the department. In a flash, a short piece entitled, "Pursuing the Star" was formed in my mind:

> *As the bell for students' going to classes is chiming*
> *Suddenly, I realize that I am knocked onto the 50th stair of the*
> *staircase*
> *Lifting up my eyes*
> *I see there will be countless stairs lying ahead*
>
> *No matter what winds and rains behind me*
> *The arrow wounds*
> *I have trained myself sinewy as the Knight of Round Table*
> *Like a bell, the harder, I get struck, the louder, I shall clang*
>
> *Ignoring those sleeping willows by Chung Kung Lake*
> *With the faint breeze in the evening*
> *After taking a mouthful of water and reposing myself a while*
> *I will surely get on this life journey again*

CHAPTER 41

THE COURSE
OF RESEARCH METHODOLOGY

In 2003, the application submitted by the Department of Applied English at Leader to the Ministry of Education for establishing a master's degree program was approved. And this program was divided into two groups: ESL, and Literary Studies. Because Research Methodology is one of the core courses, every graduate student must take it. And the candidate, who was going to teach the course of Research Methodology for Literary Studies group, became indecisive. Having weighed the pros and the cons of several other potential candidates, the then chairwoman finally decided to let me conduct it.

From my point of view, the so-called Research Methodology for Literary Studies was nothing else but to teach the students in the master's degree program to wrap up their theses. Aside from the technological stuff, the course should involve literary criticism, and thus, conducting this course by introducing literary criticim to the students should not be deviated from track.

There are countless books about literary criticism. Of them, I picked two books that matched the MA program students at Leader: One is *Beginning Literary Criticism* by Prof. Michael E. Holstein; another, *A Handbook of Critical Approaches to Literature* by Wilfred L. Guerin, etc.

Beginning Literary Criticism is not a fat and thick book but a good one, consisting only of 113 pages.[73] Initially, it begins with the first step introducing literary criticism and theory, the reading comprehension guides of the genres, drama, novel and poetry, then moves on to the second step of how to find a topic and how to organize a thesis, and finally, gets on the third step of how to make footnote and bibliography, and to the finish of a thesis. This small book is written *chang kuai lin li*, or smoothly and completely. Moreover, especially, it warns the student who is learning how to write a thesis that the most invaluable thing of a thesis lies in its originality. It entails the student studying the first-hand material, namely, the work itself, instead of the second-hand material, literary criticism. If the order is reversed, the student will only pass on what others have said. Therefore, originality tops everything else. If a right topic has been found, the thesis will be done easily.

The profundity of this book is achieved with breathtaking lightness. Readers with a few years' English education and knowledge of literature can comprehend the contents without any difficulty.

There are lots of concrete examples listed about how to write a thesis. Based on them as examples, and practicing one step after another, one should get the knowledge of wrapping up a thesis.

As for the ways of how to make the footnote and the bibliography, it shows concrete examples for the beginner to follow. If reading these exampes more times, one can certainly grasp the know-how of writing them and listing them.

This book also reminds the reader of the fact that studying literary criticism needs close reading. The reader must familiarize himself with the oft-used vocabulary and terminology. Having got this indispensable step done, he can harvest the "crop" by the Chinese proverb, "Half the work with double results." In addition, three parts of speech, prepositions, conjunctions and adverbs play the pivotal roles. The smoothness of a good thesis depends upon them. Overall, this small book introduces us to the key of success in wrapping up a thesis.

A Handbook of Critical Approaches to Literature has been highly valued by the academics in the field since its first edition was published in 1960.[74] In 2005, its 5th revised edition came out. And it has been translated into many different languages, namely, Chinese, Japanese,

Korean, Spanish and Portuguese.

The book is composed of more than 400 pages, a collective work, written and edited by five leading scholars and specialists in the field. It is characterized by the following:

1. The literary theory or research methodology is divided into nine approaches: textual, historical, philosophical, formalist, psychological, mythological, cultural, feminist, and the play of meaning.

2. Aside from the play of meaning approach, each approach uses six classics to be tested for its applicability via *Hamlet*, "To His Coy Mistress," *Huckleberry Finn*, "Young Goodman Brown," "Everyday Use," and *Frankenstein*. Therefore, students can get a clear picture of how applicable these approaches to literature are in terms of analysis. On the other hand, that these six classics in the genres of drama, poetry and novel can be served as "test tools" by the said approaches to induct, deduct, and analyze to get the climaxes of them indicate that they have characteristic features of multifarious dimensions.

3. Each literary theoretical origin and development are fully depicted in this book. Once a student has read it, he will have got the panorama view of the approach rather than *Yiguan kuibao,* or using a length of pipe to see one spot on the body of a leopard, just partly, not wholly. Moreover, listed at the end of each theory are the entries of the bibliography for those who are interested in learning more about it.

4. The structuralism and poststructuralism in Chapter 10 are the most difficult literary theories. Unless a reader who has long steeped in literary theories, one cannot understand the essence of them. But in this book, the authors use the shortest paragraphs to summarize and analyze them so clearly enabling the readers to have grasped the rough pictures of them. It is a tough job indeed.

5. This book emphasizes enlightenment rather than conclusion. It

can be said this way that the literary theories are still developing. In another word, based on these said theories, scholars can expand them and furthermore, create brand- new ones. Even a reader can create a literary theory if he has such a creativity.

6. The book is very rich in contents and the textual structure is well organized, full of beautiful sentences and witty remarks, too numerous to enumerate. While reading, readers will be extremely fascinated by it.

The course of Research Methodology for the literary studies group was conducted by me for four years. Every semester, there were always six or seven students taking it. I fully enjoyed having this small class in which I profited myself according to a Chinese saying: "To teach is to learn."

CHAPTER 42

HEMINGWAY STUDIES

In that Master's Degree Program, and in the first semester of each school year, I offered the course, Research Methodology for Literary Studies group; in the second, Hemingway Studies. In fact, in the earlier years, I offered a course called Selected Readings of American Novels at the DFLL at NCKU. And the novels I selected for teaching that course were Hemingway's major works. In my undergraduate school days, I read *The Old Man and the Sea*, which won him the Nobel Prize. Since then, I have been greatly interested in his novels, and with the time gone by, this interest doesn't fade away, but to continue growing.

Roughly, there are 18 weeks in a semester. And within this period of time, I teach students Hemingway's four major novels and two short stories: *The Sun Also Rises, A Farewell to Arms, For Whom the Bell Tolls*, and *The Old Man and the Sea*; "The Short Happy Life of Francis Macomber," and "The Snows of Kilimanjaro." Each one of these works is intriguing. But aside from *The Old Man and the Sea*, they all have something to do with death.

The title of *The Sun Also Rises* is derived from the revalation of the first chapter of *Ecclesiastes of the Old Testament of the Holy Bible*: "Meaningless! Meaningless!" says the Teacher, "utterly meaningless! Everything is meaningless. What does man gain from all his labor at which he toils under the sun? Generations come and generations go, but the earth remains forever. The sun rises and the sun sets and hurries back to where it rises."[75] In addition, the *yinwen,* or the wedge for this novel on the inside of the cover page of *The Sun Also Rises* is also from the *Ecclesiastes*: "The wind blows to the south and turns to the north; round and round it goes, ever returning on its course. All streams flow into the sea, yet the sea is never full. To the place the streams come from, there they return again."[76]

From these two quotes, we see that Hemingway's *The Sun Also Rises* and some of his other works are not deviated from "nihilism," especially, from the main theme of the *Ecclesiastes*.

The protagonist, Jake Barnes, gets injured in his loins in the war. Therefore, he can't have sex with his girlfriend, Brett Ashley. The love both of them have been pursuing changes into such a condition that though they have the romantic longing for something, yet it becomes useless and results in anything but the essence of love (their love becomes stereotypical when the novel starts in Paris, and so does it when the novel ends in Madrid). And in between, there are the complicated plots going on that Robert Cohn and Pedro Romero are courting Brett Ashley, too. Consequently, the secondary tension is created, and that keeps these three men in rivalry. Complicated as it is, eventually, everything becomes nothing and returns to its original place where it starts.

Under the sun, there is nothing new. Life keeps going on anyway. And when the sun rises in the east again, does that symbolize a new era is coming? Or is another kind of nothingness is come? This "incomplete love story," in turn, becomes the symbolizing of the saying "You are all lost generation." Exposed to us is the extreme complexity of human relationships. In the novel, there are no code heroes created by Hemingway; the heaven and the earth exist forever, and they are only code heroes.

A Farewell to Arms is a novel that describes war and love. In the first chapter, the keynote of "nihilism" has been set for this novel.

There is a group of soldiers walking along the road towards the front in the rain. After that, there is nothing left on the road. Only leaves stripped off from the trees by the wind are rolling on and on. After that, the road becomes "bare" again. In the first chapter which consists of only one and a half pages, the word, "bare," has presented seven times, and so has "nihilism" permeated everywhere, humanity and natural world.

Thus, the leading and supporting characters, Frederic Henry and Catherine Barkley, cannot get away from the destiny of "nihilism." And from their first encounter, they are doomed to "nothingness" at the denouement. What Frederic has intended in terms of courting Catherine is nothing but to substitute for his going whoring in the "Bawdy House for officers" where he plays the girls false, in fact carnally driven. In the same token, Catherine takes Frederic to fill the void left by her maiden lover who got killed in the war, and continues to play Frederic false, too. Out of expectation, this kind of sham thing later develops into a "world-shaking" love story.

However, having gone through the misfortures: choas of the military withdrawal, arrest by the military police, narrow escape from the kangaroo-court by jumping into the river, chase by gendarmes and the risk of his life with Catherine for getting in Switzerland illegally, Frederic comes to know that Catherine is an indispensable partner in his life. They are compared to "Chinese ducks" fleeing the war together. And though having not gone through a wedding ceremony, they become a wedded couple in reality living out sort of happy life somewhere in Switzerland. Nevertheless, at the end of the novel, Catherine died of childbirth. And everything returns to nothingness.

After Catherine's death in the hospital, Frederic walks back to his hotel alone with the rain which though suggests a sort of new birth, yet everything becomes a dream to him.

The novel is imbued with religious belief. Aside from what the military chaplain has preached and done rubs off onto him through osmosis. Frederic finaly grasps the essence of the religion (Christianity) and speaks out such a golden word: "In defeat, we believe in God."[77]

The difference between this novel and *The Sun Also Rises* lies in that there is a code hero in it. That is Frederic Henry. He shows contempt on the abstract nouns: "glory," "honor," "courage," "hallow," and regards them as the empty words used as tricks for hoaxing people into wrongdoings. And they are not comparable to those concrete words such as "village," "street," "river," and "troops." The former is fictive; the latter realistic.

Hemingway looks down on the concept of a big organization such as nation. By contrast, he praises "small potatoes," small units and humanism.

The scene of the chaotic retreat is written very successfully. Apart from Leo Tolstoy's big retreat in the novel *War and Peace*, no retreating scene in other novels is written as well as in *A Farewell to Arms*.

For Whom the Bell Tolls starts with how to blow up a strategic bridge. As far as time is concerned, it is a 3-day or a 72-hour story, and as the place is concerned, it is just a bridge. However, it develops into a Hemingway's the fattest and thickest book of all his works.

Ever since Robert Jorden accepted the mission of exploding the bridge, he has had a hunch that he won't return alive. (There is a similarity between him and an assassin named Jing Ke in the Qin Dynasty of China in terms of mission. When Jing Ke bid farewell to his folks, he came up with a couplet and sang: "With the wind screaming on the freezing Yi River, the fearless shall not return." Moreover, after Pilar, one of the female members of the guerrilla group, does the palm reading for him, and showed sort of an air of mystery, Robert firmly believes in what he has had on this mind.

In the mountain, he falls in love with a girl named Maria, one of guerrilla members, and in the sleeping bag outside the cave, they consummate their love on the snowy ground. And in the wilderness, while engaging in sexual intercourse, they feel that the earth is moving beneath them. That signifies that the true love is there (Robert really goes for Maria, so does Maria) according to the Gypsy's astrology. Moreover, the bond of love forged in the wartime is extremely different from the others.

With the time gone by, a stream of deaths begins occurring. At the first stage of heavy engagements, firstly, the guerrilla group led by El Sordo is stranded on the top of the mountain by the government troops, and then, as the bombers skim over the mountain and drop bombs and finally, no one survives. At the second stage, No. 1 Fernando gets hit, seriously wounded, and passes away on the declivity; No. 2. When Anselmo detonates the device to demolish the bridge, the old man Anselmo is crushed by the fallen rock. At the final stage when Robert reins his horse across the narrow gorge on which the gun fires are converging, unfortunately, his horse gets hit by a bullet, and Robert's left leg is pinned down by the fallen horse and bleeding. Consequently, he cannot make an escape with the other members. Such a miserable situation is turned out that he is left behind and alone. With his rifle in his hands, he is waiting for the enemy to come to get him. He is stuck there waiting for his death to come too.

The most moving scene of this novel is that when Robert with a broken leg bids farewell to Maria, "Listen to this well, rabbit," (Maria's nickname), …. "Thou wilt go now, rabbit. But I go with thee. As long as there is one of us there is both of us. Don't you understand?"[78] (philosophy of oneness). If there is no true love between Robert and Maria, nothingness cannot be felt so keen and deep, especially, after their moving away from each other.

A Farewell to Arms and *For Whom the Bell Tolls* are of the same nature in terms of team spirit but the difference between these two novels lies in that in the former, there are only two comrades getting killed, others run away; in the latter, besides El Sordo's group, only three, the rest totally withdraw to safety.

The title of *For Whom the Bell Tolls* is derived from one of John Donne's poetic works, the 17th century metaphysical poet, "No man is an island entire of itself; every man is a piece of the continent a part of its main; if a clod be washed away by the sea, Europe is the less, as well as if promontory were, as well as any manner of thy friends or of thine own were; any man's death diminishes me, because I am involved in mankind. And therefore, never send to know for whom the bell tolls; it tolls for thee."[79]

Without doubt, *The Old Man and the Sea* is Hemingway's masterpiece. Being akin to a Chinese proverb, *ouxinqixu,* or straining his heart till it is bleeding, he polishes it into a jem. Thus, this work brought him two big prizes, the Pulitzer Prize and the Nobel Prize.

After having got no fish for 84 days, the old man, Santiago, finally gets a huge and incomparable fish, the Marlin, in the deep waters. He fights for two days and three nights to subjugate the fish. This catch proves that he is *baoda weilao,* or a precious broadsword and though old yet not rusty, it is still sharp and capable of cutting things. It also proves that he is the greatest fisherman in the world.

The fish is longer than the fishing boat. And the old man has no other choice but to lash it to one of the sides of his boat. When he is on his way back home, he whistles and calculates how is he going to sell this fish in the fish market? Out of the blue, the side of the boat is teeming with a school of sharks that trails the Marlins' bleeding through the water gnawing the old man's "trophy" ruthlessly. Although Santiago does his utmost to engage in this fight with the unflinching sharks, he is outnumbered. In a flash, the old man's "hope" is destroyed by the huge sharks' scarlet mouths.

The old man sails back to the port where he sets out to sea. With his mast on his shoulder, he trudges uphill to his "shabby" shack. Left behind is the Marlin's skeleton beside the moored boat, the whole skeleton swaying along with the waves. Isn't this a kind of nothingness?

The other two short stories are "The Short Happy Life of Francis Macomber and "The Snows of Kilimanjaro" which end with denouements of nothingness, too. However, two questions remain unanswered: No. 1: "Does Margaret intend to murder her husband, Francis, or is he killed by an accident?" No. 2: "How does the leopard climb up to the top of 19,700 feet high in Mt. Kilimanjaro?" And there is a variety of interpretations but nobody can give definite answers even to this day.

Without doubt, the thought of nothingness permeates all of Hemingway's works. The most obvious example appears in one of his short stories, "A Clean Well-Lighted Place."[80] He used the word, nothingness, to substitute for the key words in the Lord's Prayer. It can be considered unique in writing style.

If life is futile, why do people like to keep living in this world? It dawns upon me eventually that Hemingway stresses the course of life in which people all fight for survival. Like all apprentices created by Hemingway in his novels, people try to learn how to survive in the hard times getting rid of obstacles that they have had in their daily lives. If not, how did Hemingway create such well-known quotes as follows?

"But man is not made for defeat"

"A man can be destroyed, not defeated."[81]

The quotes are the greatest revelations that I have got from reading Hemingway's works. Depending on these two quotes, I have gone through numerous difficulties and hardships in my life.

I stayed at Leader until January 31, 2008 and ended my second teaching career, seven and a half years in total. During this period of time, no matter where I was, in the Department of Applied English or in the Office of Student Affairs, my colleagues and I got along very well. Moreover, I felt respected.

One thing worthy of mentioning here is that during my last two years at Leader and with all my colleagues' concerted effort, the Department of Applied English passed the most rigorous evaluation held for the university level by the Ministry of Education. This was a huge accomplishment for a fledgling department like ours, especially, for a privately-funded college of this kind.

EPILOGUE

In 2009, I quit my part-time teaching job at NCKU and retired outright intending to enjoy my retirement. At present, I was 78, and thinking of the years ahead of me, with no offspring nearby to turn to for help if needed, I had to go to America to live with my two children. But each year, we want to come back to our family house in Tainan staying for some time and visiting our relatives, neighbors and old friends. We also hoped that in the future, as long as our health permits, we'd like, sometimes, to do the sight-seeing and pay visits in Mainland China. And there is always possibility for us to call on Zhonglan, my eldest sister in Nanjing, Yulan, half-sister in Jinan and my sister-in-law, Shumin, in the city of Mudanjiang.

In summary, the story of my entire life might still not be considered a typical one in the times of upheaval. Of my contemporaries, there are lots of more people who have been in the worse position than I. If they are willing to get their memoirs written, theirs will be a little more standardized ones to suit the purpose of writing autobiography. However, living in America, I have frequently been asked a question like this: "During the late 1940s, how did you get out of Mainland China?" I usually gave them a strained smile instead of an answer. However, once I started a conversation with somebody about the vicissitudes of odyssey that I had gone through, I couldn't make my journeying straight in a few words.

In addition, at the time I taught at NCKU, I saw some of the students who were lazy and unmotivated. And during the class time and sometimes, I talked about some of the contents of the chapters described in this memoir, for example, selling shoes in Qingtao, rough road to Fuzhou, illigally drafted into the army in the Penghu Islands after leaving from the Chinese Mainland, university days, and two trips to the U.S. to get my degrees to boost them up.

Those who had been associated with me for a while were also curious about my teenage life. How did a 17 years old boy manage to leave Mainland China? How did I survive in Taiwan? After listening to my untold stories, they thought unanimously and indicated to me, "Why don't you get the whole thing down on the paper?"

Another factor that presses me to write this memoir dated back to Double Ninth Day in 1966. (It is called Double Ninth because the festival falls on the 9th day in September, the 9th month of the year.)

The purpose of holding luncheon by the Cultural Comission on the Double Ninth Day is to show respects to senior writers and artists. My name was on the guest list.

In the course of that luncheon, I unexpectedly met Ya Huen, the chief editor of the supplementary edition affiliated with *The United Daily News*, and right at that moment when Qing Yue was returning a photo borrowed from me in which there are six young soldiers in uniforms. And I immediately handed it over to Ya Huen and asked him to identify who I was in the picture. He identified me in the photo at a glance. After carefully examining each one of us in the photo for a while, he said to me: "Please write the story about this picture. How is that?"

It took me about five days to finish writing a piece of article entitled: "My Literary Friends in the Army" and mailed it to him. Unexpectedly, on July 7, 1997, the 50th Anniversary of Victory Over Japan Day, it got published by four installments, namely, taking 4 days to run the whole thing. Without anticipation, this piece of writing caused a big sensation among the students from Shandong Province. Some of them I knew, and some of them I didn't, called me continuously and talked with me about our past. Accordingly, I got the opportunity to renew the camaraderie with the buddies of the 5th company of whom I had long lost track. Furthermore, we reminisced about our old days' dining in the open. All these "noises" gave me an immense encouragement.

Another reason is that Mr. Chuang Hsincheng of New York who, often, contacted me by sending me emails or sometimes, calling me. He said to me repeatedly that since I had the kind of "harrowing experience" while retreating to Taiwan and the hard days on the Penghu Islands, I ought to write a memoir. If done, it would be an interesting one.

The key factor for me to write this memoir is the encouragement from my family. And being a man, one must leave something like legacy to one's descendants.

Based upon all these, I decided to give a try.

At present, thinking back to those miserable days, I must attribute all those hardships, difficulties and sufferings to the times and the quirk of fate. But in my mind, I still have had the questions that remain as follows:

1. If I hadn't left Jinan in 1948, what would have happened to me?
2. If I had been intercepted by the Communists Army on the way southward to Taiwan during the upheaval of 1949, what would have happened to me?
3. At the age of 16, if I hadn't been illegally-drafted into the Nationalists Army by generals Lee Zhenqing and Han Fengyi on the Penghu Islands, what would have happened to me?

Having calculated the years of my entire life that I have had up to now, I have found that I have stayed in the Chinese Mainland 16 years; in Taiwan, 61 years; and in California, U.S.A. 3 years.

In the middle of the night when I am awake and out of a dream, I often recall my adventure of the 80-some odd difficult years. The harder events, they are, the better I can remember. They look like the brightest stars in the sky twinkling overhead occasionally.

I also often recall those who helped me out during those difficult days. I call them my saviors. Without their timely helps, the first half of my life must be more wretched; the second half of my life is not as easy as what it is. And gratitute wells up in my heart. Translating this gratitude into practice is my important work during my twilight years.

I have been running here and there throughout my life. Have I got something worthwhile done?

The answer is negative.

However, I refuse to be discouraged. What I can do now is nothing else but to read and write. And at the "stage of sunsetting," though I still want to to do what I want yet I do not want to get myself overstretched.

I have lots of opportunities to visit Fisherman's Wharf in San Francisco, and facing the vastness of the Pacific Ocean, My thoughts are racing. As for so-called "home, national and global affairs," they suddenly and seemingly were too far away from me. I can't tell them clearly, let alone comb them straight. But one point that I'd like to make here is that I wish China and Taiwan well and prosperous. No matter what the situation will be in the future, and in the 21st century, the world has gone this far in civilization, the disputes between China and Taiwan ought to be resolved by peaceful means. If antagonizing each other and starting a war, both sides will certainly fall victim to either stupidity or insanity.

BIBLIOGRAPHY
OF CHINESE WORKS CITED

1. Chen, Yunjuan, The Studies of Students from Shandong Province, 1945–1962, Taipei: Literature of Shandong Province, 1998.
2. Lui, Zemin, Free Talks about the Past, Taipei: Literature of Shandong Province, 1997.
3. Liu, Zhaoxian, The 50-Year Ups and Downs of My Life, Taipei: Self-published Edition, 2001.
4. Ma, Chungliang, "My Literary Friends in the Army," The Supplementary Edition Affiliated to *The United Daily News*, Taipei: July 7–10, 1997.
5. Pang Shouqian and Ren Mingzao, editors. The Collection of Papers for Celebrating Liu Zemin's 80th Birthday, Taipei: Self-published edition, 1991.
6. Qi, Fengjin, My Eighty Years' Even Path, Kaohsiung: Self-published edition, 2011.
7. The Preparation Committee for Zhang Minzhi's and Zhou Jiang's 40th Memorial Anniversary of Execution, the Chronicle of the Two Principals' and Five Students' Execution of the Yintai United Secondary School—A 40-year Injustice, Taipei: Self-published Edition, 1989.
8. The Preparation Committee, for Zhang Minzhi's and Zou Jiang's 50th Anniversary of Execution—the Collection of Papers in Memory of Zhang's and Zou's Deaths, Taipei: Self-published edition, 1999.
9. Wang, Peiwu, The Principal on the Cross, Taipei: Wenjing Publising House, 2000.

Bibliography
of English Works Cited

1. Barker, Kenneth, ed. Zondervan *NIV Study Bible*. Michigan: Zondervan, 2002.
2. Holstein, Michael E. *Beginning Literary Criticism*. Taipei: Bookman Books, LTD. Taipei, Taiwan 1987.
3. Guerrin, Welfred L. etc. *A Handbook of Critical Approaches to Literature*. Oxford: Oxford University Press, 2005.
4. Hemingway, Ernest. *The Sun Also Rises*. New York: Scribner's Sons, 1954.
5. ————, A Farewell to Arms. London: Arrow Books, 2004.
6. ————, For Whom the Bell Tolls. New York: Charles Scribner's Sons, 1968.
7. ————, The Old Man and The Sea. New York: Charles Scribner's Sons, 1952.
8. ————, The Short Stories of Ernest Hemingway. New York: Charles Scribner's Sons, 1966.

ENDNOTES

1. "Dongfang Shuo," Wikipedia, The Free Encyclopedia. n. d. Accessed on January 20, 2013. https//en.wikipedia.org/wiki/Donfang Shuo.

2. "Dongfang Shuo Tomb" is drawn from Chinese Baidu Web Service Company under the heading of topography. n. d. Accessed on January 20, 2013. https//baike.baidu.com/item

3. "Xia Houzhan," Baidu. n. d. Accessed on January 20, 2013. https//baike.baidu.com/item

4. "Yan Zhenqing," Wikipedia. n. d. Accessed on January 22, 2013 https//en.wikipedia.org/wiki/Dongfang Shuo

5. "Dongfang Shuo," cited as in No. 1

6. "Dongfang Shuo." cited as in No.1

7. "The Lingcheng District," the Ling County was rezoned under the jurisdiction of PRC and became a part of city of Dezou. Baidu. n. d. Accessed on January 22, 2013 https//en.Baike.baidu.Com/item

8. Letter from my immediate uncle, Ma Jiaxian, dated October 13, 1991

9. "The Lingcheng Distrist" cited as in No.7

10. "Battle of Jinan" Wikipedia, The Free Encyclopedia. n. d. Accessed on May 28, 2013 https://en.Wikipedia.org/wiki/Battle -of-Jinan

11. Qi, Fengjin, My Eighty Years' Path, Kaohsiung: Self-published, 2011

12. "Battle of Jinan," from Whipedia, cited as in No. 10

13. "Battle of Jinan," from Whipedia, cited as in No. 10

14. Liu, Zimin, Free Talks About the Past in Taiwan, Taipei: Literature of Shandong Province, 1997. 119

15. Liu 7

16. Liu 26-44

17. Liu 64-75

18. Liu 118

19. Wang, Changling, "Marching Out to the Frontier" translated by Teng Yanchang, Google Service Company, August 13, 2010. Accessed on September 5, 2013 https://www.en84 com.>article-3539-1

20. "Longyou County" (Quzhou City) Baidu Web Service Company. Accessed on September 11, 2013 https//baike. Baidu. com/item Longyou

21. "Ruannang Xiuse," Copy right, 2015 Ministry of Education, R.O.C. dict resided. moe, edu tw > cgi-bin>cbdic>gsweb

22. "The Daunting Route into the Region of Su." Google. Accessed on October 2, 2013 https://28utscprojects. Wordpress.com>2011/01/15

23. Lu Daoya, "The Storm that I Have Gone through at Changanzhen," published in the collection of Liu Zemin's 80th Anniversary of Birthday edited by Pang Shouqian and Ren Minggzao, Taipei: Self-published, 1991. 181

24. Liu 127

25. Lu 181

26. Liu 126

27. Liu 126

28. Wang, Puwu, A Principal on the Cross, Taipei: Wenjing Publishing House, 2000. 55-56

29. Chen, Yunjuan, The Studies of Shandong Students, 1945-1962, Taipei: Literature of Shandong Province, 1998. 145

30. Liu 127

31. Liu 183

32. Wang 65

33. Chen 167, Wang 66

34. Wang 67

35. Chen 167

36. Liu, Zhaoxian, The 50-Year Ups and Downs of My Life, Taipei: Self-published Edition, 2001. 168

37. "Li Zhenqing," Baidu Web Service Company, n. d. Accessed on March 20, 2014 Https//baike. Baidu. com/item/1023877

38. This information is drawn from my interviews with my classmates of the Jinan First United Secondary School. Some of them are still living in Taiwan and the U.S. Their names are Wang Chuanpu and Wu Chuangda.

39. I was told by many of my fellow students, especially by the one named Li Chi-min.

40. The Preparation Committee for Zhang Minzhi's and Zhou Jiang's 50th Anniversary of Execution—the Collection of Papers in Memory of Mr. Zhang's and Mr. Zhou's Deaths, Taipei: Self-published edition,1999.

41. Liu, Tinggong, "The Stigma of History" published in the collection of Papers commemorating Zhang Minzhi's, Zhou Jiang's and Five Students' 40th Anniversary of Injustice Case—the Chronicle of Execution of Principals and Students of the United Secondary School of Yangtai, Taipei: Self-published edition, 1889. 103

42. *The Xin Shen Pao.* December 12, 1949

43. Fu, Weining, "The Case of Wrongful Execution Still Remains in the Dark," published in the collection of the 50th Anniversary of Execution. 68

44. The Chiang's Address to the Taiwanese people on May 16, 1950. Accessed on May 20, 2014 https//zh Wikipedia. org/zh-hant/

45. Here, the wall newspaper of ours is not identical to that of the Communist's big-character poster. In the Communist world, they use it for propaganda in a movement. We use the wall newspaper to show the works of our potential writers for creative writings.

46. Chen 174

47. The Story on Sun Liren's Talk is cliché-ridden, and those who attended the assemblies knew that by then.

48. Chen 250

49. Chen 252

50. Sino-American Mutual Defense Treaty. Effective from 1955 to 1979. Accessed on May 22, 2014

51. Chen 260

52. Chen 270

53. Chen 270

54. Chen 270

55. Chen 253

56. Chen 253

57. Chen 257-258

58. Barker, L. Kenneth, et al., eds. Zondervan NTV, Study Bible, Michigan: Zondervan, 2000, Isaiah 42:3, 1457

59. Chen 267

60. Chen 266

61. Chen 266

62. This information is coming from a translated work entitled: "On Quietness" published on the Supplementary edition affiliated to *The Central Daily News*. Its author is Song Rui

63. Chen 267

64. The 1964 Baihe Earthquake, Wikipedia, the Free Encyclopedia, October 18, 2017. Accessed on March 15, 2017 https//zh.wiipedia. org/wki/1964 Baihe Earthquake

65. Barker, Romans 6:23, 2330

66. Barker, John 14:6, 2204

67. "Sturdy grass withstands a strong wind and a loyal official can be found during unrest." m. hk headline. Com. hk/daily news/content-cl/2014/11/308832 asp.

68. The chief editor, Yu Yunping of Wenyi (Literature and Arts) Magazine Monthly, sent me a short note lavishing praises on my writing style for the article published on 161 issue of the magazine in November, 1982.

69. Department of Foreign Languages and Literature edit. "A Collection of Papers Presented in the 2nd Annual Conference of English and American Literature." Taipei: Bookman Books LTD. 1987, 1-2

70. The document was issued by the Personnel Office at NCKU on January 8, 1988

71. Letter from my eldest sister, Zhonglan, dated on May 25, 1991

72. Nanjing University. https://zh.Wikipedia.org/zh-hant Nangjing University. Accessed on April 30, 2017

73. Holstein, Michael E. Beginning Literary Criticim, Taipei: Bookman Books LTD. Reprinted by permission of the copyright holder of Michael Holstein, 1987.

74. Guerin Wilfred L. etc., eds. A Handbook of Critical Approaches to Literature, 5th ed. Oxford: Oxford University Press, 2005.

75. Barker, Ecclesiastes 1:1-5, 1345

76. Barker, Ecclesiastes 1:6-7, 1345

77. Hemingway, Ernest, A Farewell to Arms, London: Arrow Books, 2004. 160

78. Hemingway, Ernest, For Whom the Bell Tolls, London: Scribner. 1968. 463

79. John Donne: https//web. Cs. Del. Ca/-John Donne/poetry/island

80. John Donne: https//web. Cs. Del. Ca/-John Donne/poetry/island

81. Hemingway, Ernest, The Old Man and the Sea, New York: Charles Scribner's Son, 1952. 103

ACKNOWLEDGEMENTS

I am greatly indebted to my sister-in-law, Bao-hwa Wang and assistant prof. Shui-mei Chung for their editing. I owe a debt of gratidude to Dr. Hsincheng Chuang for his changing the title of this memori from Up from the Rank and File into From Foot Soldier to College Professor and making substantive and stylistic suggestions. I also owe special thanks to my classmate, Fuhsiung Lin, for his time, energy and spiritual support to have read the whole thing. I am grateful to my daughter-in-law, Avian Liao, son, Taohung, for their repeat editing on the computer. Without their assistances, this book couldn't have been written. Overall, with regard to all the stuff in this memoir, I take the full responsibility on myself.

血歷史212　PC1046

新銳文創
INDEPENDENT & UNIQUE

From Foot Soldier to College Professor
A Memoir

作　者	馬忠良（James C. Ma）
責任編輯	洪聖翔
圖文排版	陳彥妏
封面設計	蔡瑋筠

出版策劃	新銳文創
發 行 人	宋政坤
法律顧問	毛國樑　律師
製作發行	秀威資訊科技股份有限公司
	114 台北市內湖區瑞光路76巷65號1樓
	電話：+886-2-2796-3638　傳真：+886-2-2796-1377
	服務信箱：service@showwe.com.tw
	http://www.showwe.com.tw
郵政劃撥	19563868　戶名：秀威資訊科技股份有限公司
展售門市	國家書店【松江門市】
	104 台北市中山區松江路209號1樓
	電話：+886-2-2518-0207　傳真：+886-2-2518-0778
網路訂購	秀威網路書店：https://store.showwe.tw
	國家網路書店：https://www.govbooks.com.tw

出版日期	2022年2月　BOD一版
定　價	420元
I S B N	978-986-5540-93-7